Research Reports ESPRIT

Project 6532 · HI FI · Volume 1

Edited in cooperation with the European Commission

W. Schuler   J. Hannemann
N. Streitz   (Eds.)

Designing User Interfaces for Hypermedia

Springer

Volume Editors

Wolfgang Schuler
Norbert Streitz
Gesellschaft für Mathematik und Datenverarbeitung mbH
Dolivostr. 15, D-64293 Darmstadt, Germany

Jörg Hannemann
empirica GmbH
Oxfordstr. 2, D-53111 Bonn, Germany

ESPRIT Project 6532, HIFI (Hypertext Interface for Information: Multimedia and Relational Databases), belongs to the Software and Advanced Information Processing sector of the ESPRIT Programme (European Specific Programme for Research and Development in Information Technologies) supported by the European Commission.

The aim of ESPRIT Project 6532, HIFI, was to create a set of tools to allow a reader to access, via a hypertext interface, a large body of information managed by external (possibly pre-existing) databases, either relational or multimedia. Methodologies to support the hypertext interface development process are also being investigated.

For three different real-life applications (for banks, hospitals and museums) prototypes have been developed and tested. The applications and the set of the HIFI tools have been fully specified and designed.

Partners in the project were:
Benaki Museum, Athens (Greece); Epsilon Software AG, Athens (Greece); GMD-IPSI, Darmstadt (Germany); Music/Forth, Chania (Greece); Politecnico di Milano, Milan (Italy); Siemens AG, Munich (Germany); Systems & Management SpA, Milan-Turin (Italy); Syntax Sistemi Software SpA, (Olivetti), Bari (Italy).

ISBN-13: 978-3-540-58489-6   e-ISBN-13: 978-3-642-45743-2
DOI: 10.1007/978-3-642-45743-2

CIP-Data applied for.

CR Subject Classification (1991): I.7.2, H.5.1, H.1.2, J.1

Springer-Verlag Berlin Heidelberg New York

Publication No. EUR 16105 EN of the
European Commission,
Dissemination of Scientific and Technical Knowledge Unit,
Directorate-General Information Telecommunications, Information Market and
Exploitation of Research,
Luxembourg.

Typesetting: Camera-ready by the editors
SPIN: 10480846   45/3140-543210 – Printed on acid-free paper

Preface

One can observe that a wide range of human activities involves various forms of design. Especially if the goal implies the creation of an artifact, design is at the very center of these activities. It is the general understanding in the public to place design especially in the context of, for example, fashion, furniture, household items, cars, and architecture or in a more general way at the intersection of art and engineering. Of course, in the field of information technology, developers of software and hardware are called system 'designers'. Design can be identified and considered in the context of many activities related to publishing: creating a product ad in a magazine, designing the layout of a newspaper, authoring a book. Summarizing these examples as 'creating documents', these are activities where two challenges with respect to design have to be met. Designing the content, its structure, and its relationship to the existing knowledge of potential readers is one, while the other refers to the 'rhetorical' aspects including designing the presentation of the material in order to communicate the content. Publishing is communicating knowledge.

Once these documents take the form of electronic documents, the original challenges are extended by additional dimensions caused by the availability of new means for content creation, structuring, and presentation. The results of these activities in terms of interactive electronic documents exist only 'in' the computer – at least with respect to the full range of their functionality – and are 'read' via user-interfaces created by special user-interface designers. Hypertext and hypermedia documents are prominent examples of these challenges. While the concept of "hypertext" with its emphasis on non-linearity provides new opportunities with respect to structuring the information, the rapid spread of multimedia technology allows also the creation and presentation of time-dependent data (e.g., audio and video) to be used as content thus going beyond text and pictures. These new opportunities and challenges with respect to structure and content characterize the design of Hypermedia = Hypertext + Multimedia. The task of designing user-interfaces for hypermedia is a crucial aspect of the creation of any but especially of large hypermedia applications in the real world. This is the topic of this book and reflected in the title: *Designing User Interfaces for Hypermedia*.

While the design of user-interfaces for interactive computer systems in general is difficult because it is usually an ill-defined problem with specifications which are never sufficient, the design of large hypermedia applications is an especially complex task. There are no design principles readily available which can be applied in a straight forward fashion. Due to the lack of a sufficient theoretical basis, a methodology for the design of hypertext and hypermedia has to be developed which can be used to guide the construction of specific hypermedia interfaces and applications. In order to address the above issues in a systematic way, we organized a *Workshop on Methodological Issues on the Design of Hypertext-based User Interfaces* which was held at GMD-IPSI in Darmstadt, Germany, on July 13–14, 1993. This workshop was part of our contributions in the ESPRIT project 6532 HIFI (Hypertext Interface For Information: Multimedia and Relational Databases). Details on the HIFI project are described at the end of this book (see section 5). The call for contributions to the workshop invited papers and participants to address the following topics:

- Design and construction process of hypertext/hypermedia-based interfaces
- Design proposals for the interface artefact
- Evaluation concepts and methods for hypermedia user interfaces
- Experiences with specific applications and practice reports.

These topics were selected to discuss quite a range of questions. Examples are: Which framework for the hypermedia interface design process has been or should be used: theory or model-based approach, or a task-artefact cycle framework? Which specific design methods have been or should be used: argumentative design, design rationale method, participatory design, rapid prototyping, human acitivity approach, traditional requirements and constraints analysis, scenario building? Which are suggestive models for hypermedia user interfaces? What kind of metaphors are useful? How useful are handbooks and guidelines for 'traditional' user interfaces? Which specific design decisions have improved the comprehensibility of hypermedia applications? In which way is it necessary to revise design decisions when an application grows larger and becomes more complex (scaling)? Which evaluation approaches have been or should be used? What are the specifics of evaluating the usability of hypermedia interfaces? Of course, the workshop did not provide definite answers to all these, in some cases very fundamental, questions. But that was not our expectation, either. Rather, the workshop proved to be a highly stimulating and effective forum for the exchange of ideas and practical experiences, for the discussion, critique, and combination of proposals for concrete designs as well as for methodological considerations.

Encouraged by the success of the workshop and the feedback, there was the feeling that the results of this workshop should be disseminated to a larger audience outside the workshop participants. Although there were already proceedings distributed on site at the workshop – containing working papers of the talks, descriptions of projects, and system demonstrations – to publish a book on the workshop required substantial revisions and reorganization of the material. One important aspect was that the revised contributions should reflect also the discussion and feedback received during the workshop. In addition, some contributions had to be regrouped according to the experience of new relationships discovered during the workshop. In order to achieve a high quality book, all authors were asked to reorganize, elaborate, and edit their initial contributions. These 'value-added' papers were again reviewed by the session chairs of the workshop. Based on this feedback, authors had to revise their papers a second time around before they were accepted for publication. In addition, each set of papers constituting one of the five sections of this book is introduced by general comments and a characterization of each paper pointing at the relationships of these papers.

The new organization of the book resulted in five sections:

1 Foundations of Hypermedia Design
2 Metaphors for Hypermedia Interfaces
3 Evaluation and Critical Aspects of Hypermedia Design
4 Detailed Design Proposals and Guidelines
5 The ESPRIT Project HIFI.

Looking at the final version of this book, we think that the result justifies the additional effort which everybody put into the revision process. We like to thank all contributors for following the recommendations of the reviewers to a high degree, the reviewers for taking the time to comment and provide valuable feedback and recommendations, the section editors for their thoughtful introductions and summaries of the papers providing a comprehensive perspective. In addition, we want to acknowledge the patience and organizational support of Mrs. Ingeborg Mayer from Springer Verlag, Heidelberg and the technical support of Uwe Pechel from GMD-IPSI in preparing the camera–ready copy. Finally, we hope that you, the readers, enjoy this book and have a chance to participate in this exchange of ideas and proposals.

Darmstadt, October 1994   Wolfgang Schuler, Jörg Hannemann, Norbert Streitz

Table of Contents

5 The ESPRIT Project HIFI   219

Appendix: Addresses of the Authors   247

1 Foundations of Hypermedia Design

Norbert A. Streitz

While there is a long tradition in the design of traditional paper-based documents, there is little or no tradition in designing hypermedia documents or more general hypermedia applications. It is obvious that how designing is done has a strong impact on what is finally produced, distributed, and used. What is needed is an orientation or even better a methodology for hypermedia designers which should be based on a thorough understanding of the new and critical aspects of this new medium for communicating knowledge. The goal is that this methodology is based on a foundation for hypermedia design. The fact that it is a software environment where hypermedia design takes place implies that one has to analyze first how to support authoring and production activities in general in such an environment. Then, one has to account for the additional requirements which result from the new product characteristics inherent to hypermedia. Both sets of requirements are equally important.

The development of the SEPIA hypermedia authoring environment (Streitz et al., 1992) provides an example of this approach. Based on a detailed analysis of the cognitive processes of writing and the features of the overall authoring situation, authoring was characterized as a design activity involving 'opportunistic' problem solving, i.e., a high degree of changing constraints and reorientation of goals. Mapping the identified problem characteristics on requirements for software components resulted in the realization of task-specific 'activity spaces' which provide dedicated functionality to authors for a number of subproblems of the overall authoring process (planning, information collection and structuring, representing arguments, rhetorical structuring). But it soon became obvious that beyond the generic authoring support there had to be components which address the additional challenges of designing the presentation of hypermedia documents. For example, creating and maintaining coherence in a hyperdocument facilitates comprehension and understanding of its content. The specific nature of coherence in hypermedia documents and new opportunities for visual presentations led to additional considerations and corresponding system features (Thüring et al. 1991; Hannemann & Thüring, this section). The conclusion is that it is necessary to provide both sets of support and functionality (generic authoring and hypermedia specific design support) and to do this in an integrated fashion.

The first four papers in this book constituting the first section address this general problem of hypermedia design and provide contributions to what could be a starting point for a foundation in this field.

The paper of *F. Garzotto, L. Mainetti, and P. Paolini* (Hypermedia application design: a structured approach) emphasizes the need for a structured approach to hypermedia design and proposes HDM as a basis. They consider design as the task of specifying representation structures, dynamic behaviour, navigation patterns, and lay-out features with respect to a hypermedia application. An important aspect is the distinction between structuring 'in the large' and authoring 'in the small'. Their work is motivated by the goal to provide a guideline which will make hypermedia design more systematic and better organized. It is aimed at support for mastering the complexity of hypermedia application development and improving consistency and usability of the resulting applications.

The contribution of *L. Hardman* (Experiences in authoring hypermedia: creating better presentations) addresses the problem in two ways. First, she describes and discusses the lessons she learned during her involvement with a number of academic and commercial hypertext projects. Based on controlled reader studies, she identifies inadequacies of different hypermedia interfaces. Her observations are then turned into a number of useful considerations for different stages of design. The second part motivates and describes a structured approach to authoring hypermedia which shares similarities to the one in the preceding paper by Garzotto et al.. In order to illustrate parts of the requirements listed before she describes an editing environment which enables authors more easily to experiment with and change both the structure and the layout of a presentation until s/he is satisfied.

In their paper (What matters in developing user interfaces for hyperdocument presentation?), *J. Hannemann and M. Thüring* observe the problem that over the last few years, the design of hypermedia interfaces has mainly focused on solving the navigation problem. They criticize that browsing has been regarded as the most central user activity and argue that there are more applications, especially beyond information kiosks or electronic advertisements, which demand more of a reader's attention. This leads to the position that navigation should not be regarded as an end in itself but as a prerequisite for the reader's actual goal: the comprehension of the hyperdocument. This results in their approach to develop design principles which focus on coherence and especially on increasing the readability of hyperdocuments. Finally, they describe an implementation of an interface which is based on these principles.

Coherence is also a topic which is addressed in the contribution by *U. Thiel* (Interaction in hypermedia systems: from browsing to conversation). His starting point is how users can be supported in the construction of coherence when interacting with a hypermedia database. He proposes to explore the potential of conversational dialogue design for hypertext systems. This approach is motivated by the fact that in large databases one cannot build upon pre-edited coherent paths or similar features for coherence enhancement. An experimental interface to a database on European projects is described in order to show how the key ideas can be applied.

In summary, the four contributions in this first section represent a stimulating opening to the book and provide a basis for the discussion of the contributions which follow in the remaining sections. They indicate clearly the intricate relationship between authoring support, the design approach adopted, and the final product.

Although all the preceding is true, there is still one important aspect missing. It is the implication of the observation that for large and complex, real life applications there has to be a team of people which work together. The range of qualifications needed for demanding hypermedia productions cannot be found in one or two persons. A final hypermedia application has to be seen as the result of the interaction between content providers, value adding editors, interface designers, and, of course, the tools and the methodology applied. This implies that the design approach and the initial methodology has to be extended in order to include styles of collaboration resulting in additional forms of system support. In order to address the collaborative aspects of hypermedia design, additional questions have to be answered. For example, what kind of additional structures are needed in the early phases of a hypermedia project, especially for brainstorming in group meetings? Partial answers include that one has to extend the range of available structures beyond those which are used in the final product. This range includes very informal scribbles, as they are frequently used by graphic designers, to more formal ones, e.g., argumentation and rhetorical structures (Haake, Neuwirth & Streitz, 1994). In addition, one has to address the question of what kind of support is needed to facilitate the collaboration in a team creating a large hypermedia application? This includes also more general issues of Computer-Supported Cooperative Work (CSCW) in terms of synchronous and asynchronous as well as same place/ different place cooperation (Streitz et al., 1994). From a more global perspective, it is this extended relationship and interaction which has to be concentrated on in order to design and produce high quality hypermedia applications.

References

Haake, J., Neuwirth, C., Streitz, N. (1994). Coexistence and transformation of informal and formal structures: Requirements for more flexible hypermedia systems. *Proceedings of the 6. ACM European Conference on Hypermedia Technology (ECHT'94)*. Edinburgh, UK (September 18–23, 1994), pp. 1–12.

Streitz, N., Geissler, J. Haake, J., Hol, J. (1994). DOLPHIN: Integrated meeting support across LiveBoards, local and remote desktop environments. *Proceedings of the 5. ACM Conference on Computer–Supported Cooperative Work (CSCW'94)*. Chapel Hill, NC (October 22–26, 1994), pp. 345 – 358.

Streitz, N., Haake, J., Hannemann, J., Lemke, A., Schuler, W., Schütt, H., Thüring, M. (1992). SEPIA: A cooperative hypermedia authoring environment. *Proceedings of the 4. ACM European Conference on Hypertext (ECHT'92)* Milano, Italy (November 30 – December 4, 1992), pp. 11–22.

Thüring, M., Haake, J., Hannemann, J. (1991). What's ELIZA doing in the Chinese Room — Incoherent hyperdocuments and how to avoid them. *Proceedings of the 3. ACM Conference on Hypertext (Hypertext '91)* San Antonio, TX (December 15 – 18, 1991), pp. 161 – 177.

Hypermedia Application Design:
a Structured Approach

Franca Garzotto, Luca Mainetti, Paolo Paolini
Politecnico di Milano, Milano, Italy

Abstract. Hypermedia design is the task of specifying representation structures, dynamic behaviour, navigation patterns, and lay-out features, of a hypermedia application. This paper describes a *structured approach* to hypermedia design, identifying the crucial steps in the design process. Our main goal is to provide a guideline to make hypermedia design more systematic and better organised, and to help mastering the complexity of hypermedia application development and improving consistency and usability of the resulting applications.

1 Introduction

Until few years ago, hypermedia application development was mainly conceived as an artisan activity, performed on the basis of individual creativity and experience. Methodologies, models, and tools, to support the development of hypermedia in a systematic, engineered, and efficient way, were absent. While this approach could still be acceptable for the kind of applications developed till few years ago, today it is more critical, due to a number of reasons:

- applications domains for hypermedia have become more complex, ranging from industrial or administrative training to technical documentation, from information points to electronic exhibitions, just to mention a few. As a consequence for developers, understanding and organising the contents, and conveying their meaning for end users, have become more difficult.
- Hypermedia applications have grown in size, moving from few dozens to many thousand of nodes and links. Hypermedia for technical documentation of large industrial plants, or to distributed hypermedia as the World Wide Web, are obvious examples.
- New media, such as video, sound, animation, are playing a more important role.

It has, therefore, become harder, today, to master the complexity of hypermedia development, and more difficult to produce applications that are of good quality, coherent, well organised, and truly usable, in a cost effective way. We need somehow to move from a pre-industrial to an industrial era of hypermedia, transforming hypermedia development from an hand-crafted activity to a more organised, engineered, efficient process.

The "life cycle" of hypermedia application development involves the "canonical" stages of application analysis, design, implementation, testing and evaluation, each of which should be engineered, taking into account the peculiarities of hypermedia with respect to other classes of software application development.

In this paper, we will discuss a specific stage, namely, *hypermedia design*, trying to suggest a systematic way to it. In hypermedia, the term *design* refers to the process of *defining* (i.e., taking decisions about) and *specifying*, in a clear and precise way, the *representation structures* of an application, their *dynamic behaviour*, their *visualisation features*, their *navigation properties*, abstracting as much as possible from implementation aspects.

Until few years ago, scarce attention was paid to hypermedia design; given the limited size and complexity of applications, nodes and links could be built on the fly, and a careful pre-planning of the application in all its aspects was not strictly needed. Today, the role of design cannot be neglected, since the efficiency and quality of the development process (and of the resulting applications) are largely affected by the quality of design [3, 7, 8, 9, 26, 27, 29, 35, 36, 37].

Systematic design forces a team of developers to focus on the rationale of the application to be developed, to discuss it in terms of the regularities and the global properties of the application, and to take decisions at the proper level of abstraction. Most of the "conceptual" (i.e., technology-independent) problems and inconsistencies can be potentially detected and resolved at design level, before actually implementing the application. Precise and coherent design may reduce implementation mistakes, and, in principle, the better the design the higher the quality of the final application, in terms of coherency and consistency with respect to its requirements.

2 "Structured" Hypermedia Design

Our goal is to identify the main activities that are involved in the design process, and to provide a check list of tasks that can guide designers in performing their work more systematically. Our approach to hypermedia design is *structured*, in the sense that it considers the design process as a sequence of distinguishable, albeit interdependent, phases, that mostly proceed in a top-down fashion, from higher to lower level of abstraction and detail.

Structured design has been defined for, and tested on, a specific class of applications, which we will call *structured hypermedia*. Their main feature is the need of *coherent structuring* of the information [37], both at logical and at visualization level. This means that a structured hypermedia application is not an arbitrary set of nodes and links. Information is instead organised according to regular patterns, precisely pre-defined by the designer, is presented by visual structures that convey the information organisation and semantics to end users.

Furthermore, its dynamic behaviour and its navigation paths are regular and predictable. These properties can potentially reduce the risk of disorientation, help users to understand the application, and improve usability.

The degree of application "structure" may vary from domain to domain. We can find examples of structured hypermedia in fields such as technical documentation, front-ends to information systems, information points, electronic exhibitions, industrial or administrative training, and many others, where regularity, consistency, and predictability are crucial requirements. Typically, hypermedia applications in domains such as electronics fiction, games, literature, are much less structured, since unpredictability, surprise, and disorientation, are part of the intended effects. Therefore there is not a strong need of predictable navigation paths and of a strictly coherent organisation of logical and visual structures.

3 Structured Design Phases

A structured hypermedia application can be regarded from various perspectives:
1) in terms of the *statics* of the application, i.e., of the *representation structures* that describe the information.
2) In terms of the *dynamics* of the application. This refers both to the way users interact with the application (essentially, by navigating across the various pieces of information), and to the way these pieces of information behave (i.e., change their state along the time) either independently or as a response to user's actions.
3) In terms of the *lay-out* of the application, i.e., the way to present information on the screen.
4) In terms of the *functionalities* of the application other than navigation (e.g., printing facilities or integration with external, pre-existing applications).

These different dimensions of a hypermedia application correspond to different tasks, or phases, of structured design, discussed in the rest of this section, and graphically illustrated in the following figure 1. The tasks "hyperbase schema design", "reading schema(s) design", "instances design", and "access structures design", address the *static* aspects of a hypermedia application. The other tasks - "dynamics design", "additional functionalities design" and "lay-out design" - correspond, respectively, to the design of the dynamic, functional, and lay out features of a hypermedia application.

The input to the design process is the set of application requirements returned by the process of application analysis. The output is a set of (formal or semi-formal) specifications defining the various aspects of the hypermedia application to be developed. The order among the various phases is not strict, in the sense that, in general, each phase gives feedbacks to previous ones, and might involve revisions of decisions already taken in a previous step. Arcs in figure 1 denote possible dependencies among design phases.

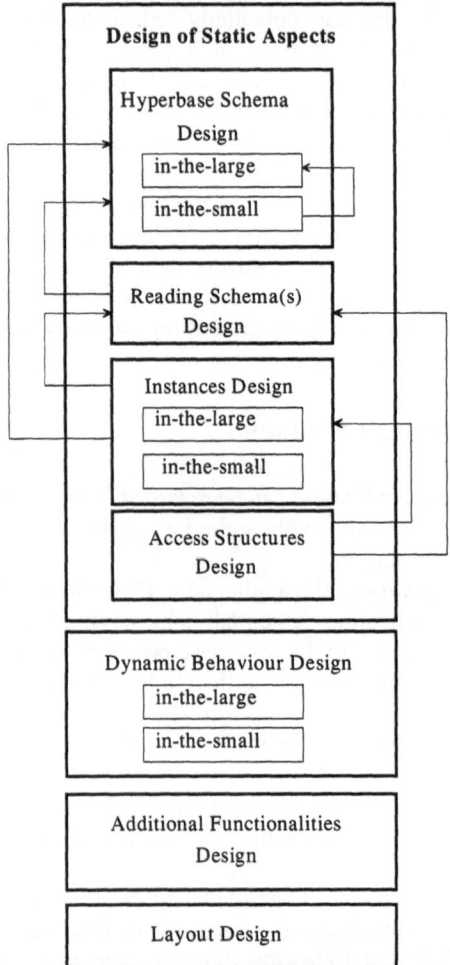

Figure 1. Structured design phases

3.1 Hyperbase schema design

This phase defines the *classes,* or *types,* of information objects and relationships. The collection of these specifications represents what we call *hyperbase schema.*

A hyperbase schema distinguishes between two levels of definitions, *in-the-large* and *in-the-small.* In-the-large definitions specify how objects of the various types are organized in logical constituents, and how objects are mutually interrelated. In-the-small definitions specify the actual structure of each individual constituent, and the types of their data values. The notion of hyperbase schema design is similar to the concept of schema design as it is found in the data base world. Data base schemas, however, are more fine-grained and do not clearly separate in-the-large definitions from in-the-small definitions.

Hyperbase schema design usually proceeds in a top-down fashion. First, it identifies the classes of information objects and relationships the application will deal with (which can be represented with Entity-Relationship diagrams, for example). Then it defines the structure of the objects of the various types, specifying which are the constituents of the objects, and which constituents are interrelated by the various relationships. Finally, it specifies the structures in-the-small, that is, the types of data values contained in each the constituents of the various objects.

In a hypermedia for technical documentation, for example, the designer may start defining that the application will deal with equipments, repair procedures, tools to be used, equipment faults, and that the relevant relationships are among equipments and repair procedures, procedures and needed tools, etc. The designer can then proceed by specifying that repair procedures are defined by a general introduction and a sequence of steps, and that each step is related to its own set of tools. In-the-small, he can specify that the introduction constituent of a repair procedure contains just a piece of text, and that each step contains a small text description of maximum ten lines, a list of critical physical parameters about the equipment to be fixed, a picture and a small video that exemplify how to perform that step.

Hyperbase schema structures represent information according to the designer's view point. As such, they tend to be minimal, for efficiency of design, and to avoid redundancies. Hyperbase schema structures are not necessarily the optimal representation for the end user. In general, they must be re-organised in such a way that they result more efficient for the intended use by the end-users, as discussed in the following phase.

3.2 Reading schema(s) design

Roughly speaking, this phase is the hypermedia counterpart of view design in the data base field. During this phase, hyperbase schema structures are re-arranged in a reader oriented perspective, by filtering and re-structuring (portions of) the hyperbase schema. We will call *reading schema* the set of resulting representation structures. Reading structures can be *derived* from the hyperbase schema, by specifying rules to select portions of hyperbase structures and to re-organize them into new structures. In general, if the application is devoted to several classes of users, there might be several reading schemas, one for each class of users.

If we compare reading structures with hyperbase schema structures, the latter are mainly designer-oriented, and are organised in a neutral, objective way with respect to all the possible organizations that the various classes of readers would desire. Reading schema(s) structures, instead, are closer to reader's requirements and perception, and are more specialised for the specific intended uses of the (various classes of) readers. As such, they might be redundant. Let us assume for

example that the designer has defined the hyperbase schema for technical
documentation discussed in the previous section. For a given class of readers, he
might decide that a repair procedure is better defined by aggregating the whole
list of tools needed for that repair, to the introductory component of the
procedure itself. This new representation of procedures can be derived (i.e.,
computed) from hyperbase structures, and has some redundancy, since the
detailed description of tools, and their relationships with the individual steps of a
procedure still co-exists. However, the new reading structures allow the provision
of a synthetic representation of what is needed for a given procedure *inside* the
description of the procedure itself (which is what the user may actually need).

It should be finally remarked that the new structures defined in a reading
schema can be obtained by altering the in-the-large structure of hyperbase objects
(i.e., by aggregating object constituents in a different way) and/or by altering the
in-the small-structure (i.e., by aggregating the content of constituents in a
different way), as exemplified by the above example.

3.3 Instances design

Instances design defines the actual objects and relationships that must appear in
the application, among all the possible ones in the application domain, as well as
their contents. They are instances of the reading schema types, i.e., their
representations satisfy the reading schema definitions. Again, we can split
instance design in two sub-phases: in-the-large and in-the-small.

Instance design in-the-large is the process of identifying which are the actual
objects and relationships that the user will find in the application. In a
hypermedia for technical documentation, for example, this phase specifies that
the application will contain equipments E1, E2, E3, and E4 (where E1,.., E4 are
the names of the choosen equipments), repair procedures P1, P2, and P3, tools
T1, T2, T3, T4, T5, and T6, equipment faults F1, F2, F3, and F4, and that a
relationship R1 hold between E1 and P2, E4 and P3, and so on.

The result of instance design in-the-large is a sort of *skeleton* of the application.
The internal structure of each information object, as well as their mutual
connections are defined, but the actual data contents, i.e., the fragments of text,
images, videos, formatted data, are still missing, since they refer to instance
design in-the-small.

Instance design in-the-small is the process of producing (or identifying, when
pre-existing), the data values that are contained in the various constituents of
each object, according to the definitions in the small of the reading schema. In the
above example, the decision that a given picture will be used in the first step of
fixing procedure P1 concerns with instance design in-the-small.

Instance design might have a significant impact on previous design choices,
since it might raise representation requirements that become clear only when
actual objects and their contents are created.

3.4 Access structures design

In hypermedia applications, it is useful to identify "sets of interest", i.e., collections of pre-existing structures that are of special interest for the user. Related collections in turn can be grouped in "super-collections", at any level of nesting. For example, it might be useful to collect, for each piece of equipment, all its most common faults, and then to group such collections into a higher level collection.

These "sets-of-interest" not only provide ways to classify domain information under "opportunistic" criteria that are alternative or complementary to the classification provided in the reading schema. Their main use is as *access structures,* i.e., entry points to start navigating in the application. Reader's navigation should not start arbitrarily, from any piece of information defined in the application. The user should instead be presented with some entry points defined by the designer according to the user's interest, and from here he or she should be allowed to make his or her selection and to access any of the listed items. Typical access structures are, for example, guided tours [38], or "indexes of topics" (sometime also called "tables of contents"). Typically, index of topics list the main subjects of a given application (say, "equipments", "faults", "tools", "repair procedure"), and, for each subject, they "point" to a second level access structure listing all pieces of information corresponding to a given topic, each of which can be then accessed directly.

3.5 Dynamic behaviour design

This phase defines the *behaviour* of the application [1, 2, 15, 17, 18, 24, 39], i.e., the ways by which users interact with the application, the application responses to user's actions, or the way it evolves along the time in a user- independent way.

The main way, for users, to interact with a hypermedia is by navigating across the various information structures. Navigation, however, can be more complex than mere traversing of static connections. Thinks for example of trace and backtracking mechanisms, which allow to inspect the navigation history of a session, or of context dependent navigation [40].

Another example is provided by navigation on guided tours. In [11, 13], guided tours are intended to be linear structures across which the user can navigate in sequential order. The designer can take a number of different decisions about navigation control on guided tours. He can choose that non-guided tour links should be hidden (or de-activated), and become available only upon an explicit user's request. This decision allows to guide navigation in a rigid way, and it is especially useful for novel users, since it provides a "protected" navigation environment that reduces the risk of disorientation. Alternatively, the designer may decide that all links are active at any time. Another decision may concern the possibility of temporarily suspending the guided tour, and to allow users to return to it later, after traversing non-guided tour links and exploring related items. This choice implies that the application should keep track of the item from which the guided tour was temporarily left, allowing the user to resume to it at any time after a deviation. The situation becomes more complex when there are nested guided tours, i.e., some guided tour items are guided tours in turn. The designer must decide what happens when the user reaches an item of a nested tour, and, for example, wants to "go next". "Next" can be interpreted as "go to the next item at the current level" or "go the next item at a higher level". A multiple interpretation offers the advantage of an efficient interaction for the user, if he/she wishes to change subject of the navigation session; it has the disadvantage, however, of adding additional complexity to the interaction.

All the above tasks can be referred as designing the *dynamic behaviour in-the-large*. They specify the high level behaviour of a hypermedia application, but not the local behaviour, i.e., what happens when a link is activated and a given item ("node", in the current hypermedia terminology) is accessed or left during navigation. Defining these aspects is a task that we will refer to as *dynamic behaviour design in-the-small*. It can be as complex as its counterpart in-the-large, since a variety of behaviours can be envisioned, especially in presence of multimedia, time-based information (e.g., video, animation, sound, etc.).

Multimedia are intrinsically *active* and *re-active*. The re-active nature of a piece information implies that it is sensitive to external "events", or "stimuli". While static media can have a limited re-activity (scrolling a text or zooming a picture are examples of response to a stimulus), the reactivity of dynamic media is more sophisticated, and its design is more complex. A video, for example, can be stopped, paused, re-started, moved forward or backward; sound features can be controlled ("modify the volume level", "start", "replay", etc.) and so on. The designer must therefore decide, for example, what is the degree of user's control when the user has access to an item containing a piece of text, a video, and an animation. The active nature of dynamic media has two aspects: the dependency on time and the capability of an object to influence the behaviour of other objects. The evolution of the state of an active object can be dependent on time-based behaviour, and independent from the user interaction. Multiple active media must be coordinated, or *synchronised* (even without an explicit user's request of the user or his will of interacting with the application). Synchronisation can be defined among multimedia items within the same node, or across different nodes. For example, a music piece contained in a node can continue playing even after the user has activated a navigation link and another node has become the current one [19].

Dynamic behaviour design in-the-large and in-the-small must be coordinated by the designer, in such a way that the overall effect is meaningful and consistent. Good design of the dynamics of a hypermedia is crucial for the usability of the application, and for reducing the risk of disorientation, since incoherence and unexpected behaviours of the application can be particularly frustrating, especially when a massive use of multimedia is involved.

3.6 Additional functionalities design

A hypermedia application, in a broader sense, might include a number of functionalities other than pure navigation. They might significantly help for the success of a hypermedia, and their design should not be neglected, even if it can be carried on as in traditional software applications. Examples of these functionalities are: query based access, printing of visited node, possibility for the user of creating guided tours and access structures on the fly, integration with external, pre-existing applications. In general, these features depend on the specific application domain and on the needs of end users.

3.7 Lay-out design

This phase [28] defines the aesthetic appearance of the application: for example, the way information must be arranged on the window(s) displayed on the screen, the way links and functionalities are visualised (e.g., through active icons), their placement on the window, etc. A typical style of approaching the design of these aspects is to create *visual templates* [14, 35], i.e., graphical objects (created either on the computer or on paper) that provide the look-and-feel of the application, showing the lay-out of visual pages that correspond to the various types of objects and of related links.

Lay-out design should convey as much as possible the intended semantics of the information structure(s) and connections that are to be displayed on the screen. For example, it should try to define visual effects that make explicit the distinctions among different classes of information objects and different categories of links.

4 Conclusions

Hyperbase schema design in-the-large, reading schema design, instances design in-the-large, and access structures design, are largely independent from the specific systems chosen to develop and to deliver the application. On the contrary, all other phases or sub-phases are dependent, at different degrees, on implementation choices. It is obvious, for example, that including multimedia material in a given application, designing special visual effects or sophisticated dynamic behaviour in-the-large or in-the-small, and providing special functionalities, cannot abstract from the actual power of the available implementation system. It is therefore difficult to define *a priori* the actual constraints of these latter design tasks, and it might happen that some choices concerning in-the-small aspects, lay-out design, dynamics design and functionalities design, have to be revised at implementation time, after the actual development system has been chosen.

Hypermedia structured design is founded on a critical reflection on our experiences in developing medium and large size hypermedia applications in a variety of fields [4, 22, 24, 30, 33], and on the analysis of hypermedia development works carried on by other partners of ESPRIT projects HYTEA [26], HIFI [5, 22], and MINERS [30]. Our experience has shown that significant gains in the quality of hypermedia applications, and a tangible reduction in costs and effort, can be achieved with a systematic, structured approach to design. It allows a better planning of the overall activities involved in the development process, and improvement of communication and cooperation among the various members of a project. At the same time, the various phases of structured design can be viewed also as a check-list of tasks to be performed, thus provide ways to evaluate the work done or in progress.

On the other hand, it is obvious that some tools should be provided to the designer to support the various phases of structured design. Some work in this direction has been done by the ESPRIT project HYTEA, which has defined and implemented a set of tools that explicitly support the design of hyperbase schemas, reading structures, instances, and access structures. The HIFI project has continued the HYTEA work in the direction of supporting the design and creation of dynamic hypermedia interfaces to data bases. Its main difference with respect to HYTEA is the goal of supporting the creation of instances at execution time, by dynamically retrieving their content from pre-existing information bases.

All these tools are based on HDM (Hypertext Design Model) [7, 8, 9, 10, 12, 34] and on its updated version, HDM+ [23]. HDM provides primitives to define entity types (representation structures for domain objects), web types (connection structures representing domain relationships and access structures), instances of these types, derivation expressions to define reading structures, and access structures ("indexes" and "guided tours"). HDM+ also supports authoring-in-the-small, by providing primitives to structure information contents at node level. Within the MINERS project, the general approach has been specialised for supporting design and creation of hypermedia publishing platforms.

HDM and HDM+ have reached some sort of maturity, and can provide significant guidelines in designing static aspects of hypermedia applications. Dynamic behaviour design and lay-out design still need to be supported. Lay-out design is mostly an "creative" task, which can be hardly standardised and modelled in a "scientific way". Our believe is that it should be addressed by specialists in visual communication, rather than in computer science. By the way, this also implies that hypermedia design will become, more and more, a team work in which different, heterogeneous expertises are necessarily involved. Recent researches have addressed the problem of modelling dynamic behavior, mainly focusing on in-the-small dynamic aspects of multimedia behaviour [6, 16, 20, 21, 31, 32]. To our knowledge, however, a model and a complete methodology that support all aspects of hypermedia application design is still absent.

Acknowledgements: This work has been partially supported by the Commission of European Communities within ESPRIT projects HYTEA, HIFI, and MINERS. We are grateful to all partners of these projects, and to the past and present members of the Multimedia Laboratory at Politecnico di Milano. We thanks the reviewers of this paper for their helpful comments and suggestions.

References

[1] Buchanan M.C., Zellweger P., (1992) "Specifying Temporar Behaviour in hypermedia Documents". In Proc. ACM ECHT '92, Milano, Dec. 1992
[2] Buchanan M.C., Zellweger P., (1993) "Automatic Temporal Lay-out Mechanisms". In Proc. ACM Multimedia '93, Anaheim, 1993
[3] Bush V., (1945) "As We May Think", In The Atlantic Monthly, Jul. 1945
[4] Caloini A., Garzotto F., Paolini P., (1991) "Hypermedia Course Notes: The Experience of Politecnico di Milano". In Proc. Italian Conf. on Hypertext in Education and Research, Torino, 1991, pp. 35-42
[5] Cavallaro U., Garzotto F., Paolini P., Totaro D., (1993) "HIFI: Hypertext Interface for Information Systems". In IEEE Software, Nov. 1993
[6] De Mey V., Gibbs S., (1993) "A Multimedia Component Kit". In Proc. ACM Multimedia '93, Anaheim, 1993
[7] Garzotto F., Paolini P., Schwabe D., Berstein M. (1991) "Chapter 13: Tools for Designer". In "Hypertext/Hypermedia Handbook" Berk E. Devlin J. eds., McGraw Hill, 1991
[8] Garzotto F., Paolini P., Schwabe D., (1991) "HDM - A Model for the Design of Hypertext Applications". In Proc. ACM Hypertext '91, S. Antonio, Dec. 1991. ACM-Press, New York.
[9] Garzotto F., Paolini P., Schwabe D., (1991) "Authoring-in-the-large: Software Engineering Techniques for Hypermedia Application Design". In Proc. 6th IEEE Int. Workshop on Sw Specification and Design, Oct. 1991
[10] Garzotto F., Paolini P., Schwabe D., (1993) "HDM - A Model Based Approach to Hypermedia Application Design". In ACM Trans. Off. Inf. Systems, Vol. 11, N. 1, Jan. 1993
[11] Garzotto F., Mainetti L., Paolini P., (1993) "Navigation Patterns in Hypermedia Data Bases". In Proc. 26th IEEE Int. Conf. on System Sciences, Maui, Jan. 1993
[12] Garzotto F., Mainetti L., Paolini P., (1993) "HDM2: Extending the E-R Approach to Hypermedia Application Design". In Proc. 12th Int. Conf. on the Entity-Relationship Approach, Arlington, Dec. 1993
[13] Garzotto F., Mainetti L., Paolini P., (1994) "Navigation in Hypermedia Applications: Modelling and Semantics". In Journal of Organizational Computing (to appear)
[14] Gibbs S., Breiteneder C., Tsichritzis D., (1993) "Data Modeling of Visual Objects". In "Visual Objects" Tsichritzis D. eds., Universite' de Genève, 1993

[15] Halatz F., Schwartz M., (1994) "The Dexter Hypertext Reference Model". In Comm. ACM, Vol. 37, N. 2, Feb. 1994

[16] Hamaka R., Rekimoto J., (1993) "Object Composition and Playback Models for Handling Multimedia Data". In Proc. ACM Multimedia '93, Anaheim, 1993

[17] Hardman L., Bulterman D.C.A., Van Rossum G., (1993) "The Amsterdam Hypermedia Model: Extending Hypertext to Support Real Multimedia". In Hypermedia, Vol. 5, N. 1, 1993

[18] Hardman L., Van Rossum G., Bulterman C.A., (1993) "Structured Multimedia Authoring". In Proc. ACM Multimedia '93, Aug. 1993

[19] Hardman L., Bulterman D.C.A., Van Rossum G., (1993) "Links in Hypermedia: the Requirement for Context". In Proc. ACM Hypertext '93, Seattle, 1993

[20] Hardman L., Bulterman D.C.A., Van Rossum G., (1994) "Adding Time and Content to the Dexter Model". In Comm. ACM, Vol. 37, N. 2, Feb. 1994

[21] Hardman L., (1994) "Experiences in Authoring Hypermedia: Creating better Presentations". This volume, 1994

[22] HIFI Working Group, (1993) "Specification and Design of a Hypertext Interface to a Banking Information System", Tech. Annex, ESPRIT Project P6532 HIFI, 1993

[23] HIFI Working Group, (1993) "HDM+ User Manual", Deliverable 12 ESPRIT Project P6532 HIFI, 1993

[24] Hira K., Hara Y., Shibata N., (1993) "Media-based Navigation for Hypermedia Systems". In Proc. ACM Hypertext '93, Nov. 1993

[25] HYTEA Working Group, (1992) "A Hypermedia Database for On-line IVECO Technical Documentation", Tech. Rep. ESPRIT Project 5252 HYTEA and FIAT-IVECO Department of Technical Documentation, 1992

[26] HYTEA Working Group, (1993) "The HYTEA Authoring Tools", Final Report. ESPRIT Project 5252 HYTEA, 1993

[27] Jordan D., Russel D., (1989) "Facilitating the Development of Representations in Hypertext with IDE". In Proc. ACM Hypertext '89, Pittsburgh, 1989

[28] Kahn P., Lenk K., (1992) "Designing Information for the Computer Screen", Tutorial held at ACM ECHT '92, Milano, 1992

[29] Marshall C., Halasz F., Roger R., Janssen W., (1991) "Aquanet: A Hyepretx Tools to hold Your Knowedge in Place". In Proc. ACM Hypertext' 91, S. Antonio, 1991

[30] MINERS Working Group, (1993) "MINERS: An Editorial Platform for Electronic and Traditional Publishing", Tech. Annex ESPRIT Project 6530 MINERS, 1993

[31] Ogawa R., Harada H., Keneto A., (1990) "Scenario-based Hypermedia: A Model and a Systems". In "Hypertext: Concepts, Systems, and Applications" Rizk A. Streitz N. Andre' J. eds., Cambridge University Press, 1990

[32] Prabhakaran B., Rahavan S.V., (1993) "Synchronization Models for Multimedia Presentation with User Participation". In Proc. ACM Multimedia '93, Anaheim, 1993

[33] RAI - Radio Televisione Italiana (1991) "The Multimedia Encyclopedia of Philosophical Sciences", Tech. Rep. RAI-DSE (Department of School and Education) presented at "International Grand Prix Italia for Video Communication," Sep. 1991

[34] Schwabe D., Caloini A., Garzotto F., Paolini P. (1992) "Hypertext development using a Model-based Approach". In Software Practice and Experience, Vol. 22, N. 11, 1992

[35] Smith Katlin K., Garret N.L., (1991) "Hypermedia Templates: an Author's Tool". In Proc. ACM Hypertext '91, S. Antonio, 1991

[36] Streitz N., Haake J., Hanneman J., Lemke A., Schuler W., Schütt H., Thüring M., (1992) "SEPIA: A Cooperative Authoring Environment". In. Proc. ACM ECHT '92, Milano, 1992

[37] Thüring M., Haake J.M., Hannemann J., (1991) "What's Eliza Doing in the Chinese Room? Incoherent Hyperdocuments - and How to Avoid Them". In. Proc. ACM Hypertext '91, S. Antonio, 1991. ACM-Press, New York.

[38] Trigg R.H., (1988) "Guided Tours and Tabletops: Tools for Communicating in a Hypertext Environment". In ACM Trans. Off. Inf. Systems, Vol. 6, N. 4., Oct. 1988

[39] Van Rossum G., Jansen J., Mullender K.S., Bulterman C.A., (1993) "CMIFed: A Presentation Environment for Portable Hypermedia Documents". In Proc. ACM Multimedia '93, Aug. 1993

[40] Zellweger P.T., (1989) "Scripted Documents: A Hypermedia Path Mechanism". In Proc. ACM Hypertext '89, Pittsburgh, 1989

Experiences in Authoring Hypermedia: Creating Better Presentations

Lynda Hardman
CWI, Amsterdam, The Netherlands

1 Introduction

The first part of this chapter discusses the lessons that have been learned by the author during her involvement with a number of academic and commercial hypertext projects. This experience has been gained through conducting controlled reader studies, where inadequacies of the final document interface can be found, and through observations of authors trying to create material in the new medium and not being aware of sources of applicable design knowledge. This part concentrates on what needs to be considered during the different stages of design and assumes that the author is following some form of structured design process, such as that described in (Garzotto et al. 1994). The second part motivates and describes a structured approach to authoring hypermedia. While the editing environment described does not explicitly support the requirements discussed in the first part, the author can more easily experiment with and change both the structure and layout of the presentation until s/he is satisfied. A final section looks to further possible improvements in simplifying hypermedia authoring.

2 Designing for the Reader

Although creating hypermedia presentations is a complex task there exists little advice about what factors authors need to take into consideration when designing and creating such presentations. Authoring hypermedia information can be compared with other creative processes, such as writing a book, structured programming, designing an exhibition or making a film. In all these cases authors need to be clear about the ideas they want to get across, how these will be structured, the best media for expressing each idea, how these will be layed out, and navigation routes through the material. Before embarking on the creation process, authors need to consider all of these diverse design aspects.

Three main issues of hypermedia design are addressed in this section:
- How should information be structured?
- How should the information be presented?
- What tools do readers need for exploring the information?

2.1   Information structure

An obvious advantage of using hypermedia is that it can reflect the "natural" structure of the subject matter being dealt with. For example, the medical domain often uses distinct functional and anatomical structures for classifying information, and one, or indeed both, of these structures can be reflected in the hypermedia structure. This advantage is more apparent in complex domains where there are multiple ways of structuring the material. It was for this reason that the creator of the neuroanatomy tutorial in (Hardman 1988) chose to use hypertext as the communication medium. She found it difficult to explain all the different related aspects of neuroanatomy to her students and sought a way of more directly communicating the different approaches and their connections.

Given that this is what the author wishes to achieve, how does an author know when hypermedia information is "well-structured"? At a high level this can be expressed as giving a coherent reflection of the subject matter, that there are sufficient options for navigation and that the structure supports the task the user is carrying out. While this does not take us much further towards concrete design rules, we *can* learn from analysing what has worked, or not, in previous designs, as discussed in this section.

Effective structure

Many systems enable the creation of hypertext structure but give an author no support in determining what would be the most effective structure to create. Creating successful structure is often still a matter of seeing what works, but a small number of studies have been carried out to look at the positive and negative effects of different approaches to structuring in hypertext. For example, the study described in (Edwards & Hardman 1989) was devised to look at how hypertext structures can help or hinder readers in accessing information. Different groups were exposed to the same information structured in three different ways: a hierarchy access structure, an index structure and a dual access structure (index plus hierarchy). The hope was that the dual access structure would be the preferred form of structuring, because it offered more ways of accessing the information. In fact this was perceived by the readers to be the least helpful of the structures, probably because they had too little time with the material to be able to adjust to the extra complexity.

This experiment warns against the use of too many links which, while bringing the advantages of more flexible access structures, have to be weighed against the cost of the extra complexity. This finding is confirmed by Wright (1991), who demonstrated that "one click away" is not always as close for the reader as the designer may think— for inexperienced computer users accessing information via a link involves a cognitive load, thus disturbing readers in their train of thought.

An example of successful consistent structuring of information is the Glasgow Online hypertext (Hardman 1989). The hypertext has several different sections with information about the city of Glasgow, and by using the same types of structuring throughout the hypertext readers could easily use sections they hadn't previously visited based on their experience with sections they had.

Content-based vs. navigational structures

When designing hyper-structure it is useful to distinguish between different types of structure — in particular content-based and navigational structures. A similar distinction is made by (Hannemann & Thuring 1994) as *factual* and *rhetorical* structuring, and by (Garzotto et al. 1994) as *hyperbase schema design, reading schema(s) design, instance schemas design* and *authoring in the small*, versus *access structure(s) design*. The content-based and navigational-based structures are illustrated by the hierarchy and index access structures, respectively, in the Edwards & Hardman experiment. The hierarchical structuring is a content-based structure since it gathers parts of the material into meaningful groups. The index is a navigational structure in that it gives the reader access to the information but implies no further relation between the source and destination of the link. The design process should start by considering the content-based structures, since these reflect the material the reader is interested in, and then adding the navigational structures "on top" of these.

Application of HCI principles

Just as in the building of any computer application, a hypermedia author can be helped by considering human computer interaction principles and guidelines. (Hardman & Sharratt 1989) give a distillation of these which have been specialised to hypertext design[†]. Examples of design principles applied to hypertext are (paraphrased):

Mental processing The hypertext should not complicate the reader's information gathering tasks nor impose excessive mental processing requirements. The author should: (i) minimize the overall mental load by reducing the requirement for readers to remember objects, actions, codes and abbreviations; (ii) minimize the task-specific mental processing by arranging for efficient completion of a typical reader task.

Flexibility The hypertext should: (i) be capable of adaptation to the needs of readers of different types and levels of experience; (ii) provide multiple paths that allow readers to by-pass parts of the hypertext.

A selection of these design principles have been applied in the creation of a hypermedia document describing a tour of Amsterdam (Figure 1): the amount of information presented is kept to a minimum; different routes are provided (the reader is always able to return to the initial screen, can choose to go back to the beginning of the walking tour, or can go on to the next stop on the tour).

---

†. The principles and guidelines discussed in the paper need to be extended to hypermedia presentations which also include dynamic media such as sound and video.

Although the design can be improved by the application of these principles and guidelines, the most influential factors on hypertext usability are individual differences among users, so that, disregarding how much effort went into "good" design, the system still needs to be evaluated with representative users (Nielsen 1989).

2.2   Information presentation

However good the structural design of a hypertext document is, it still needs to be expressed using good presentation. There are two separate aspects of information presentation which need to be addressed. First, exactly what information needs to be present on the screen, for example, sufficient contextual information at the destination of a link for readers to be able to orient themselves. Second, the (typo)-graphic design of this information, for example, titles should be placed at the top of the window in a large, bold font.

When deciding on what and how much information should be presented, issues such as screen clutter have to be weighed against the cognitive overhead of not having the information visible. (Hardman & Sharratt 1989) contains a relevant selection of guidelines (distilled from existing human computer interaction guidelines), for example, in paraphrased form:

- Necessary information, for example, the name of the current section, a title, the information of interest, and the link markers should be displayed.
- Different link types, for example those leading to a small note or those that jump to an entirely new section, should be apparent (before the reader is committed to following the link).

Having decided upon what information is to be presented this has to be translated into some visual form that allows the reader to interact with it. For example, that a link can be followed has to be apparent to the reader. This requires either some form of visual encoding for the link-ends, or informing the reader which objects are likely to form the ends of links. When a visual encoding is taken from existing typographic conventions readers have problems recognising

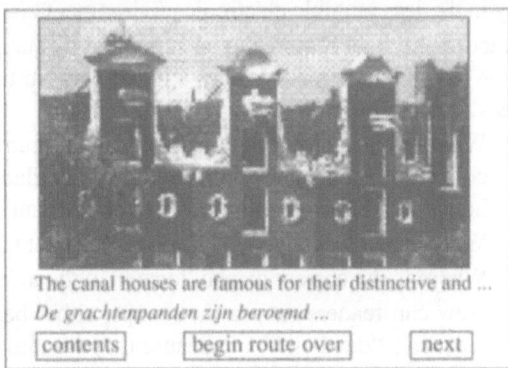

Figure 1. The gables clip from a walking tour in Amsterdam.

the link-ends. Advantages of this approach, however, are that no new symbols or markup are required and that the screen remains relatively clutter-free. Most systems introduce new symbols or box items to denote link-ends (where some are more aesthetically pleasing than others). Creative approaches to designing link markers are described in (Evenson & Rheinfrank 1989) and (Kahn 1994).

Some consequences of confronting readers with less than optimal presentation conventions are described in (Hardman 1989). For example, linked items and non-linked items were often confused because inconsistent typographic styles were used. Some conclusions about presentation issues from this study are the following:

• Conventions can be used to convey information and reduce screen clutter.
• Conventions need to be explained to the reader and used consistently.
• Contextual information can be passive, or active, allowing readers to use it to move to different sections (for example, a list of section headings indicating the current section could be used to jump to the other sections).
• Readers should be able to tell which screen items are link-markers.
• Inactive items that require emphasis should not look like link-markers.
• Different styles of link-markers (indicating different link types) can be used at the cost of added complexity.

For information about on-screen design in general (Kahn & Lenk 1993) pulls together a wealth of experience in the area.

2.3   Navigation tools

In the online environment there is no physical presence of stored information; it is difficult to give an overview about how much information there is, or "where" some pieces of information lie with respect to each other. To overcome some of the shortcomings of the electronic environment the reader needs to be provided with, for example, a suite of (simple to use) navigation tools. These could provide functions similar to those readers are already familiar with in a paper environment (e.g. bookmarks, margin notes, paper clips) along with new functions which become necessary in the less tangible electronic environment.

The type of functionality that requires to be supported by such a suite of tools can be based on the notion that a reader traces a linear path (in time) through the material (chapters 4, 5 and 6 of (Kibby et al. 1991)):

Looking forward	What subject areas are available in the current information collection, how much information is available in each, and how much information is likely to be relevant?
Moving forward	Where can readers go, and how they can get there?
Current position	Where is the current display located in the information space?
Moving back	How can readers retrace their steps, either because they have reached a "dead-end", or because they want to revisit a screen?
Looking back	Which material, and how much, has already been covered?

Some form of graphical overview diagram would be able to convey much of this information, by representing the information space in some way and to show whether they have been visited or not, for example by shading-in different areas; possible future routes (perhaps derived from a query) could also be shown. The reader's current position can be given through the use of sufficient context information, or also by annotating an overview diagram. Other possible tools are bookmark and annotation lists.

An example of a suite of tools built in a working system can be seen in the NCSA Mosaic (Hughes 1994) program which has been created to allow the reader to browse through information distributed throughout the (internationally networked) world. It thus has to cope with handling a very large information space. There are specific navigation tools for going back and forth through already-visited nodes, and a separate, persistent list of bookmarks (called the Hotlist). For showing where the reader has already been (independent of the particular path taken) link markers are shaded differently.

The experiences gained from using a different, prototyped, suite of tools is given in chapter 10 of (Kibby et al. 1991). This suite of tools consisted of a history list, a means of marking the current screen in order to come back to it later ("bookmark"), the ability to view the list of marked screens (and go to a selected screen), and an indication in the history list of which screens were marked. When a screen was marked, for inclusion in the bookmark list, a symbol was also drawn on the screen itself. The conclusions from this work are that such tools are needed, but that in this particular study the readers did not spend sufficient time with the material, so they rarely needed to find their way back to previously studied sections. A probable explanation for this is that the tasks they were given were easily carried out with only the standard hyperlinks and no need was found to use the tools which had been supplied. This agrees with one of the conclusions in (Wright 1991), which states that users were grateful for the introduction of new tools only when they were given a problem that their current tool set was too weak to offer assistance.

3   Improvements to authoring paradigms

When designing a hypermedia presentation for the reader the author has to supply a good structure, a clear and aesthetically pleasing presentation and an adequate means of moving around and annotating the information. Given all these differing requirements, how can we make life easier for the author? We discuss briefly the requirements for authoring hypermedia after which we describe our hypermedia authoring system CMIFed.

3.1   Authoring environment requirements

Early hypermedia authoring systems did not support easy restructuring of the hypertext information— once the information structure had been created it was difficult to reorganise it. For example, the design of the tutorial in (Hardman 1988) was changed a number of times because the author was exploring the possibilities of the system she was using — Guide (OWL 1986). This meant that the information which had already created had to be laboriously cut and pasted into a new structure. Because of these inflexible authoring systems authors were constrained to get the hypertext design right the first time.

Another constraint imposed by most hypermedia authoring systems is that there is no separation of structure from layout — by placing an item on the screen the author specifies both its position in the presentation's structure and its layout attributes. The authoring process is simplified considerably if the layout of the items is under separate control. This is analogous to most word processors which allow the definition of different paragraph styles associated with different structure levels in the text.

A third feature which is often lacking in authoring systems is the ability to display the final presentation on a number of different platforms. This is a highly desirable feature — especially after the considerable amount of work the author has put into the creation of the presentation. This requires a platform independent representation of the presentation and the ability to re-create the author's intended layout styles for any end-user platform.

In summary, when creating a hypermedia presentation, including multiple, dynamic media such as sound and video, authors need to be able to combine items in a presentation, and to link from one presentation to another. Authors require some way of grouping nodes together, specifying timing constraints among the media items, creating links to a complete presentation and specifying screen layout.

3.2   A Hypermedia Editor: CMIFed

The CMIFed (CWI Multimedia Interchange Format editor) hypermedia authoring system (Van Rossum et al. 1993) was developed to satisfy the above requirements. It gives an author the ability to create explicit structure and timing relationships in a complex hypermedia document, and allows the editing of these in a straightforward way. The system uses a structured authoring approach (Hardman et al. 1993) where the author can create structure which can be filled in later with media items, or media items can be created and then later collected into one or more structures (although this flexibility does not preclude the need for a good design).

It is based on a platform-independent model of hypermedia (Hardman et al. 1994). This can be compared with the Dexter model (Halasz & Schwartz 1994) which provides a similar level of description for hypertext, but does not include dynamic media, or the notion of combining nodes into presentation layouts (though does not exclude the latter).

The CMIFed authoring environment separates out different tasks of the authoring process and presents the corresponding information in three separate, but connected, views. The *hierarchy view* allows the author to define the structural relations between the media items making up the presentation. This structure is used to derive basic timing information which is displayed in the *channel view*. The channel view shows the resource usage of the media items composing the presentation, and allows precise synchronization relations to be specified. The *player* is used to preview the presentation.

In order to describe the authoring environment of CMIFed we discuss it in terms of the following example. Figure 1 shows a "typical" multimedia presentation—a clip from a walking tour of Amsterdam. The presentation is formed from a collection of media items displayed on the screen, in this case an image and some text items. A spoken commentary, in either Dutch or English, is also given, and the subtitles change in time with the spoken words. The boxed text items (link markers) are linked to other parts of the multimedia presentation.

Hierarchy View

The hierarchy view, figure 2, is the primary authoring view, allowing the author to create multimedia presentations using a top-down or bottom-up approach. The hierarchically structured nodes of the presentation are represented as nested boxes, where children of a node are played either sequentially or in parallel.

Authoring is carried out by creating parallel and sequential structures (composite nodes) and assigning media items as the leaf nodes of this structure. Media items assigned at higher levels of the structure are displayed for the duration of the structure in which they are defined, e.g. the *contents...* and *begin...* items in figures 1, 2 and 3.

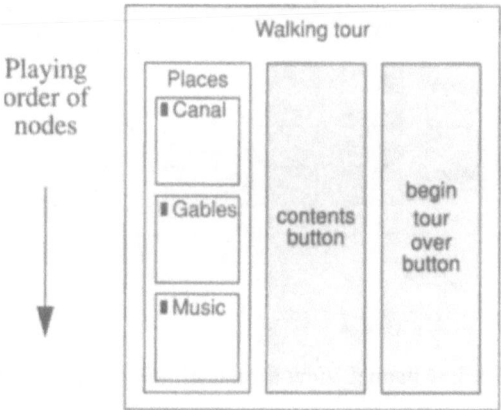

Figure 2. **Hierarchy view for the *Walking tour* sequence.**

Places, contents... and *begin...* are played in parallel. *Canal, Gables* and *Music* are played one after the other. A small dark box indicates hidden sub-structure.

Channel view

CMIFed uses channels, logical output devices, upon which visual items can be displayed and audible items played. The channel view, figure 3, shows the logical resource usage of a presentation, including timing relations derived from the structure defined in the hierarchy view. More complex timing constraints can be specified using synchronization arcs (the arrows in the figure). The media items making up the presentation are shown in the channel view with their precise durations and timing relationships.

A channel enables the author to define high-level presentation characteristics for each media type, so that presentations can be composed without having to specify details for each item: for example, a text channel defines a rectangular area on the screen and a font. Also, if the style of, for example, a heading is to be changed throughout the presentation then the change need be made only once for the relevant channel.

Player

The player allows the author to play a selection from the hierarchy or channel view, without having to go through a complete sequence. The author or end user can turn channels on and off, for example allowing the selection of alternative languages, e.g. UK and NL in figure 3.

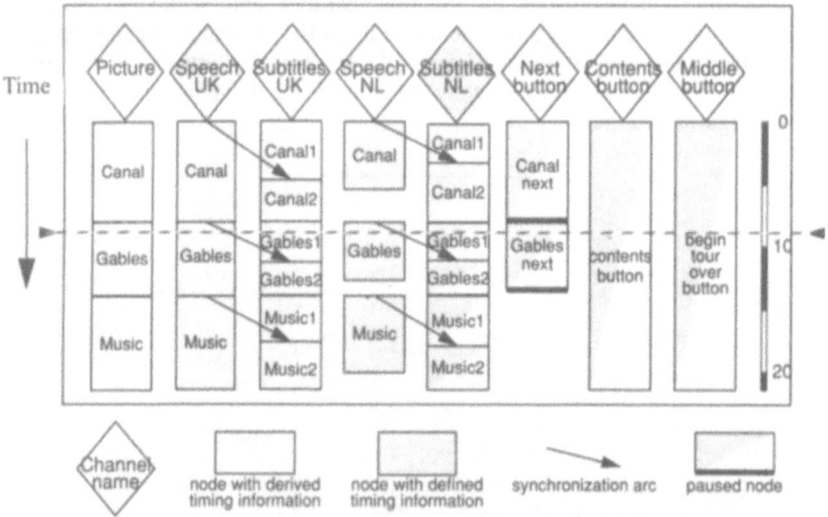

Figure 3. Channel View for the *Walking tour* sequence.

The diamonds at the top of the figure show the channel names (inactive channels are shaded). The data nodes assigned to the channels are represented as boxes beneath the diamonds. The height of a box represents its duration. A fully-shaded box has its duration explicitly defined, either through its data type, for sound and video, or through the author assigning a specific duration. A box with a shaded triangle has inherited its duration from its parent in the presentation's structure.

4 Future of Hypermedia Authoring

From the work presented here we can analyse what is expected of a well-designed hypermedia presentation, we can separate out the different tasks required of the author, and we can produce an authoring system support these tasks explicitly. The author, however, is still required to do all the authoring work. A following step would be to allow the author to specify high-level requirements for the information and layout, and have the system generate the details of the presentation from this. The ultimate goal for high-volume applications, such as the daily news, would be that the end user becomes the author — defining their information requirements and having the system present the information with no further human intervention. (Haake et al. 1994) have already investigated this approach and related work is reported in this volume (Kamps & Reichenberger 1994).

With automatic methods we cannot hope to replicate human creativity, but for large volume, lower quality applications we can aspire to reduce the tedium of the hypermedia author's task.

References

Edwards, D. M. & Hardman, L. (1989). 'Lost in Hyperspace': Cognitive Mapping and Navigation in a Hypertext Environment. In R. McAleese (Ed.) *Hypertext: theory into practice*, pp. 105-125. Oxford: Intellect, 1989.

Evenson, S. & Rheinfrank, J. (1989). Towards a Design Language for Representing Hypermedia Cues. In *Proceedings of the 2nd ACM Conference on Hypertext (Hypertext '89)*, pp. 83-92, Pittsburg, PA, Nov. 5-8, 1989.

Garzotto, F., Mainetti, L. & Paolini, P. (1994). Hypermedia Application Design: A Structured Approach. This volume.

Haake, A., Hüser, C. & Reichenberger, K. (1994). The Individualized Electronic Newspaper: An Example of an Active Publication. To appear in Special Issue of *Electronic Publishing: Origination, Dissemination and Design* on Active Documents.

Halasz, F. & Schwartz, M. (1994). The Dexter Hypertext Reference Model. *Communications of the ACM*, 37(2): 30-39.

Hannemann, J. & Thüring, M. (1994). What Matters in Developing User Interfaces for Hyperdocument Presentation? This volume.

Hardman, L. (1988). Hypertext Tips: Experiences in Developing a Hypertext Tutorial. In Jones, D. M. & Winder, R. (Eds.) *People and Computers IV*, pp. 437-451. Cambridge: Cambridge University Press (1988).

Hardman, L. (1989). Evaluating the usability of the Glasgow Online hypertext. *Hypermedia 1(1)*: 34-63.

Hardman, L. & Sharratt, B. (1989). User-Centred Hypertext Design: the application of HCI design principles and guidelines. In R. McAleese and C. Green (Eds.) *Hypertext State of the Art* , pp. 252 - 259. Oxford: Intellect 1990.

Hardman, L., Van Rossum, G. & Bulterman, D. C. A. (1993). Structured Multimedia Authoring. In *Proceedings of the 1st ACM Conference on Multimedia (Multimedia '93)*, pp. 283-289, Anaheim, CA, Aug 1-6, 1993.

Hardman, L., Bulterman, D. C. A. & Van Rossum, G. (1994). The Amsterdam Hypermedia Model: Adding Time and Context to the Dexter Model. *Communications of the ACM*, 37(2): 50-63.

Hughes K. (1994). Distributed Systems. *SIGLink Newsletter*, 3(1): 4-8.

Kahn, P. & Lenk, K. (1993). Typography for the Computer Screen: Applying the Lessons of Print to Electronic Documents. *Seybold Report on Desktop Publishing*: 7(11): 3-16.

Kahn, P. (1994). Three Fundamental Elements of Visual Rhetoric in Hypertext. This volume.

Kamps, T. & Reichenberger, K. (1994). A dialogue approach to graphical information access. This volume.

Kibby, M.R., Hardman, L., Tanner, G., Mayes, J.T., Knussen, C. & Grant S. (1991). Final report on user interfaces for hypermedia. DELTA Project P7061 (D1014), The SAFE Project, HYP/21, March 1991. (Available from author.)

OWL (1986). Guide Users Manual. OWL International Inc., Bellevue, Washington, USA, 1986.

Nielsen, J. (1989). The Matters that Really Matter for Hypertext Usability. In *Proceedings of the 2nd ACM Conference on Hypertext (Hypertext '89)*, pp. 239-248, Pittsburg, PA, Nov. 5-8, 1989.

Van Rossum, G., Jansen, J., Mullender, K. S. & Bulterman, D. C. A. (1993). CMIFed: A Presentation Environment for Portable Hypermedia Documents. In *Proceedings of the 1st ACM Conference on Multimedia (Multimedia '93)*, pp. 183-188, Anaheim, CA, Aug 1-6, 1993.

Wright, P. (1991). Cognitive Overheads and Prostheses: Some Issues in Evaluating Hypertexts. In *Proceedings of the 3rd ACM Conference on Hypertext (Hypertext '91)*, pp. 1-12, San Antonio, TX, Dec. 15-18, 1991.

What Matters in Developing Interfaces for Hyperdocument Presentation?

Jörg Hannemann, Manfred Thüring
empirica GmbH, Communications and Technology Research, Bonn, Germany

1 Introduction

For the last few years, interface design in the domain of hypertext has mainly focused on the solution of the navigation problem. Moreover, browsing has been regarded as the most central user activity. While this claim may hold for hypertexts that do not demand a reader's full attention, such as information kiosks or electronic advertisements, its validity must definitely be doubted for the majority of hyperdocuments. "Reading ... hypertext about matters that deeply matter to us" (Bernstein, 1991b, p.365) requires a lot more concentration and mental effort than careless node hopping. Therefore, navigation should not be regarded as an end in itself but as a mere precondition for the reader's actual goal: the comprehension of the hyperdocument. Interface design focusing on this neglected issue may help to avoid what Foss (1989) has termed the "Art Museum Phenomenon" of hypertext, i.e., that "after you have spent a long day in a large art museum gazing a hundreds of paintings . . . at the end of the day you may not be able to tell someone what you have seen" (p. 408). To overcome this phenomenon interfaces are required which significantly increase the readability of hyperdocuments.

A first step towards that goal is the generation of a comprehensive **design space** representing the central problems that must be solved in developing interfaces for hyperdocument presentation. In this paper, we will propose such a design space in terms of a **hierarchical issue structure**. Moreover, we will discuss several design decisions that might provide adequate answers to some of the issues. We hope that our approach will inspire other designers and will help to focus the discussion on design issues which are essential for developing interfaces that will increase the readability of hyperdocuments.

2 Issues for the Design of Presentation Interfaces for Coherent Hyperdocuments

One major purpose - or even *the* major purpose - of reading is comprehension. In cognitive science, comprehension is often characterized as the construction of a mental model which represents the facts and semantic relations described in a text (Johnson-Laird, 1983; van Dijk & Kintsch, 1983). The readability of a document depends on the mental effort spent on the construction process. This relationship is addressed by the first two issues in figure 1, i.e. if we want to increase the readibility of a hyperdocument (I1) the main issue is how to support readers in the construction of their mental models (I2).

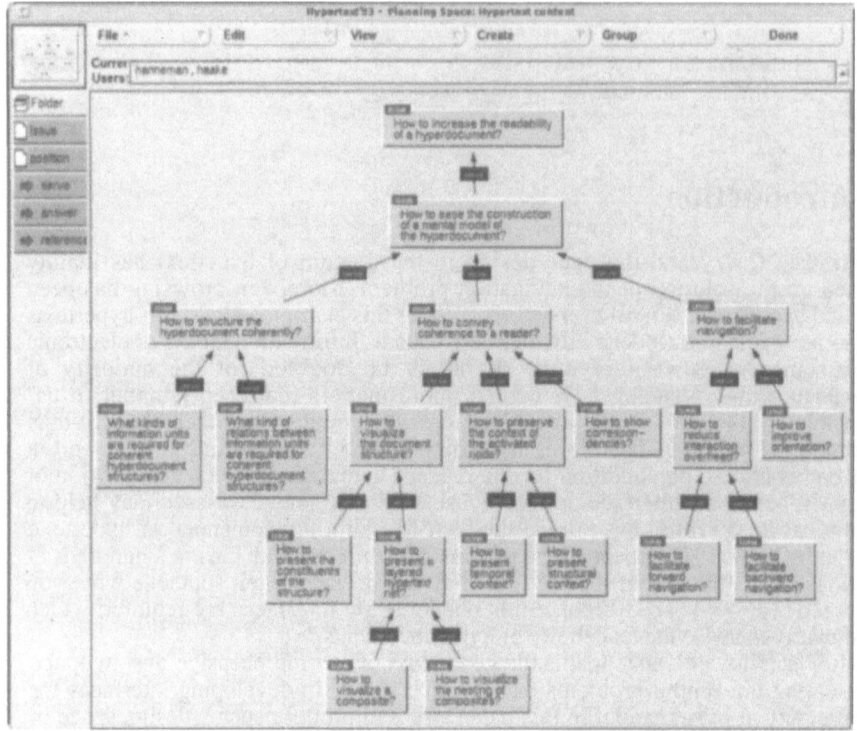

Figure 1: Issues for designing coherent hyperdocuments

Empirical studies have shown that a reader's ability to understand and remember a text depends on its degree of **coherence**. In psycholinguistics coherence is not regarded as an isolated text feature, but as the result of a cognitive construction process (see VanDijk & Kintsch, 1983): A document is coherent if a reader can derive a mental model from it that corresponds to facts and relations in a possible world. This construction process is facilitated when the document is set out in a well-defined structure and provides rhetorical cues reflecting these structural properties. Hence, for reducing the mental effort of comprehension, it is not sufficient to impose a coherent structure on a document; it is also necessary to *convey* that structure to the reader by means of appropriate cues (Charney, 1987).

Beside these two factors, another determinant directly affects the construction of a mental model which is related to the limited capacity of human information processing. Every extra effort required in the course of processing a document reduces the mental resources available for comprehension. Therefore, all additional activities create an extra workload which the reader has to cope with. With respect to hypertext, additional activities mainly concern the reader's navigation. Empirical research indicates that these additional activities may "interrupt the train of thought" (Gordon, Gustavel, Moore & Hankey, 1988; Monk Walsh & Dix, 1988) activities create an extra workload which the reader has to cope with. With respect to hypertext, additional activities mainly concern the reader's navigation. Empirical research indicates that these additional activities may "interrupt the train of thought" (Gordon, Gustavel, Moore & Hankey, 1988; Monk Walsh & Dix, 1988) and by this way may impede the comprehension process. Hence, navigation in a hyperdocument should be convenient and require as little effort as possible.

In summary, the issue of facilitating the construction of a mental model (I2) can be refined into three interrelated subissues which are discussed in the next sections:

- How to create a coherent hyperdocument (I3)

- How to convey coherence in hyperdocument presentation (I4)

- How to facilitate navigation (I5).

2.1 How to create a coherent hyperdocument

In producing a coherent hyperdocument, an author must master two problems: the creation of a coherent document structure (I6) and the appropriate naming of the created structural elements (I7).

2.1.1 How to establish coherence by structuring

Two different activities may be involved in creating the structure of a hyperdocument which we call **factual structuring** and **rhetorical structuring**. Factual structuring identifies the information units which form the building blocks of the hyperdocument as well as the semantic relations between these units. As an example, consider two hypertext nodes: "Expert systems" and "MYCIN". While the first one gives an overview of the major characteristics of expert systems, the second one contains a short description of MYCIN (an expert system in the domain of medicine (Buchanan & Shortliffe, 1984). Several semantic relations between both texts may exist, e.g., the characteristics of expert systems may be "illustrated by" the MYCIN description or features of MYCIN may be "summarized in" the text about expert systems. Information units and relations of that kind establish a structure that is basically focussed on the semantics of the document, but does not specify in which way its elements should be processed by a reader. This requires a specific rhetorical structuring: Depending on the author's anticipation of his readers' interests and background, different reading structures are needed in which selected parts of the factual structure are presented in a linear or non-linear order. While linear rhetorical structures may be sequential, branching or conditional paths (Zellweger, 1989), non-linear ones take the form of partial nets derived from the factual structure and do not specify a particular reading-sequence, i.e. the reader can browse freely.

The distinction of factual and rhetorical structures leads to the issue of how these structures can be created-(I13 and I14). One solution is offered by **SEPIA's construction kit** (Thüring, Haake & Hannemann, 1991) which provides a set of design objects particularly dedicated to establish coherent hyperdocument structures. It consists of two parts:

(1) The content part offers design objects for creating factual structures. Its information units are atomic nodes and composite nodes. Atomic nodes represent chunks of information (e.g., text, graphics, audio, video). Composite nodes comprise references to other infomation units and are used for aggregating atomic nodes or other composites. In addition, two types of relations between information units are supported: "Node-node-links" connect two entire nodes (atomic or composite). Embedded links connect a select part of a node with another node ("embedded links"). Together these design objects enable authors to create different kinds of factual structure, i.e., hierachies as well as flat and layered nets (the latter resulting from nesting composites).

(2) The organizational part offers design objects for rhetorical structuring, called structure nodes and structure links. Structure nodes are composite nodes containing references to design objects of the content-based structure. In addition, each structure node specifies an atomic start node which is automatically opened when a reader enters the structure node. Two kinds of structure nodes are provided by the kit, each allowing different degrees of freedom with respect to navigation: While sequencing nodes represent author-defined reading sequences, exploration nodes represent a subset of the factual structure without specifying an additional ordering. Instances of both node types can be connected by structure links: Sequencing links define sequences among content or sequencing nodes. Exploration links provide access to an exploration node and are usually embedded into a sequencing node.

These design objects can be summarized in a hierarchy of associated design object classes (see figure 2). Along the hierarchy, every subclass inherits properties from its superclass.

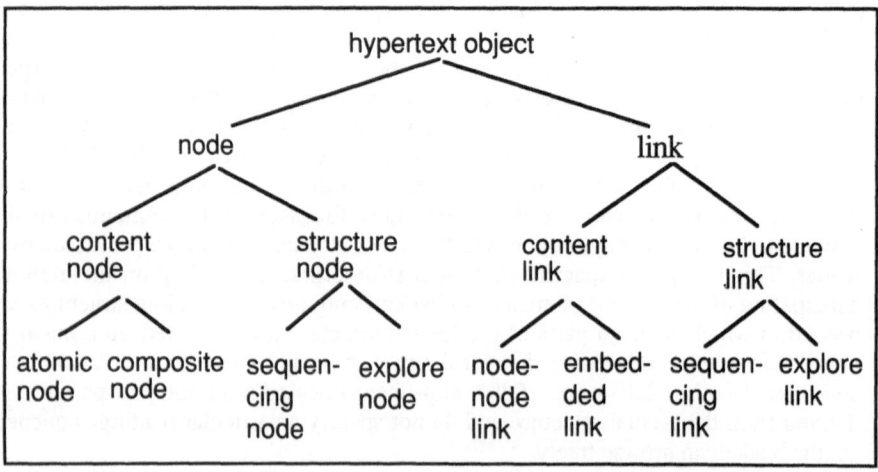

Figure 2: Hierarchy of design object classes

Providing design objects for both, factual as well as rhetorical structuring, offers an important advantage. The factual structure can be created by the author without accounting for reader-specific needs in detail. In fact, the author can use this part of the construction kit for the mere purpose of expressing his view of the domain that he writes about. Of course, the structure emerging from this process of identifying information units and semantic relations can also be presented to a reader. Nevertheless, different groups of readers may require different pieces of information as well as different orderings. In this case, the author can create reader-based, rhetorical structures by using the design objects from the organizational part the construction kit. Thus, multiple reader-specific versions can be derived from a single factual structure.

2.1.2 How to establish coherence by naming

Structure is a necessary but insufficient precondition for coherence. It informs the reader that a hyperdocument consists of separate information units some of which are related to each other, but it tells nothing about the *meaning* of these units and relations. Information of that kind can only be conveyed to a reader by appropriately naming the structural elements thus leading to the issues of how to label nodes (I15) and links (I16).

In general, a node label should represent the content of the node, i.e., it should trigger expectations about the kind of information to be found when the node is opened. A link label, on the other hand, should express a semantic relation between link source and link destination thus helping the reader to understand *why* there is a connection between both nodes.

So far, no conventions have evolved in the hypertext community which could serve as orientation for appropriate naming. In order to support authors in choosing names which increase the coherence of hyperdocuments SEPIA's construction kit therefore proposes a simple guideline for labelling: The names of source, link and destination should form a short sentence which characterizes the content of both nodes and their relationship. The example given in the previous section demonstrates this principle: "Expert systems" (source) "illustrated by" (link) "MYCIN" (destination). If this information is adequately presented to a reader, e.g., in a graphical browser (see below), it triggers a variety of inferences which increase coherence and thus support comprehension.

In addition to this guideline the construction kit offers a taxonomy of link labels which represent typical relationships between information units in a hyperdocument. The author can choose one of these labels, but is also free to create a name on his own.

2.2 How to convey coherence in hyperdocument   presentation

In order to convey the coherence of a hyperdocument to his readers, the author cannot solely rely on conventional cues, such as indicating semantic relations between pieces of information (see also Charney, 1987). Instead, he must deal with new forms of structural indicators that aim at helping readers to construct a mental model of the content of the document. Three subissues are related to this task:

- How to present the structure of a hyperdocument (I8)
- How to present the content of a hyperdocument (I9)
- How to indicate correspondencies between presented information units (I10).

2.2.1 How to present the structure of a hyperdocument

An answer to this issue is to present hypertext structures in maps or graphical browsers. Although this solution is apparently not favored by all designers of hypertext systems, several empirical studies show that content maps improve understanding (Monk, Walsh & Dix, 1988; De Lucas & Larkin, 1991). Maps and browsers provide an overview of central topics and important relationships thus increasing the global coherence (see van Dijk & Kintsch, 1983) of a hyperdocument. They support the development of a mental macrostructure which represents the gist of what is read. Into this gist, all information acquired from the document can be integrated thus gradually building up a coherent mental representation. Moreover, a gist that is derived from a graphical structure can serve as a cognitive map which eases orientation. On account of this facilitation, cognitive resources that would otherwise be bound to navigation are set free for comprehension.

The graphical presentation of structure greatly depends on the kind of design objects that are used to *create* structure. Since we are concerned with the presentation of hyperdocument structures that are developed in SEPIA (Streitz, Haake, Hannemann, Lemke Schütt, Schuler & Thüring, 1992) we will focus on the presentation of objects belonging to SEPIA's construction kit. Two subissues are important in this context: how to present a layered hypertext net arising from nesting composite nodes (I17) and how to present nodes and links in a graphical browser (I18).

With respect to issue 17, several approaches have been developed to facilitate the presentation of layered hypertext nets such as the fisheye view (Furnas, 1986) or dynamic zooming functionalities. A more suitable alternative for layered nets are mulitple browsers which allow for displaying information from more than one level of the net simultaneously. Multiple browsers can be used to preserve the context for a reader who switches from one level of the net to another, e.g., browser A may display the user's position in the current layer while browser B shows the layer he came from. This is likely to facilitate the construction of macrounits which are important to establish coherence at a global level.

With respect to positioning multiple browsers on the screen, there is strong emprirical evidence that a tiled window layout is better than overlapping windows since it leads to higher reader performance on different tasks (Instone, Teasley & Leventhal, 1993). Therefore, a stable screen layout should be choosen to prevent the overlapping of browsers.

Since structure nodes may either be sequencing nodes or exploration nodes, two situations have to be distinguished for displaying structural information in multiple browsers: In case of a sequencing node, the reader sees the graphical presentation of a reading path. In case of an exploration node, he sees the graphical presentation of a net in which he can freely browse. In both cases, the reader is also provided with information about the context of the currently activated node at the next higher level in a separate browser.

With respect to issue 18, nodes are usually displayed as objects using a special shape (boxes, circles etc.) which carry short names to describe their content and icons or color to indicate their type. In addition, cues for the amount of the content can be given using different degrees of shades or border width. Links are usually displayed as edges or arrows combined with special icons or labels to hint at their type as specified in the course of factual structuring. Thus, the display of structure provides information about the content of nodes as well as information about their relations establishing by this way coherence at the local level.

2.2.2 How to present the content of a hyperdocument and how to preserve contextual information

The issue of presenting content (I19) is related to the amount of information that may be stored in an atomic node. Usually the content of a node is displayed in a dedicated window on the screen. Since atomic nodes can contain fairly large chunks of information, the window may not suffice to display the complete content at a time. In this case, facilities must be provided which enable the user to process the information step by step. For example, scrollable windows can be used to display long pieces of text or large graphics.

The segmentation of information into nodes and their display in separate windows mainly contribute to "the fragmentation characteristic of hypertext" (Marshall & Irish, 1989, p.22). On behalf of the reader, fragmentation may result in a lack of interpretive context (Landow, 1987) and thus lead to the impression that the hyperdocument is merely an aggregation of loosely linked pieces of information rather than a coherent entity. To prevent this impression, the content of a node should not be presented in isolation but in a context which enables the reader to connect the content to other information outside the activated node. In order to clarify how the context of a node can be preserved (I20), two different kinds of contextual information can be distinguished which we call structural context and temporal context. This distinction gives rise to issue 23 and 24.

Structural context can be provided by a presentation style in which graphical information about the document structure is presented together with the content of an activated node (see also Nielsen, 1988). In this case, the reader can locate the node in the environment of neighboring nodes and links and can relate its content to this structure. Obviously, this increases coherence and supports the comprehension of important semantic relations.

Additionaly, the impression of fragmentation can be reduced by a **temporal context** in which the actual node is displayed together with its predecessor. This conveys a sense of continuity across nodes which is very important for comprehension: In attempting to understand the content of a new node, a reader tries to extract its information and relate it to the content of nodes which he has visited before. In psycholinguistics, this is called "given-new-strategy" (Clark & Haviland, 1974) and is regarded as a basic process in comprehension. With respect to hyperdocuments, it leads to an integrated mental representation of information which is distributed over different nodes. Preserving the content of the predecessor of the actual node is one possibility to support this strategy. Since the reader can see the ´given´ information of the old node he can detect semantic relations between both sources. As a result, he can join the content of both nodes in a coherent mental representation.

An additional way to support this strategy is to support backjumps to any location visited before by giving access to an **active reading history** which allows the reader to simply click on an already visited node to get immediately the desired information. This type of computer-supported retrospection is especially important if a reader wants to inspect a previously not fully or misunderstood information (Alessi, Anderson & Goetz, 1979). Looking back at such information units, a reader is able to correct his old view and to integrate it with newly acquired knowledge in order to establish coherence at a global level.

2.2.3 How to show correspondencies between presented information units?

The presentation of *structural* context implies that an activated node is displayed together with the structure in which it is embedded. The presentation of *temporal* context implies that an activated node is displayed together with its predecessor. In both cases, two windows are required: one showing the current node, the other showing the contextual information. In order to reduce the impression of fragmentation, readers must be enabled to recognize correspondencies between these different windows. For example, it should be possible to read the content of the activated node in window A and at a glance identify its position in the structure displayed in window B. Considerations of this kind lead to the issue of how to show correspondencies between information units across windows (I10).

For indicating such correspondencies, referential devices such as arrows or asteriks can be used (Marshall and Irish, 1989) thus establishing relations similar to deictic references in guided tours as proposed by Trigg (1988). Alternatively, **color** can be imposed as a cue for correspondencies between objects on the screen, i.e., identity of nodes displayed in different windows can be indicated by the same color. The use of identical colors for identical objects helps readers to detect correspondencies at first glance and increases the coherence of a document at a perceptual or visual level. Therefore, color can serve as a valuable supplement to linguistic cues in order to point out relations which are crucial for comprehension. In addition, **spatial cues** can be provided. If contextual information is always displayed in a window at a fixed position, the reader can use this cue to identify correspondencies.

2.3 How to facilitate navigation

For the majority of readers, navigating through a hyperdocument is not only a novel and unusual activity, it is also a demanding tasks which requires a lot of concentration. Since navigation can result in a considerable mental effort, it may occupy a significant part of the reader´s information processing capacity. Actually, some readers seem to navigate *instead* of reading, i.e., they get so absorbed in "browsing" that they hardly stop to *process* any information so that navigation challenges in a hyperdocument "interrupt their train of thought" (Gordon, Gustavel, Moore, & Hankey, 1988; Monk, Walsh & Dix, 1988).

Two tasks must be accomplished as part of navigation: First, the reader must "move" through the document in order to get any information. For this purpose, he must get familiar with the interface of the document and use its functionality for navigating. Second, the reader must be informed about his current position and about his options for proceeding back or forth in the document. Depending on the complexity of the interface and on the quality of orientation support, both tasks can be rather demanding. In order to reduce the capacity that is required for their accomplishment, two design issues are of crucial importance: the reduction of interaction overhead (I11) and the improvement of orientation (I12).

2.3.1   How to reduce interaction overhead

To reduce the potential interaction overhead, it is necessary to take a closer look at the kinds of navigational needs that may occur during reading. These needs can concern the direction as well as the distance of a move.

With respect to direction, one can distinguish between forward and backward navigation. While **forward navigation** occurs when a reader seeks new information by moving to a node he has not yet opened, **backward navigation** occurs when he tries to find old information by moving to a node which has already been visited. Relevant issues in this context are how to facilitate forward navigation (I21) and backward navigation (I22).

With respect to distance, one can distinguish between local and global navigation. In **local navigation**, the reader simply wants to follow a link, i.e., he wants to move from his current node to a node that is directly linked to it. In **global navigation**, the reader wants to reach a node that is *not* directly linked to his current position. Two cases are relevant for this type of navigation: (a) The desired node has not been opened before, but is currently visible, e.g., as part of a graphical browser. (b) The desired node has already been visited by the reader, but is not directly linked to the node which is currently activitated. In this case, it may or may not be visible on the screen.

The combination of these types of moves leads to four types of navigational situations each requiring specific support to reduce navigation overhead (compare I28 to I31). With respect to interface design, a variety of navigational devices can be used for this purpose. For example: Standard facilities, such as 'next buttons' and 'back buttons' allow for local forward and backward navigation; histories and bookmarks can be used for global backward navigation; and indeces as well as graphical browsers can be used to support all four types of navigational moves. In agreement with Whright and Likorish's (1990, p. 93) empirical results, it can be concluded that "different navigation systems appear suitable in different circumstances."

2.3.2   How to improve orientation

With respect to improving orientation, Bernstein (1991a, p. 295) has claimed that a severe and/or prolonged disorientation is uncomfortable but the complete absence of orientational challenges is dull. Hence, he argued for a "mild disorientation" which "can excite the readers, increasing their concentration, intensity, and engagement." Whatever a mild disorientation might be and how it could be accomplished, we aggree with him to the extent that hyperdocuments should not bore the reader. But there is no need to reach this goal by means provoquing disorientation since a variety of other factors can be used for arousing curiosity - as for instance Berlyne (1960) has shown in his well known theory of epistemical behavior.

For improving orientation graphical facilities, such as maps and browsers, can be used. How well a map supports orientation may be characterized in terms of the reader's ability to answer three questions: where am I, how did I get here, and where can I go next? To support orientation, interface design should therefore address the following issues:

- how to indicate the reader's current position with respect to the overall structure of the document (I23)

- how to show the way that led to his current position (I24) and

- how to present navigational options for the next move (I25).

In a layered hypertext net, the indication of the reader's current location should show his position in the hierarchy of layers as well as his position within the layer itself. Depending on the degree of nesting of composites, the complexity of the document structure may make it very difficult to show the reader's location on both of these dimensions. Due to the limitations of the screen, a large and complex layered net cannot be displayed as a whole in a graphical browser. Since it is often impossible to indicate the reader's position with respect to the *complete* document, it is necessary to provide a browser that displays only a segment of the overall structure, but nevertheless provides enough information about the current layer and the current node.

A similar difficulty arises for showing the way that led to the reader's current position: in order to enable the reader to reconstruct his moves, it is probably not very helpful to tell him which nodes he has already opened. A simple history function which leaves the structural information about layers and neighboring nodes aside is obviously not sufficient in documents of great complexity.

In order to cope with the problems arising from issue 23 and 24, we propose a combination of graphical browser and history function: The browser displays the reader's position in the current layer and also shows the relation of this layer to the one above. The history function shows the overall number of layers of the document, lists all nodes (composite as well as atomic) that have already been opened and indicates their position with respect to the level of layers. Moreover, it should enable the reader to use it for navigation, e.g., by selecting an item from the history and by activating it, the reader is taken to the selected destination. In combination, both facilities not only provide the required information about the reader's position and recent navigation, but also indicate all available options for his next move: The browser displays the current node together with all departing and arriving links and thus supports forward and backward navigation *within* the present layer. The history, on the other hand, lists all nodes already visited and thus supports global backward navigation *across* layers.

3 Summary and Conclusions

To improve the readability of hyperdocuments, it is not sufficient to concentrate on navigation without supporting comprehension. Moreover, recent research has pointed out that the ability to navigate through a document greatly depends on the reader´s *understanding its content* (McKnight, Dillon & Richardson, 1991). Taking this into account, the navigation problem has to be reconsidered (Bernstein, 1991a) under the perspective of easing the comprehension of hyperdocuments.

A deeper understanding of a document can be accomplished by imposing a coherent structure on it, conveying this structure to the reader and providing adequate navigation facilities. In this paper, we have shown that this approach leads to a variety of issues which are of crucial importance in the design of hyperdocument interfaces. The general design idea for answering these issues is a unique combination of structure and content with additional orientation cues and facilities for convenient navigation.

Since we believe that only a tight coupling of adequate structural elements to interface components for presentation can improve the readability of hyperdocuments, we have advanced an approach which explicitly addresses this issue (see also Waterworth, 1990). The development of our approach has proceeded in two steps:

1. Based on the hypermedia authoring system SEPIA (Streitz, Hannemann & Thüring, 1989) we have built a **construction kit** for creating coherent hyperdocuments (Thüring, Haake & Hannemann, 1991). Using SEPIA' construction kit, an author can generate a factual hyperdocument structure which represents semantic relationships between nodes and can then establish a variety of rhetorical structures which offer reading paths for sequential reading or exploration nodes for free browsing.

2. To convey the rhetorical structures to a reader, we have developed a **presentation interface** which relates the design elements of SEPIA's constrution kit to presentation elements on the screen (Hannemann, Thüring & Friedrich, 1992). A static screen layout has been proposed which supports both, the detection of correspondencies between content and structure of the hyperdocument, and orientation by providing contextual information. It uses a combination of graphical browsers presenting nested hypertext nets and content windows displaying the content of atomic nodes to preserve the structural and temporal context of a node. To facilitate navigation, we proposed to reduce interaction overhead by supporting multiple ways of moving through the document: clicking on nodes in browsers, following embedded links in content windows, selecting links in the button panel, and using a device called "the Navigator" for global backward navigation. Orientation is improved by indicating the reader´s current position in the graphical browsers and the Navigator. The reader´s navigational options are consistently presented in the browsers, the button panel and the Navigator. Orientation is further supported by the regular navigation semantics of the interface which maintains the structural and temporal context of the current node.

So far, we have not investigated the adequacy of our interface in a systematic empirical study, but first experiences with several readers support at least some of our design decisions. Especially, the graphical browsing facilities and the navigator seem to give valuable assistence. Of course, evidence from these first observations is not sufficient for evaluating our design decisions. Therefore, a major part of our future work will consist of empirical studies testing the interface that was described in this paper. These studies will investigate which of the interface components support the construction of a coherent mental represenation and thereby improve comprehension and navigation. This line of research will provide more guidelines for the design of reader-oriented interfaces which is part of a corresponding activity in the ESPRIT Project HIFI (1992): The development of a methodology for hypermedia interface design.

Beside these evaluative and methodological investigations, we will expand the current version of the presentation interface by integrating index as well as search and query functionality and by providing active components which enable the reader to take notes and make comments. These devices may be very useful to foster a personalized view of what the reader has processed and may therefore contribute to the formation a coherent mental representation of the hyperdocument (Foss, 1989). We hope that such interfaces are not only very helpful for comprehension and effective browsing, but will also make exploration and reading more enjoyable.

Acknowledgements: This work is part of a larger effort in the WiBAS department at the Integrated Publication and Information Systems Institute (IPSI). We wish to thank our collegue Jörg Haake for very helpful discussions. More over, we would also like thank Christian Schuckmann und Boris Bokowski for their support to implement the reader-interface in HyperNews and for their stimulating ideas about the graphical browsers and navigation facilities.

References

(Alessi, Anderson & Goetz,1979) S. M. Alessi, T.H. Anderson, & E.T. Goetz. An investigation of lookbacks during studying. Discourse Processes, 2,1979, 197-212.

(Berlyne, 1960) D.E. Berlyne. Conflict, arousal, and curiosity. New York: McGraw-Hill, 1960.

(Bernstein,1991a) M. Bernstein. The navigation problem reconsidered. In E. Berk, J. Devlin (Eds), Hypertext/Hypermedia Handbook, pages 287-287. New York: McGraw-Hill, 1991.

(Bernstein, 1991b) M. Bernstein. Structure, Navigation, and Hypertext: The status of the navigation problem. In *Proceedings of the 3nd ACM Conference on Hypertext (Hypertext `91)*, pages 363-367, San Antonio, Texas, Dec. 15-18, 1991.

(Buchanan & Shortliff, 1984) B.G. Buchanan & E,H. Shortliff. Rule-based experts systems: The MYCIN experiments of the Stanford Heuristic Programming Project. Reading, Mass.: Addison-Wesley.

(Charney, 1987) Comprehending non-linear text: The role of discourse cues and reading strategies. Proceedings of the 1st ACM Conference on Hypertext, pages 109-119, Chapel Hill, North Carolina, Nov. 13-15, 1987. New York: ACM Press, 1987.

(Clark & Haviland, 1974) H. H. Clark & S.E. Haviland. Psychological processes as linguistic explanation. In D. Cohen (Ed.), Explaining linguistic phenomena. Washington: Hemisphere, 1974.

(Dee-Lucas & Larkin, 1991) D. Dee-Lucas & J.H. Larkin. Content map design and knowledge structures with hypertext and traditional text. Poster at the 3rd ACM Conference on Hypertext, San Antonio, Texas, December 15-18, 1991.

(Foss, 1989) C.L. Foss. Tools for reading and browsing hypertext. Information Processing & Management, 25(4), 1989, 407-418.

(Furnas, 1986) G.W. Furnas. Generalized fisheye views. Proceedings of the ACM CHI '86, pages 16-23. Boston, MA, 13-17 April, 1986. New York: ACM Press, 1986.

(Gordon, Gustavel, Moore, & Hankey, 1988) S. Gordon, J. Gustavel, J. Moore, and J. Hankey. The effects of hypertext on reader knowledge representation. Proceedings of the Human Factors Society 32nd Annual Meeting, pages 296-300.

(Hannemann, Thüring & Friedrich, 1992) J. Hannemann, M. Thüring, and N. Friedrich. Hyperdocuments as user interfaces : Exploring a browsing semantic for coherent hyperdocuments. In R. Cordes & N. Streitz (eds.) Hypertext und Hypermedia 1992, pages 87-102. Heidelberg : Springer, 1992.

(HIFI, 1992) HIFI: Hypertext Interface For Information: Multimedia and relational databases. Technical Annex of the ESPRIT Project 6532.

(Johnson-Laird, 1983) P.N. Johnson-Laird. Mental models. Cambridge: Cambridge University Press, 1983.

(Landow,1987) G.P. Landow. Relationally encoded links and the rhetoric of hypertext. Proceedings of the 1st ACM Conference on Hypertext (Hypertext '87), Chapel Hill, North Carolina, November 13-15, 1987. New York: ACM Press, 1987.

(Marshall, Irish, 1989) C. C. Marshall & P. M. Irish. Guided Tours and On-Line Presentations: How Authors Make Existing Hypertext Intelligible for Readers. In Proceedings of the 2nd ACM Conference on Hypertext (Hypertext `89), pages 15 - 26, Pittsburgh, PA, November 1989.

(McKnight, Dillon & Richardson, 1991) C. McKnight, A. Dillon & J. Richardson. Hypertext in Context. Cambridge University Press, 1991.

(Monk, Walsh & Dix , 1988) A. Monk, P. Walsh & A. Dix. A comparison of hypertext, scrolling, and folding as mechanisms for program browsing. In D. Jones & R. Winder (eds.) People and Computers IV. Cambridge: Cambridge University Press, 1988.

(Nielsen, 1988) J. Nielsen. Trip Report: Hypertext '87. ACM SIGCHI Bulletin, 19 (4), 27-35.

(Searle, 1980) J. R. Searle. Minds, brains, and programs. The Behavioral and Brain Sciences, (3):417-457, 1980.

(Streitz, Hannemann, & Thüring, 1989) N. Streitz, J.Hannemann, & M. Thüring. From ideas and arguments to hyperdocuments: Traveling through activity spaces. In Proceedings of the 2nd ACM Conference on Hypertext (Hypertext `89), pages 343-364 , Pittsburgh, PA, November 5-8,1989. New York: ACM Press, 1987.

(Streitz et al., 1992) N. Streitz, J. Haake, J. Hannemann, A. Lemke, H. Schütt, W. Schuler & M. Thüring. SEPIA: A cooperative hypermedia authoring evitonment. In D. Lucarella, J. Nanard, M. Nanard, P. Paolini (Eds.), *Proceedings of the 4 th ACM Conference on Hypertext (ECHT `92)*, pages 11-22, Milano, Italy, November 30 - December 4, 1992, New York: ACM Press, 1992.

(Thüring, Haake & Hannemann, 1991) M. Thüring, J. M. Haake & J. Hannemann: What's ELIZA doing in the Chinese Room? Incoherent hyperdocuments - and how to avoid them. In *Proceedings of the 3nd ACM Conference on Hypertext (Hypertext `91)*, pages 161-177, San Antonio, Texas, December 15-18, 1991.

(Trigg, 1988) R. H. Trigg. Guided Tours and Tabletops: Tools for Communicating in a Hypertext Environment. *ACM Transactions on Office Information Systems*, 6(4): 398-414, 1988.

(van Dijk & Kintsch, 1983) T. A. van Dijk & W. Kintsch. *Strategies of Discourse Comprehension*. Orlando: Academic Press, 1983.

(Waterworth, 1990) J.A. Waterworth. Hypermedia interfaces for hypermedia documents. In A. Rizk, N. A. Streitz & J. Andre´ (Eds.), *Hypertext: Concepts, Systems and Applications, (Proceedings of the European Conference on Hypertext, ECHT '90, Paris, France, November 1990)*, pages 356-358. Cambridge: University Press, 1990.

(Whright & Likorish, 1990) P. Wright & A. Lickorish. An empirical comparison of two navigation systems for two hypertexts..In R. McAleese and C. Green (Eds.) *Hypertext: State of the art*, pages 84-93. Oxford: Intellect, 1990.

(Zellweger, 1989) P. T. Zellweger. Scripted Documents: A Hypermedia Path Mechanism. In *Proceedings of the 2nd ACM Conference on Hypertext (Hypertext `89)*, pages 1-14, Pittsburgh, PA, November 5-8, 1989.

Interaction in Hypermedia Systems:
From Browsing to Conversation

Ulrich Thiel
GMD-IPSI, Darmstadt, Germany

Abstract. In this paper, we address the problem of how a user can be supported in his/her *construction of coherence* during interaction with a hypermedia database interface. We discuss the approaches to assist the user taken in navigation-based hypertext systems and contrast this with the proposals for "conversational hypertexts." Since hypertext systems accessing large databases cannot build upon pre-edited coherent paths or similar features for coherence enhancement, the potential of conversational dialogue design for hypertext systems should be explored. In an experimental interface we employed a variety of dialogue features, including dynamic planning of paths using a case-based approach, meta-information, and access to previous dialogue states. The interaction is modelled in terms of a multimodal conversation. MERIT ("Multimedia Extensions of Retrieval Interaction Tools") provides a user-centered interface to a database covering European research programs, projects, and consortia in the field of information technology. The system supports the user by offering a selection of sample retrieval strategies, called "cases," which are modifiable to meet situation requirements. Based on the resulting dialogue plans, MERIT generates situation-dependent query forms and visualizations of information objects. The system generates graphical presentations of retrieval results which support a survey or detail-oriented reception of the retrieved data, thus providing visual cues for the user's relevance assessment. Additionally, the system employs interactive maps to display geographical data, and can provide scanned-in documents.

1 Introduction

From the viewpoint of interface design, the most salient aspect of hypermedia is the browsing facility provided in hypermedia systems. This can be applied not only to inspect non-linear documents, but also every collection of displayable items stored in a database (e.g., pictures, videos, voice documents, animations, facts). However, in most cases it does not suffice to provide a browsing option, since the users almost inevitably face the risk of getting "lost in hyperspace" (Conklin 1987). Why? And what can be done about it? In order to get a deeper understanding of this problem, we start with a closer look at the notion of hypertext/hypermedia.

At the first glance, the notion of "hypertext" is easily understood: nodes, links, and browsing. However, a more detailed look reveals that there are at least two readings, or interpretations, which stress different aspects. According to Landow and Kahn (Landow & Kahn 1992) we can regard hypertext either as a "*technology*" or as a "*thing*". Whereas the first view is system-oriented and stresses the navigational aspects, cf. e.g. Conklin, 1987, the second, somewhat older, reading centers around the notion of a non-linear document as put forward by V. Bush and T. Nelson. More recent proponents claim that "a hypertext is an *intentional interactive document*, providing a non-linear, dynamic analogue to the traditional notion of structured document" (Stotts, Furuta & Ruiz 1992, p. 273). Obviously, such "non-linear interactive document" possesses – or should possess, at least – a structure, which allows a reader to regard it as a whole, and to relate its parts in a meaningful way.

Adopting a term from the field of text linguistics, we will refer to this quality as the *coherence* of the hyperdocument. The coherence of a text – the notion applies to (monological) texts as well as dialogues – is mainly regarded as a product of the interplay of semantic and pragmatic aspects. The semantic analysis reveals the so-called *coherence relations* among text units (cf. e.g. Mann & Thompson 1988). There are further approaches (cf. e.g. Charolles 1981) that emphasize the importance of the reception process arguing that text coherence is constituted by the interpretation of the reader in a given situation. Some empirical investigations support such positions (cf. Danks & Ritman 1986, Colley 1987); they give evidence about the influence of situational context on the construction of *cognitive coherence*. As a consequence, integrated conceptions of coherence (cf. Lundquist 1985, Viehweger 1989) aim at combining semantic and pragmatic components. In the case of dialogical texts such as conversations the participants' discourse goals are of major influence on the mutual construction of a coherent understanding, cf. Craig & Tracy 1983).

In the remainder of this paper we will first sketch some of the approaches to support the user in establishing coherence that have been taken in hypertext research so far. Next, we will discuss the approach taken in the MERIT system, which employs a case-based approach to the dynamic planning of guided tours and uses a conversational interaction model. We then illustrate the effects of the dialogue design by discussing the dialogue options in a typical situation. We briefly sketch related ideas which have been put forward in the broader area of human-computer interaction research. We conclude the paper with a short summary of ideas presented here.

2   How to Support a Coherent Reception of Hypertexts

The recipient – the reader of a traditional text as well as the user of a hypertext system – is in charge of constituting coherence in her mind, mainly by interpreting the contents and drawing inferences from the relational cues. So far, this image complies with the notion that the compound comprising the user and the hypertext system can be regarded as an "intelligent system" : The hypertext system provides a "knowledge base", and the human plays the part of the "inference engine" (cf. Moulthrop 1992, Parunak 1991). Taking into account the users' limited ability to reason over large amounts of data, this does not necessarily imply that hypertext systems should be conceived as passive data stores. Instead, the user *has to be supported by the provision of cues* that allow her to establish coherence relationships. A variety of approaches to achieve this goal have been proposed, e.g.:

- Using concepts like "paths" (cf. Zellweger 1989) or "guided tours" (Trigg 1988, Marshall & Irish 1989); the author of the hypertext can guide the recipient in order to reduce the navigation space and decrease the danger of disorientation and navigational problems.

- Regarding a hyperdocument as a finite automaton, the browsing options available at a given node can be specified. Thus, it is possible to verify the resulting paths with respect to formal conditions (cf. Stotts, Furuta, & Ruiz 1992).

- The explicit representation of rhetorical links (cf. Marshall 1987, Streitz, Hannemann & Thüring 1989, Thüring, Haake & Hannemann 1991) among text components intends to facilitate the user's reconstruction of a given (hyper)text structure.

- Other approaches represent semantic relationships between text units (cf. e.g. Collier 1987, Hammwöhner & Thiel 1987) which allow the user to choose between navigation options based on the contents of the accessible nodes.

While these techniques are based on the notion of a hypertext as a (coherent) non-linear *monologue*, which is explored by the reader, other proposals aim at establishing coherence in the process of interaction by regarding it as a *dialogue*, where the system's task is to present nodes from a hyperbase that are meaningful continuations of the ongoing interaction:[1] For instance, Whalen & Patrick (1988) argue for a *"conversational hypertext"*, where a user can access further nodes in the hypertext base by typing in natural language queries or comments. These are matched against so-called *parse templates*, which are lists of index terms associated with each node. Whereas this pattern matching approach does not involve any kind of natural language understanding, more sophisticated techniques for the automatic indexing of large hyperbases are proposed by Osgood & Bareiss (1993). The browsing interface to a such an indexed hyperbase allows the user to select conversational links like *"Refocussing, Causality, Comparison* and *Advice"* (Osgood & Bareiss 1993, p. 310).

However, the provision of semantic links or indices in advance seems to be restricted to applications which involve hypertext *authors*, or require a semantic parsing and automatic indexing of the text units (cf. Hammwöhner & Thiel 1987, Osgood &Bareiss 1993). The first approach, although promising for the future, has to cope with several drawbacks, e.g. the need for providing and maintaining a comprehensive domain model as a knowledge base. Automatic indexing is mainly based on statistical methods which are designed for textual data. Although current approaches to tackle non-textual information, like data mining or content-based retrieval, may solve the problem of determining the semantics of data items – at least

---

1. In the area of information retrieval, a similar approach was put forward by Oddy 1977.

to a certain degree –, they are far from providing a viable solution to the problem of generating meaningful hyperlinks or paths like a human author.

In the case of hypermedia interfaces to *large* databases, there is no way to provide authored paths, due to the sheer amounts of data. Approaches trying to overcome this obstacle combine hypertext browsing with information retrieval functionality, e.g. by devising "query links" (Frisse 1988, Golovchinsky & Chignell 1993), or "dynamically planned guided tours" (Guinan & Smeaton 1992). These techniques are used to determine a subset of the accessible nodes according to a query which imposes restrictions on the contents of the nodes.

In the MERIT system ("Multimedia Extensions of Retrieval Interaction Tools")[2] (Stein, Thiel & Tißen 1992, Stein & Thiel 1993) we apply similar techniques, however, the concepts of context-sensitive queries and plan-based user guidance are combined with a conversational dialogue design. The system allows casual users to access a database containing factual and textual information about research projects funded by the European Community. Although the database was conceived and implemented as a hypertext base (cf. Gu & Thiel 1993), the interface does not rely on navigation facilities alone. In order to support the user in establishing a coherent mental representation of the retrieved data, it often does not suffice to let her investigate the hypertext along certain paths – although this is better than unrestricted browsing. Instead, the user may need a more flexible way of interaction, allowing her to request meta-information, to go back to previous dialogue situations, to reject information items offered by the system, or to change their presentation forms. In contrast to conventional path mechanisms, these options need not be devised by a path author, since they are provided automatically by the system in accordance to a given dialogue situation. As this degree of flexibility requires an expressive interaction metaphor, the interaction in MERIT is closely modelled along the patterns of a *conversation* between an information seeker and an information provider.

3 MERIT: A Hypermedia Information System

MERIT provides a graphical interface to a database covering European research programs, projects, and consortia in the field of information technology. The system supports the user by offering a selection of sample retrieval strategies, called *cases,* which are modifiable to meet situational requirements. The dialogue is focussed by object perspectives, i.e. sets of features relevant to a problem, which define its thematic structure. For instance, the user may select a case like "Finding a partner" or "Searching a project that addresses a given problem." These cases differ obviously in the relevant attribute fields of the project entries, e.g. the "partner problem" requires to retrieve contact addresses etc. whereas the second information need will be satisfied by inspecting detailed project descriptions. Hence, the system adopts different perspectives on the data objects and activates appropriate dialogue plans.

---

2.   MERIT runs on SUN color workstations and is written in CommonLISP. Its dynamic and static knowledge bases are based on CLOS, the object-oriented extension of CommonLISP, and on CRL, which is part of Knowledge Craft. It has an interface to the relational database system SYBASE, which is a C program. As its graphical interface, it uses HyperNeWS.

Based on these dialogue plans, MERIT generates situation-dependent query forms and visualizations of information objects. The process of selecting search terms is assisted by a semantic component proposing additional search terms that are derived from an initially given one by associative reasoning. The system generates graphical presentations of retrieval results which support a survey or detail-oriented reception of the retrieved data, thus providing visual cues for the user's relevance assessment (cf. fig. 1).

In order to achieve this flexible and adaptive dialogue behaviour, MERIT employs a _case-based dialogue manager_ (CADI, cf. Tißen, 1991, 1993, Stein, Thiel & Tißen, 1992). CADI can be seen as a special adaptation of a case-based reasoner for the generation of dialogue plans. On the implementation level, CADI represents dialogue plans as sequences of _dialogue steps_. The internal structure of a dialogue step is given by two parameters: The _perspective_ of the step, and its _implementation_. The perspective – by focussing the interaction on relevant aspects of the information items – determines the topical spectrum that can be addressed in this step without destroying the thematic coherence of the dialogue in general. Similar notions have been proposed by McCoy (1986) in the area of natural language interfaces and Reichman (1986, 1989) who takes a discourse analytical approach to multimodal dialogues. The second component of a step describes the possible and actual ways to implement the corresponding dialogue step. It may be implemented by a single dialogue contribution, or – in terms of speechact theory – a _dialogue act_. In this case the variety is given by the different forms this "utterance" may have. For instance, the presentation of a certain set of data may be a list of the data records, a table, or a graphical presentation. However, the step may also be performed by a certain sequence of interactions which then build a subdialogue that may replace the single act. Thus, we have a means to prescribe a certain act as appropriate in the given situation, but allowing the user to apply this in a way she prefers, e.g. by first requesting context or help information.

In sum, the user of MERIT engages in a _visual dialogue,_ in which the interaction, although realized by graphical means, complies with conversational patterns of exchange (cf. Stein, Thiel, and Tißen 1992). Like similar approaches to flexible graphical interaction based on the _conversational metaphor_ (cf. Hutchins 1989, Reichman 1986, 1989, Thiel 1990), we treat user inputs such as mouse clicks, menu selections, etc. not as invocations of methods that can be executed without regarding the dialog context, but instead as dialogue acts expressing a discourse goal of the user.

The specification of possible sequences of dialogue acts that can be used to realize a step relies on a conversational dialogue model which captures all well-formed, i.e. cooperative, patterns of interaction that may occur in an information seeking dialogue. The model – called "Conversational Roles Model" (COR, cf. Sitter & Stein 1992; Maier & Sitter 1992, Stein & Thiel 1993) – describes negotiation tactics in information-seeking dialogues between humans or between a human information–seeker and an information system. It is based on the _role expectations_ of the dialogue participants, which can be accepted, rejected or withdrawn. COR also describes subdialogues which have the purpose to either support the role expectations expressed or to justify rejections/withdrawals.[3]

The model focuses on the illocutionary aspects of dialogues, abstracting from the content aspects. It models the dialogue participants' expectations about the "ideal" course of an information-seeking dialogue (e.g., question –> answer –> contentment) and possible deviations from that course (e.g., question –> reject question), if certain conditions are not fulfilled. In this respect, it is very similar to the approach put forward by Winograd & Flores 1986. However, the COR model is able to cope with situations in which a subdialogue is initiated by one of the partners. In such a subdialogue, the participants' roles may change, e.g. the information seeker temporarily becomes an information provider when she is asked to modify or clarify a request.

The user interface of MERIT reflects the conversational model of interaction in two ways: First, the layout focuses on the current dialogue act and the possible continuations of the dialogue. As a consequence, graphical objects belonging to previous dialogue acts are removed from the screen. However, as in verbal conversations, it is possible to refer to utterances made in earlier stages of the dialogue by using MERIT's history mechanism. A second mayor impact of the conversational metaphor is an integrated view on both the expected continuation as well as a meaningful deviation from the current topic. In the following section we will illustrate this by summarizing the user's options in a typical dialogue situation.

4   The User's Options in a Given Dialogue Situation

By choosing a case in the beginning of the dialogue, the user determines the overall topic of the dialogue, which is usually a domain concept, e.g. *project*, and a selection of attributes which is represented by the associated perspective (e.g. all information relevant to the project organization). Most cases require a further restriction of the set of information items by filling out a query form (cf. Stein, Thiel & Tißen 1992). The cases may as well contain further steps with a different perspective, or even include steps focussing on other concepts, if appropriate. This complex thematic structure, although helpful when solving a problem similar to the one which lead to the case, may not always be appropriate. Therefore, the user interface must provide a variety of means to deviate from the case in a natural and easy way. In MERIT, the user is given the following choices when investigating a set of retrieved items:

1. Figure 1 shows one of the presentation forms employed in MERIT: Each of the retrieved information items is presented on a *card*. The user may explore the stack of cards via the **next** and **previous** buttons, or may navigate to associated information items, e.g. map or pictures, by clicking on the card's buttons. Alternative presentation forms present relational information, e.g. the relationship between *projects* and *organizations*, as a system generated graph or table.

---

3. For COR's theoretical foundation in sociology and philosophy of language cf Sitter & Stein 1992.

2. In order to continue the selected case, the user clicks on the **continue**-icon
   (arrow on the right corner on the bottom of figure 1). Before doing so, she may
   use the **info-next-step** button to request a verbal preview of the remaining steps
   of the case.

So far, the options comply with the usual notion of browsing. The current version
of MERIT only provides "area–to–area" links that comply with the conversational
style of interaction.[4] Additionally, the user has the possibility to leave the suggested
sequence by dialogue acts which change the anticipated course of interaction:

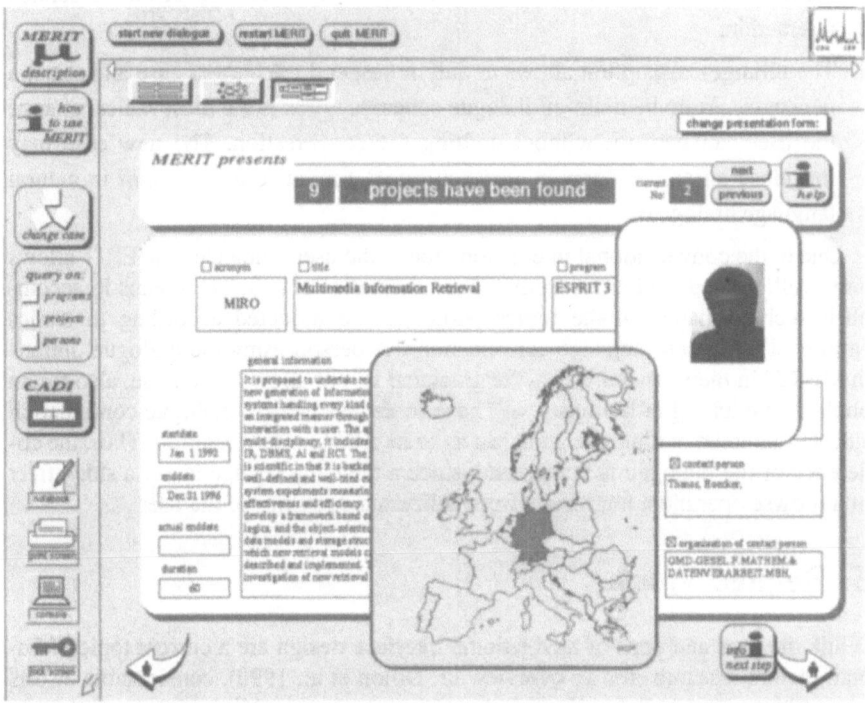

Fig. 1 A Sample Screen of MERIT

3. The user may withdraw her commitment made in her last dialogue step (**arrow**
   in the lower left corner), e.g. as reaction to an inappropriate retrieval result. In
   our example situation, the withdrawal brings her back to the query form, which
   then may be changed accordingly. In this case, the object perspective remains
   the same.

---

4. Future versions (or similar interfaces) will have to provide more browsing options (e.g.
allow for highlighted cluewords as anchors). In our prototype, however, we concentrated on
the provision of conversationally motivated interaction options which offer flexibility without
destroying the coherence.

4. Alternatively, the user can suspend the current case and restore a previous dialogue state by clicking on one of the icons in the **history** row directly above the current presentation. In our example, the user can choose between a query and two different presentations of retrieval results. In terms of conversation theory, this option is the equivalent to a *reintroduction of a previous topic*.

5. In order to suspend the current case and insert a sequence of a single **query** and presentation, the user may click on one of the topics offered. This event is modeled as a *subdialogue* (cf. Sitter & Stein 1992), which temporarily alters the thematic structure of the dialogue, but returns to the context of the suspended interaction.

6. The **change-case** option allows to quit or suspend the current case and select a new case. From the point of dialogue coherence, this is the most radical change the user can perform without quitting the conversation. The new case may introduce an entirely new context, an effect similar to a *topic shift* in natural language dialogues.

Due to the conversational interaction model, the user guidance in MERIT allows only well defined deviations from a given thematic context. The means to accomplish such a change in the topical structure are modeled according to tactics employed in natural language conversations. A person using the dialogue options in MERIT in the intended way – the graphical layout allows, of course, also for an unplanned clicking of buttons – will have to decide which dialogue continuation suits her interest, or dialogue goal, just as in an ordinary conversation. Thus, the coherence of the dialogue is maintained, since a thematic change is *not* a side-effect of a browse operation, but results from deliberate decisions of the user.

5 Related Work

While the pros and cons of navigational interface design are a current topic of human factors research (for an overview cf. Dillon et al. 1990), considerable efforts are made to enhance the navigational process, e.g. by providing overview information intended to reduce the conceptual confusion of the user (Carey et al. 1990). Other approaches address the disorientation problem by providing means for user guidance (e.g. Trigg 1988, Zellweger 1989). A way to avoid pre-editing of "paths" while nonetheless providing some helpful orientation to the casual user consists of preserving the experiences of previous users and make them explicit to the current one. In the context of document processing, Hill et al. (1992) propose the notion of *computational wear*, i.e. a recording of the frequency of usage of the document's parts. Based on Schoen's metaphor of a *reflective conversation* between a user and her environment, they stress the importance of a familiar environment. In the case of text editing, the environment is mainly constituted by the text that is worked on, and the relationships between different versions, parts etc. In the case of information systems, however, this way of constituting familiarity is not appropriate. The user, when posing a query, (usually) expects something new. Therefore, familiarity should at least be provided by well-known interaction patterns or metaphors. Among the metaphors known to almost every user, the concept of *conversation* is one that is applicable in a variety of ways. Besides the abstract notion of a situation that "talks back" to a user, (cf. Hill et al.1992), it may also be understood in a more concrete way, as e.g. in agent-based interfaces (Thorisson 1993), or conversation aids for impaired people (Alm et al. 1993). These and other conversational interfaces make explicit use of the aspects of conversations that can be formalized (the question to what degree real-life dialogues can be modeled by a "dialogue grammar" is an unsolved linguistic problem). In most cases, conversational interaction models employ network based notations (cf. Winograd & Flores 1986, Fawcett et al. 1988).

7 Conclusions

As hypermedia systems impose a high cognitive load on a user, the task of establishing coherence in the navigation process has to be supported by the system. We claimed that this cannot be done using navigational aids like paths, etc., alone, especially in applications that do not involve hypertext authors. We proposed to provide a flexible and cooperative interface capable to engage in a conversational interaction with the user. This means that the system can react to the user's requests with appropriate information offers, and provide contextual information in clarifying subdialogues. Such a conversational style of interaction is used in the hypermedia database interface MERIT.

Acknowledgements: The author would like to thank D. Effenberger, J. Gu, M. Hemmje, A. Kerner, M. Kracker, S. Sitter, A. Stein and A. Tißen for their valuable contributions to the MERIT prototype.

References

Alm, N., Todman, J., Elder, L. & Newell, A.F. (1993). Computer Aided Conversation for Severely Physically Impaired Non-speaking People. In: Ashlund, S. et al. (eds.): *INTERCHI'93 Conference Proceedings*. New York, NY: ACM Press & Reading, MA: Addison Wesley, 1993, pp. 236-241.

Carey, T.T., Hunt, W.T. & Lopez-Suarez, A. (1990). Roles for Tables of Contents as Hypertext Overviews. In: Diaper, D. et al. (eds.): *Human-Computer Interaction – INTERACT'90*, Amsterdam: North-Holland, 1990, pp. 581-586.

Charolles, M. (1981). Coherence as a Principle in the Interpretation of Discourse. *Text*, 3, 1981, pp. 71-99.

Colley, A.M. (1987). Text Comprehension. In: J.R. Beech & A.M. Colley (Eds.) *Cognitive Approaches to Reading*. New York, NY: John Wiley, pp. 17-41.

Collier, G.H. (1987) Thoth-II: Hypertext with Explicit Semantics. In: *Hypertext'87 Papers*. Chapel Hill, NC: University of North Carolina, pp. 269–290.

Conklin, J. (1987). Hypertext: A Survey and Introduction. *IEEE Computer*, 20, 1987, pp. 17-41.

Craig, R.T. & Tracy, K. (eds.) (1983) Conversational Coherence: Form, Structure, and Strategy. Beverly Hills: Sage Publications, 1983.

Danks, J.H., & Ritman, M.P. (1986). Constructing Coherent Representations from Inconsistent Texts. In: I. Kurcz et al. (eds.) *Knowledge and Language.* Amsterdam: North-Holland, pp. 259-276.

Dillon, A., McKnight, C. & Richardson, J. (1990): Navigation in Hypertext: A Critical Review of the Concept. In: Diaper, D. et al. (eds.): *Human-Computer Interaction – INTERACT'90*, Amsterdam: North-Holland, 1990, pp. 587-592.

Fawcett, R.P., van der Mije, A. & van Wissen, C. (1988) Towards a Systemic Flowchart Model for Discourse. In: R.P. Fawcett & D. Young (eds.): *New Developments in Systemic Linguistics. Vol. 2: Theory and Application.* London: Pinter, 1988, pp. 116-143.

Frisse, M.E. (1988) Searching for Information in a Hypertext Medical Handbook. *CACM*, 31, 1988, pp. 881-886.

Gu, J. & Thiel, U. (1993) Automatically Converting Linear Text to Hypertext. A Case Study. In: Frei, H.P. & Schäuble, P. (eds.): Proc. of the Hypermedia '93, *Zürich, Switzerland, March 2-3, 1993.* Berlin: Springer, 1993, pp. 220-231.

Guinan, C., & Smeaton, A. (1992) Information Retrieval from Hypertext Using Dynamically Planned Guided Tours. In: Lucarella, D., Nanard, D., Nanard, M., & P. Paolini (eds.): *ECHT' 92*, Proc. 4th ACM Conf. on Hypertext, Milano, Italy, Nov. 30 – Dec. 4, 1992. New York, NY: ACM Press, pp. 122-130.

Hammwöhner, R., & Thiel, U. (1987). Content oriented Relations between Text Units – A structural Model for Hypertexts. In: *Hypertext '87 Papers.* Chapel Hill, NC: University of North Carolina, pp. 155-174.

Hill, W. C., Hollan, J.D., Wroblewski, D. & McCandless, T. (1992). Edit Wear and Read Wear. In: Bauersfeld, P. et al. (eds.): *CHI'92 Conference Proceedings*, New York, NY: ACM Press, 1992, pp. 3-9.

Hutchins, E. (1989) Metaphors for Interface Design. In: Taylor, M.M., et al. (eds.): *The Structure of Multimodal Dialogue.* Amsterdam: North-Holland, 1989, pp. 11-28.

Landau, G.P. & Kahn, P. (1992) Where is the Hypertext? The Dickens Web as a System-Independent Hypertext. In: Lucarella, D., Nanard, D., Nanard, M., & P. Paolini (eds.): *ECHT' 92*, Proc. of the 4th ACM Conf. on Hypertext, Milano, Italy, Nov. 30 – Dec. 4, 1992. New York: ACM Press, pp. 149-160.

Lundquist, L. (1985). Coherence: From Structures to Processes. In: E. Sözer (Ed.) *Text connexity, text coherence – aspects, methods, results.* Hamburg: Helmut Buske (Papiere zur Textlinguistik, Vol. 49), pp.151-175.

Maier, E. & Sitter, S. (1992) An Extension of Rhetorical Structure Theory for the Treatment of Retrieval Dialogues. In: *CogSci '92, Proceedings of the 14th Annual Conference of the Cognitive Science Society, Bloomington, Indiana, July 1992.* Hillsdale, NJ: Lawrence Erlbaum, 1992, pp. 968-973.

Mann, W.C., & Thompson, S.A. (1988). Rhetorical structure theory: Toward a functional theory of text organization. *Text*, 8, 1988, pp. 243-281.

Marshall, C.C. (1987). Exploring Representation Problems Using Hypertext. In: *Hypertext '87 Papers*. Chapel Hill, NC: University of North Carolina, pp. 253-268.

Marshall, C.C., & Irish, P.M. (1989). Guided tours and on-line presentations: How authors make existing hypertext intelligible for readers. In: *Proceedings of the Hypertext '89*. New York: ACM Press, pp. 15-26.

McCoy, K.F. (1986) The ROMPER System: Responding to Object-Related Misconceptions Using Perspective. In: *Proceedings of the 24th Ann. Meeting of the Association for Computational Linguistics, New York.*

Moulthrop, S. (1992) Toward a Rhetoric of Informating Texts. In: Lucarella, D., Nanard, D., Nanard, M., & P. Paolini (eds.): *ECHT' 92, Proc. of the 4th ACM Conf. on Hypertext, Milano, Italy, Nov. 30 – Dec. 4, 1992.* New York, NY: ACM Press, pp. 171-180.

Oddy, R.N. (1977) Information Retrieval through Man-Machine-Dialogue. In: *J. Docum.* Vol. 33, No. 1, 1977, pp. 1-14.

Osgood, R. & Bareiss, R. (1993) Automatic Index Generation for Constructing Large-scale Conversational Hypermedia Systems. In: *AAAI '93, Proc. of the 11th National Conference on Artificial Intelligence, Washington DC, USA, July 11-16, 1993.* Menlo Park: AAAI Press/ The MIT Press, 1993, pp. 309-314.

Parunak, H. (1991) Toward Industrial Strength Hypermedia. In: Berk, E., & J. Devlin, J. (eds.): *The Hypertext/Hypermedia Handbook*. New York, NY: McGraw-Hill, 1991, pp. 381-397.

Reichman, R. (1986) Communication Paradigms for a Window System. In: Norman, D.A. & Draper, S.A. (eds.): *User Centered System Design: New Perspectives on Human-Computer Interaction.* Hillsdale, NJ & London, England: Lawrence Erlbaum, 1986, pp. 285-313.

Reichman, R. (1989) Integrated Interfaces Based on a Theory of Context and Goal Tracking. In: Taylor, M.M., Neel, F. & Bouwhuis, D.G. (eds.): *The Structure of Multimodal Dialogue.* Amsterdam: North-Holland, 1989, pp. 209-228.

Sitter, S., & Stein, A. (1992) Modeling the Illocutionary Aspects of Information-Seeking Dialogues. In: *Information Processing and Management*, Vol. 28 (2), 1992, pp. 165-180.

Stein, A., Thiel, U., & Tißen, A. (1992) Knowledge-Based Control of Visual Dialogues in Information Systems. In: Catarci et al. (eds.): *AVI '92, Proceedings of the International Workshop on Advanced Visual Interfaces, Rome, Italy, May 27-29, 1992.* Singapore: World Scientific Press, 1992, pp. 138-155.

Stein, A. & Thiel, U. (1993) A Conversational Model of Multimodal Interaction in Information Systems. In: *AAAI'93, Proc. of the 11th National Conference on Artificial Intelligence, Washington DC, USA, July 11-16, 1993*. Menlo Park: AAAI Press/ The MIT Press, 1993, pp. 283-288.

Stotts, P.D., Furuta, R., & Ruiz, J.C. (1992) Hyperdocuments as Automata: Trace-based Browsing Property Verification. In: Lucarella, D., Nanard, D., Nanard, M., & P. Paolini (eds.): ECHT' 92, Proc. of the 4th ACM Conf. on Hypertext, Milano, Italy, Nov. 30 – Dec. 4, 1992. New York, NY: ACM Press, pp. 272-281.

Streitz, N.A., Hannemann, J., & Thüring, M. (1989). From Ideas and Arguments to Hyperdocuments: Travelling through Activity Spaces. In: Proc. *Hypertext '89*. New York, NY: ACM Press, pp. 343-364.

Thiel, U. (1990) Conversational graphical Interaction in Information Systems: A Speech-Act Theory Approach (in German). PhD Dissertation, Konstanz, FRG: Univ. of Konstanz, 1990.

Thorisson, K.R. (1993) Dialogue Control in Social Interface Agents. In: Ashlund, S. et al. (eds.): *INTERCHI'93 Adjunct Proceedings*. pp. 139–140.

Thüring, M., Haake, J., & Hannemann, J. (1991) What's Eliza doing in the Chinese Room? – Incoherent Hyperdocuments – and how to avoid them. In: Proceedings of the 3rd ACM Conf. on Hypertext *(Hypertext '91)*, New York, NY: ACM Press, 1991, pp. 161-177.

Tißen, A. (1991). A case-based Architecture for a Dialogue Manager for Information-seeking Processes. Proceedings of *SIGIR '91*, October 13-16, 1991, Chicago/ USA, New York, NY: ACM Press, 1991, pp. 152-161.

Tißen, A. (1993) Knowledge Bases for User Guidance in Information Seeking Dialogues. In: Wayne, D.G. et al. (eds.): *IWIUI '93, Proceedings of the International Workshop on Intelligent User Interfaces. January 4-7, 1993, Orlando, FL, 1993*. New York, NY: ACM Press, pp. 149-156.

Trigg, R.H. (1988). Guided tours and tabletops: Tools for communicating in a hypertext environment. *ACM Transactions on Office Information Systems*, 6, 1988, pp. 398-414.

Viehweger, D. (1989). Coherence – Interaction of Modules. In: W. Heydrich et al. (eds.) *Connexity and coherence. Analysis of text and discourse*. Berlin: de Gruyter, pp. 256-274.

Whalen, T. & Patrick, A. (1988) Conversational Hypertext: Information Access through Natural Language Dialogues with Computers. In: K. Bice & C. Lewis (eds.): *CHI'88 'Wings for the Mind' Conference Proceedings*, New York, NY: ACM Press, 1988, pp. 289-292.

Winograd, T., & Flores, F. (1986). *Understanding Computers and Cognition*. Norwood, NJ: Ablex.

Zellweger, P. (1989). Scripted Documents: A Hypermedia Path Mechanism. In: Proceedings of the *Hypertext '89*. New York, NY: ACM Press, 1989, pp. 1-14

2 Metaphors for Hypermedia Interfaces

Uli Glowalla

Whenever we want to describe something new we tend to do this by reference to something familiar. This is the prototypical case for using a metaphor, since they are very powerful devices to communicate even a complex, structured set of properties in a shorthand that is easily understood by all members of a speech community who share the relevant mutual knowledge (Black, 1962). When I for instance say that my job is a jail, I communicate all properties of the superordinate category jail with just that statement. You know without any additional word that my job is like those entities that confine one against one's will, are unpleasant, are difficult to escape from, and so forth. I need not – indeed, I probably could not – list each of those properties exhaustively. Therefore, my use of the metaphor is more efficient and more precise than any partial listing of the properties of the superordinate jail. In other words, if the attribution of all those properties is the communicative purpose, then the appropriate communicative form is the metaphor. In that sense, as Ortony (1975) argued, metaphors are not just nice, they are necessary.

This becomes readily apparent in all sciences where it is quite common to use metaphors for conceptualizing abstract concepts in terms of the apprehensible (cf. Gentner, 1982). Not surprisingly, then, there is quite a tradition to use metaphors helping people to construct an appropriate cognitive representation of computing systems in general (Carroll & Thomas, 1982) and user interfaces in particular (Carroll, Mack & Kellog, 1988; Erickson, 1990). Consequently, it was quite natural to include three chapters focussing on metaphors in a volume on designing user interfaces for hypermedia.

In the first chapter of this section *Matthias Rauterberg* and *Markus Hof* present their participatory approach on metaphor engineering. They address the problem of finding a suitable metaphor for a particular application domain. Rauterberg and Hof argue a straightforward way to achieve this goal is to ask domain experts to describe their target domain to novices in a metaphorical language.

To demonstrate the usefulness of their approach the authors conducted a little study in which six male students of physics participated as domain experts. Their task was to explain both the Doppler effect and the process of generating light to different groups of novices, namely male and female school children as well as male and female adults. The results presented by Rauterberg and Hof indicate that metaphors are used more frequently when describing physical phenomena to children and female adults compared to male adults. Based on their results the authors recommend to work with either children or women as 'catalysts' in metaphor engineering sessions.

In the second chapter *Kaisa Väänänen* presents a metaphor–based authoring tool for multimedia environments called ShareME. ShareME is intended to improve the usability of hypermedia information systems in two ways. First, the authoring tool should support authors to construct hypermedia applications and second it should help users to navigate within these hyperspaces.

The approach taken in ShareME is to offer a variety of user interface metaphors from which authors may choose the one that best suits both their particular application domain and target user group. The users then view the information via the same metaphor as the author. Moreover, they may interact with the information by manipulating the objects constituting the metaphor. Väänänen estimates that a fully implemented metaphor–based authoring tool should contain between 20 and 30 different metaphors for user interfaces. The goal of ShareME is to implement a testbed consisting of 5 to 7 different metaphors. Furthermore, the author plans to work with different groups of users in order to reveal which of the metaphors turn out to be most effective for various kinds of application, user groups, and usage situations.

Finally, in the third chapter of this section *Andreas Birk, Bidjan Tschaitschain, Franz Schmalhofer, Manfred Thüring* and *Heiner Gertzen* present an intelligent documentation system called IDEAS to support the explanation of adverse events in clinical studies conducted to test new drugs. To decide whether a particular adverse event is caused by the drug under investigation or some other factor is both an important and complex problem: a multitude of heterogeneous data and numerous knowledge sources have to be considered.

The IDEAS system is presented to users via the spreadsheet metaphor. The authors argue convincingly that this approach has several advantages. For one thing, it is quite common to use spreadsheets in the pharmaceutical industry to document the results of clinical studies. Consequently, the target user group is quite familiar with this metaphor. Also, the dynamic nature of spreadsheet systems may be used quite efficiently for both updating data and filtering information. This last feature in particular helps to reduce the problems of disorientation and cognitive overload that users face quite frequently when dealing with large hypertext systems. Consequently, I expect that systems like IDEAS will improve the efficiency of decision processes in the pharmaceutical industry.

In conclusion, I am quite convinced that metaphors will help users to navigate through large hyperdocuments successfully. Moreover, the increasing capabilities of multimedia systems will allow to not only make reference to metaphors in order to explain the contents and structure of hyperdocuments to users but visualize these metaphors quite effectively. All three papers constituting this section on metaphors for hypermedia interfaces provide useful insights to this very active and promising area of system engineering.

References

Black, M. (1962). Models and metaphors. Ithaca, NY: Cornell University Press.

Carroll, J.M. & Thomas, J.C. (1982). Metaphor and the cognitive representation of computing systems. IEEE Transaction on Systems, Man, and Cybernetics SMC–12(2), 107–115.

Carroll, J.M., Mack, R.L. & Kellog, W.A. (1988). Interface metaphors and user interface design. In M. Helander (Ed.), Handbook of Human–Computer Interaction (pp. 67–85). Amsterdam: North–Holland.

Erickson, T.D. (1990). Working with interface metaphors. In B. Laurel (Ed.), The art of human–computer interface design. Apple Computer Inc.

Gentner, D. (1982). Are scientific analogies metaphors? In D.S. Miall (Ed.), Metaphor: Problems and perspecitives (pp. 106–133). Brighton, Sussex, England: Harvester Press.

Ortony, A. (1975). Why metaphors are necessary and not just nice. Educational Theory, 26, 395–398.

Metaphor Engineering: a Participatory Approach

Matthias Rauterberg and Markus Hof
Work and Organisational Psychology Unit, ETH, Switzerland

Abstract. A method for 'metaphor engineering' is introduced in the context of participatory multimedia design. Our hypothesis, that adults talk to children more with a metaphorical language than to other adults, was empirically verified. Especially male adults do not qualify for the job as metaphor engineers. Metaphors are powerful, but not sufficient to come up with a good interface. Single, over-detailed metaphors can be too restrictive and unwieldy. Effective interface metaphors often evolve over time through design, evaluation and redesign. The approach presented in this paper guarantees that the starting point of the design cycles can be optimised.

Keywords. Metaphor, multimedia, hypertext, user interface, participatory design

1 The Interface Metaphor

The construction of hypertext systems needs several design solutions, "which re-quires dedicated methodological support". One important design problem is finding a metaphor for the interface architecture, which is the design basis for the screen layouts and the dialogue structure (Carroll 1982) (Carroll 1985) (Chauvet 1991). This approach leads directly to the usage of multimedia interface technology (Carroll 1988) (Eberleh 1991) (Shum 1990).

Waterworth (1992) distinguishes four different levels of analogy in interface de-sign (cf. Hutchins 1989). The *conceptual model* is the overall view of the system, or part of the system, as conceptualised by the design team. This may comprise one overall metaphorical view or several metaphors and also non-metaphorical aspects. *Mental models* describe how users view the system, which of course will vary with the sophistication and experience of the user. This should hopefully be reasonably compatible with the conceptual model, but will not be identical in detail nor will it be complete. "A metaphor in this context is a mapping relation between aspects of the conceptual model and the world at large (e.g., a desktop). *Interaction modes* are details of user operations that are included in the conceptual model and may corre-late with metaphors (clicking to open a file, dragging to move from one folder to another, uttering a word to place a marker, for example)" (Waterworth 1992, p. 91).

Waterworth (1992) illustrates furthermore the different levels at which system func tionalities and metaphor characteristics correspond to each other in Table 1 (see also Hammond and Allison 1987). A metaphor need not be appropriate at all levels of description. Different metaphors at the same level of description may be appropriate and multiple metaphors may often be useful (Weyer 1985).

Level	Interaction events	Example metaphor	System perspective
Pragmatic	Tasks	Finding out about a topic	User session(s)
Semantic	Ways of doing tasks	Going on a library tour	Organised set of traversals
Syntactic	Combinations of mo-ves/items	Selecting a book and 'opening' it	Displayed node
Lexical	Items/moves (icon, clicks, pointing, etc.)	Pointing at a picture	Input/output token re cog-nised

Table 1. Levels of system-metaphor mapping (Waterworth 1992).

Metaphors are not 'right' or 'wrong' descriptions: rather they are 'stimulating' invitations to see a target domain in a new light (Richards 1936) (Haverkamp 1983). But, where do metaphors come from? As Carroll, Mack and Kellog (Carroll 1988) claimed, that "there is not now (and likely never will be) a discovery procedure for metaphors," we try to overcome this position. In the context of a participatory approach (Rauterberg 1992) we are looking for a method which generates a metaphor by the domain expert himself. This participatory approach ensures that the generated metaphor fits the application domain. If we try to design a multimedia information system for a new domain (e.g., proofs in philosophical theories), then we need a lot of different and unknown design concepts. We cannot continue to use well-known metaphors (see Figure 1) (Henderson 1986) (Carroll 1988) (Gould 1990). One way to discover these concepts is to ask domain experts. So, we are looking for a method, which stimulates the domain expert to describe his target domain in a metaphorical language.

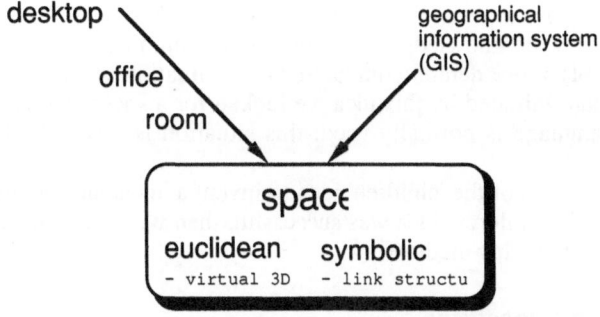

Figure 1. Historical influences for the Euclidean and symbolic space concept.

The domain knowledge of an expert is directly·communicable only to other experts with the same domain knowledge. If we try to understand a foreign domain then we need a mapping or transformation of the unknown knowledge into our own knowledge structure. Incidentally, each teacher looks for these mappings (the arrows in Figure 2). Hammond and Allison (1987) make a distinction between mapping abstraction of primary metaphor entities and mapping invocation, of secondary metaphor entities. Primary metaphor entities are activated initially in an all-or-none fashion. The secondary metaphor entities are generated later, when a lack of knowledge is perceived. To avoid unnecessary problems Waterworth (1992) recommends to omit secondary metaphor entities.

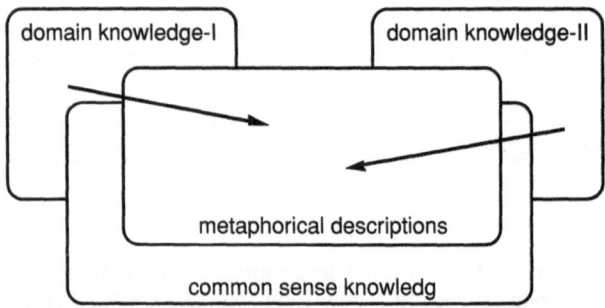

Figure 2. Communication of domain specific knowledge through mapping to a metaphorical description as part of the common sense knowledge.

'In the knowledge lies the power' has become a popular maxim in the context of artificial intelligence. 'In the metaphor lies the power' will become a popular maxim in the context of hypertext and multimedia system design. But, how can we discover suitable metaphors? The conventional way is to choose a metaphor from the set of known metaphors. Another design strategy is to develop a metaphor and look how it works (Carroll 1988). Only a domain expert himself, however, can correctly build all necessary mappings. He is the only one who has full control over his domain knowledge as well as the appropriate metaphorical descriptions of the common sense knowledge. This is the core of our approach: to look for a metaphor engineering method in the framework of a participatory design approach.

To optimise knowledge engineering methods, the following observation was quite interesting: if the knowledge engineer is a woman, then male experts do explain considerably more details compared to the situation where the knowledge engineer is a man. Initiated by this idea we looked for a social context in which a metaphorical language is normally used: this situation is given if adults explain something to children.

First we have to proof the 'children' idea to invent a 'metaphor engineering' method. Second, if the 'children' idea was successful, then we have to develop a practical metaphor engineering method.

2   Validation Procedure

To proof and validate our 'children' idea as a basis for a metaphor engineering method we carried out an empirical investigation. Domain experts explained parts of their domain knowledge to both adults and children. We recorded all explanations of the domain experts on video and analysed this material in terms of the amount of metaphorical descriptions.

2.1   Subjects and Experimental Setting

A total of 6 male students of physics participated as domain experts in this experiment. Twelve children were schoolboys (N=6) and schoolgirls (N=6) of a primary school in Basel (N=8 with age among 8 and 13 years, N=4 with age among 12 and 13 years). Twelve adults (male N=7, female N=5) were students of computer science or physics (N= 9, age 20-25 years) or people with an other educational background (N=3, age 40-50 years).

Each expert had about 10 min explanation time for two different domains. To control sequential effects each expert has to explain both domain problems twice to 2 children and 2 adults in two different orders ([D1 –> D2], [D2 –> D1]), so that each expert explained the two domains to 4 different 'metaphor engineers' (see Table 1). A total of about 40 min explanation time per expert was recorded on video.

2.2   Target Domains and Procedure

The domain experts were instructed to explain the following two problems (domains): (D1) "Why does the sound of a car change, if the car passes by?" (Doppler effect); (D2) "What happens in a bulb, if someone closes the circuit?" (Light generation).

We used a 3-factorial test design with the following three independent variables. Factor A is 'naivety': the presumed knowledge of the 'metaphor engineers' (child, adult). Factor B is 'sex': the sex of the 'metaphor engineers' (male, female). Factor C is 'domain': two domains "Doppler effect" and "light generation." The factor 'sex' was approximately balanced. The factor 'naivety' and 'order' were completely balanced.

To analyse the video sequences we derived categories from the literature (Haverkamp 1983) (Lakoff 1980) (Lieb 1967) (Richards 1936) (Wiedemann 1986). We used 3 fixed categories 'onomatopoeia', 'gesticulation', 'drawing', and open metaphorical categories, which were protocolled during analysing the videos.

A metaphor is defined as follows (Lakoff 1980) (Lieb 1967): (1) If we interpret a word or a syntactical structure of words of an explanation in their ordinary, context free sense ("common sense"), then the meaning of this part of the explanation is senseless or impossible. We call this first condition the "internal incompatibility." (2) If we relate the context free interpretation of a part of an explanation to the context of the whole explanation, then the meaning of this relation is senseless or impossible. We call this second condition the "external incompatibility." We classified parts of an explanation as metaphors, if we found an internal or an external incompatibility.

We discuss one example of a metaphor classification. One domain expert used the metaphorical description of "balls" for atoms to explain domain D2. He said: "All balls strike together." We have no internal incompatibility, but an external incompatibility in the context of electricity in a bulb. Metaphors with an internal incompatibility are often used in poems (e.g., "the green moon sang a sad song"). Sometimes we use this type of metaphor to describe special aspects of user interfaces (e.g., "the interface looks like a transparent house").

2.3   Dependent Variables and Results

Two trained raters (students of computer science at the ETH) analysed 48 video sequences - one for each experimental condition- in 15 seconds' intervals. In this paper we present the results of three dependent variables.

(1) The 'percental ratio of metaphors overall' used in each explanation trial is the
sum of all 15 seconds' intervals, which included the usage of any type of metaphor.
This measure is calculated over all metaphorical categories (fixed and open) cor-
rected by the individual duration of explanation time.

(2) The 'percental ratio of different metaphors' is the sum of all 15 sec. intervals,
which included the usage of different metaphors.

(3) The 'percental ratio of repetitions' of metaphors is the difference between the
'percental ratio of metaphors overall' and the 'percental ratio of different metaphors'.

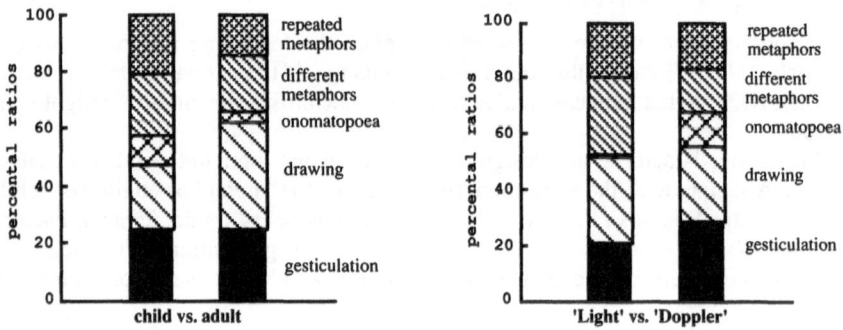

Figure 3. Percental ratios of the behavioural categories differentiated for the factor 'naivety'
and the factor 'domain.'

We analysed the data with a 3-factorial analysis of variances. To give an overview of our results we present the percental ratios of our categories, which describe
the most interesting aspects of the experts' behaviour. The portions of each category
in Figure 3 give only the relative relations among the depicted categories and not
the absolute values among all categories.

2.3.1 Percental Ratio of Metaphors Overall

The percental ratio of metaphors overall is an absolute measure to describe how
much time each domain expert explains the problem to the 'metaphor engineer' with
metaphorical terms. The main effect 'naivety' is significant ($p \leq .016$, see Table 2).
We can observe a moderate difference between both domain problems ($p \leq .067$, see
Table 2). The six experts tried to illustrate the domain "Doppler effect" using
metaphorical terms on average 35.7% of their explanation time. To illustrate the
domain "light generation" they used metaphors in 28.3% of their explanation time.

The domain experts used significantly more metaphors explaining to children
(mean 37.8% of explanation time, N=24, see Table 2) compared to talking to adults
(26.3%, N=24, see Table 2). We did not find a significant effect of the sex of the
'metaphor engineers,' but a significant interaction between the factors 'naivety' and

'sex' (p≤ .017, see Table 2). Basically, the experts used the maximum of metaphorical terms talking to boys and the minimum of metaphors talking to men. The domain experts differed in their use of a metaphorical language. So, we got a significant difference between the 'metaphorical' language of the 6 experts (p≤ .001; result
of an additional analysis).

Source	df	F-test	prob		male (%)	female(%)	total	N
A naivety	1	6.226	.017	child	39.7±13.7	35.8±12.7	37.8	24
B sex	1	2.337	.134	adult	19.6±14.9	35.7±14.5	26.3	24
C domain	1	3.539	.067					
A x B	1	6.176	.017	total	28.9±17.4	35.813.2	32.0	
A x C	1	1.288	.263	N	26	22		48
B x C	1	.015	.902					
A x B x C	1	.213	.647	(group means of metaphors overall)				

Table 2. ANOVA results of the dependent variable 'percental ratio of metaphors overall' with
factors 'naivety', 'sex', and 'domain', and the absolute means for the factors 'naivety' and 'sex.'
[Cell mean ± standard deviation]

2.3.2 Percental Ratio of Different Metaphors

The experts used significantly more different metaphors talking to a female (19.6%,
see Table 3) than talking to a male person (14.7%, p≤.014, see Table 3). The
domain "light generation" evoked on average 20.7% metaphors, the domain
"Doppler effect" only 13.3% (p≤.009, see Table 3). We see a clear minimum of
different metaphors in the cell 'male-adult' (significant interaction 'naivety' and 'sex',
p≤ .001, see Table 3).

The experts differ in explaining both domain problems. Two experts (33%) prefer
significantly the female 'metaphor engineers.' Also, to illustrate the 'light' problem
the experts use significantly more different metaphorical categories than to illustrate the 'Doppler' problem. To demonstrate the Doppler effect most of the experts
used onomatopoeia (Light generation: 1%, Doppler effect: 11%, p≤ .001, see Figure
3).

Source	df	F-test	prob		male (%)	female(%)	total	N
A naivety	1	2.726	.107	child	19.1± 5.6	18.7± 6.7	18.9	24
B sex	1	6.667	.014	adult	11.0± 8.0	20.8± 8.4	15.0	24
C domain	1	16.928	.001					
A x B	1	7.596	.009	total	14.7± 8.0	19.6± 7.4	17.0	
A x C	1	.615	.438	N	26	22		48
B x C	1	.502	.483					
A x B x C	1	.037	.847	(group means of different metaphors)				

Table 3. ANOVA results of the dependent variable 'percental ratio of different metaphors'
with factors 'naivety', 'sex', and 'domain', and the absolute means for the factors 'naivety' and
'sex.' [Cell mean ± standard deviation]

2.3.3 Percental Ratio of Repeated Metaphors

The experts used significantly more repetitions talking to a child (18.8%) than talking to an adult (11.3%, p≤ .020, see Table 4). We see a clear minimum of repeated metaphors in the cell 'male-adult' (8.6%, no significant interaction 'naivety' and 'sex', p≤ .095, see Table 4).

```
-------------------------------------     -------------------------------------------
 Source            df   F-test   prob        male (%)    female(%)   total  N
-------------------------------------     -------------------------------------------
 A naivety          1   5.884    .020      child 20.6±11.6  17.1± 8.7    18.8  24
 B sex              1    .241    .626      adult  8.6± 9.5  15.0± 8.5    11.3  24
 C domain           1    .001    .993      -------------------------------------------
    A x B           1   2.928    .095      total 14.2±12.0  16.2± 8.5    15.1
    A x C           1   1.171    .286         N   26          22                 48
    B x C           1    .076    .784      -------------------------------------------
    A x B x C       1    .271    .606      (group means of repeated metaphors)
-------------------------------------     -------------------------------------------
```

Table 4. ANOVA results of the dependent variable 'percental ratio of repeated metaphors' with factors 'naivety', 'sex', and 'domain', and the absolute means for the factors 'naivety' and 'sex.' [Cell mean ± standard deviation]

2.3.4 Discussion

Our main hypothesis was confirmed (see Table 2). If the domain experts explain their domain problems to children, then we can observe that they repeat their introduced metaphors (see Table 4) and do not generate new metaphors within the context of a metaphorical category (see Table 3). In many cases the domain experts prefer to change the metaphorical category (see Table 3). So, children are suitably to play the role of a 'metaphor engineer', of course not exactly the same role as a 'knowledge engineer'; they function more like a 'catalyst' in a metaphor extraction session.

We can conclude from our results, that male adults are definitely not appropriate to play the role of a 'metaphor engineer' (see Table 3). The most appropriate persons are children or female adults (see Table 3 and Table 4).

What else do we need further on for a metaphor generation method? We have the verification that male domain experts use a more metaphorical language explaining something to children or women than talking to other men.

The final and till now unsolved step is to develop a guide, which describes the whole procedure: (1) criteria for selection of the domain expert, (2) criteria for selection of the 'metaphor engineer', (3) requirements for the interview session, (4) criteria for the analysis phase, and (5) a set of rules to convert narrative metaphors into design metaphors.

3   Multimedia Interface Design: an Example

What kinds of metaphors are generated by the domain experts? How can we transform these metaphors to multimedia design? We try to give preliminary answers to these questions in this section.

First, we present three examples, and then we discuss the transformation of these examples to multimedia design. One domain expert used the following description to explain the Doppler effect (D1): "Imagine you stand at a highway and you hear a car passing you: Iiiioouum!" The expert introduced the context 'highway with cars' and used an onomatopoeia to demonstrate the Doppler effect.

Figure 4. An interface design for the 'light generation' domain based on the 'people – road' metaphor.

Another domain expert described the light generation (D2) with the following words: "Imagine the circuit as a river or a brook. A power plant pumps water on a high level. At your home the water falls down and drives a water wheel." Another expert explained the same domain with the following metaphor: "Imagine a demon-stration of people on a large road in a city. The head reaches a narrow lane. To avoid jams in the narrow lane the people have to hurry up. They slow down again when they reach a large road."

As one can see from these three examples, the transformations to the design of multimedia interfaces appear to be quite simple and straight forward. The first ex-ample leads us to the implementation of a sound track. The second example shows a more complex metaphor. We can transform water, power plant, house, and water wheel directly into a dynamic animated environment. With this metaphorical de-scription, however, we can not explain the effect of resistance. From the third me-taphorical description we can derive immediately an appropriate extension for the last metaphor. Consequently, we better change completely the design from passive 'water' to active 'people' (see Figure 4).

4   Conclusion

Let us summarise the main results of our study. We were interested in finding a method for metaphor generation, which is practicable in a participatory design mo-del (Rauterberg 1992). According to our results, children and female adults are sui-tably to play the role of a 'catalyst' in a metaphor engineering session. We presented the following two practicable criteria, which are helpful to detect metaphors in a narrative interview (Lieb 1967): (1) If we interpret a word or a syntactical structure of words of an explanation in their ordinary, context free sense ("common sense"), then the meaning of this part of the explanation is senseless or impossible. (2) If we relate the context free interpretation of a part of an explanation to the context of the whole explanation, then the meaning of this relation is senseless or impossible. Finally, we illustrated the way from metaphor extraction to multimedia interface design. In this paper we presented the epistemological basis for this approach.

Metaphors are powerful but not sufficient to come up with a good interface. Single, over-detailed metaphors can be too restrictive and unwieldy (Waterworth 1992). Carroll (1988) is right that "effective interface metaphors often evolve over time through design, evaluation and redesign." We could show that the approach presented in this paper leads to a promising starting point of the cyclical design process.

5   References

(Carroll 1982) Carroll J. M. & Thomas J. C. (1982) Metaphor and the cognitive representation of computing systems. IEEE Transactions on Systems, Man, and Cybernetics SMC-12(2):107-115.

(Carroll 1985) Carroll J. M. & Mack R. L. (1985) Metaphor, computing systems, and active learning. International Journal of Man-Machine Studies 22:39-57.

(Carroll 1988) Carroll J. M., Mack R. L. & Kellog W. A. (1988) Interface metaphors and user interface design. In Handbook of Human-Computer Interaction. (M. Helander, ed., pp. 67-85) Amsterdam: North-Holland, 1988.

(Chauvet 1991) Chauvet J-M. (1991) Graphical user interfaces: metaphors we compute by. In Human Aspects in Computing: Design and Use of Interactive Systems and Work with Terminals. (H-J. Bullinger, ed., pp. 308-313) Amsterdam: Elsevier, 1991.

(Eberleh 1991) Eberleh E. (1991) Browsing cognitive task spaces instead of working on the desktop: an alternative metaphor. In Human Aspects in Computing: Design and Use of Interactive Systems and Work with Terminals. (H-J. Bullinger, ed., pp. 419-423) Amsterdam: Elsevier, 1991.

(Gould 1990) Gould M. D. & McGranaghan M. (1990) Metaphor in geographic information systems. In Proceedings of the 4th International Symposium on Spatial Data Handling. (K. Brassel & H. Kishimoto, eds., pp. 433-442) Columbus: Ohio State University, 1990.

(Hammond 1987) Hammond N. & Allison L. (1987) The Travel Metaphor as Design Principle and Training Aid for Navigating around Complex Systems. In People and Computers III. (D. Diaper & R. Winder, eds.) Cambridge: Cambridge University.

(Haverkamp 1983) Haverkamp A. (1983, ed.) Theorie der Metapher. Darmstadt: Wissenschaftliche Buchgesellschaft, 1983.

(Henderson 1986) Henderson D. A. & Card S. K. (1986) Rooms: the use of multiple virtual workspaces to reduce space contention in a window-based graphical user interface. ACM Transactions on Graphics 5(3):211-243.

(Hutchins 1989) Hutchins E. L. (1989) Metaphors for Interface Design. In The Structure of Multimodal Dialogue. (D.G. Bouwhis, M.M. Taylor & F. Neel, eds.) Amsterdam: North Holland.

(Lakoff 1980) Lakoff G. & Johnson M. (1980) Metaphors we live by. Chicago: The University Press, 1980.

(Lieb 1967) Lieb H-H. (1967) Was bezeichnet der herkömmliche Begriff Metapher? Muttersprache 77:43-52.

(Rauterberg 1992) Rauterberg M. (1992) An iterativ-cyclic software process model. In Proceedings of the 4th International Conference on Software Engineering and Knowledge Engineering. (pp. 600-607) Los Alamitos: IEEE Computer Society Press.

(Richards 1936) Richards I. A. (1936) The Philosophy of Rhetoric. Oxford: Oxford University Press, 1936.

(Shum 1990) Shum S. (1990) Real and virtual spaces: mapping from spatial cognition to hypertext. Hypermedia 2(2):133-158.

(Waterworth 1992) Waterworth J. A. (1992) Multimedia Interaction with Computers - Human Factors Issues. New York: Ellis Horwood.

(Weyer 1985) Weyer S. A. & Borning J. (1985) A Prototype Electronic Encyclopedia. ACM Transactions on Office Information Systems 3(1):63-88.

(Wiedemann 1986) Wiedemann P. M. (1986) Erzählte Wirklichkeit – zur Theorie und Auswertung narrativer Interviews. Weinheim München: Psychologie Verlags Union, 1986.

Metaphor–based User Interfaces for Hyperspaces

Kaisa Väänänen

Computer Graphics Center (ZGDV), Darmstadt, Germany

Abstract. This paper describes an approach to improve usability of hypermedia information systems by using concrete user interface metaphors. Metaphors are recommended to be used here in two ways: Firstly, to support authors who construct hypermedia applications, and secondly, to support the users who navigate within these hyperspaces. Various types of metaphors must be offered in order to support the goals of different users. An authoring tool can embody these metaphors thus making them available to the authors who can then perceive the system in much the same way as the users. This paper first discusses the motivation for using metaphors in the user interfaces to hyperspaces. A prototype of a *metaphor–based authoring tool* for multimedia environments – called ShareME (Shared Multimedia Environments) – is presented and its metaphors discussed.

1 Introduction

Hypermedia information systems considered here are information retrieval applications where multimedia information (text, graphics, video, audio etc.) is arranged in conceptually well–defined *information spaces* (Brown 1990), (Väänänen 1993). This concept is partially based on the hypermedia–type node and link structures, and partially on the wider concept of *interactive multimedia* (Ambron & Hooper 1990), (Marmolin 1991). Users of these interactive multimedia environments, or hyperspaces, must be able to (inter)act in these spaces – to *navigate* within them – in intuitive ways, without a high cognitive load (Dyke Parunak 1989), (Andersen 1990).

Within such hyperspaces, multimedia can be used in two ways. Multimedia can be used either as information contents (application–dependent information) helping the user understand the *meaning* of the retrieved information, or multimedia may be used in the user interface (application–independent system feedback) thus helping the user in *navigating* through the information. Ideally, both aspects of multimedia usage should be integrated seamlessly, at the same time taking care of application– and user–specific needs on different media types and combinations.

There are two types of human operators involved in development and use of hypermedia systems for information retrieval. The *author* first constructs the hyperspace using computer–based *authoring tools*. The *user* then acquires information by moving around in the hyperspace using various *navigation methods* offered in the user interface. Therefore, there are two view points to the issues of multimedia spaces: the user's view, and the author's view.

The significance of this work lies in attempts of solving two problems. Firstly, current multimedia authoring tools offer hardly any high–level interface objects to be used in the applications under construction. Also, these tools normally require some form of programming. Secondly, when information environments which are modelled according to some machine–oriented concept such as node and link network, the users may easily "get lost" in the information structures. This may lead to the rejection of the entire system as being difficult and frustrating to use.

Next section analyzes the goals and problems of the two types of users: authors and users. The following section then discusses the metaphor approach, and considers specifically what kind of metaphors are most appropriate for hyperspaces. The section after that presents the system ShareME that has been implemented according to the presented metaphor principles. The final section discusses experiences and problems that arise from this metaphor–based approach.

2 Goals and Problems of Hypermedia Systems

The user's main goal is to find all information relevant to their interest, and to do this in a reasonable amount of time. Furthermore, the user should find this interaction process enjoyable and engaging. The author's main goal is to communicate some planned information contents to the users. This should be done in a way that the author's intended meaning of the information will be transmitted, and at the same time the user's goals becomes fulfilled.

A hypermedia system should

- allow successful acquisition of all relevant information as well as an easy authoring process
- convey information in the "right" medium (and redundantly when needed)
- support various types of users
- be easy, intuitive, attractive, entertaining and engaging to use
- encourage exploration

2.1 Users' problems

The user's main problem in interacting with hypermedia is the difficulty in understanding the structure and contents of the information space, that is, not knowing *what* is there, and *how* to access it.

Users' problems are due to the lack of

- views on different levels of detail — the user should be able to "zoom" to the details of information, as well as to get overviews on the various topics
- appropriate navigation methods — the user should have various means to get to their goal, depending on their navigation strategy
- system feedback — the user should be given immediate, visual and consistent cues of what is happening as the result of their actions

♦ content–based retrieval methods — the user should be able to get information based on the semantic and syntactic contents of multimedia information

♦ multimodality — the users should have various means for interaction, to be used either simultaneously or in sequence

The work described in this paper attempts to offer support for the first three items on this list. For solutions to the two last items, see (Burrill et al. 1993) and (Blattner and Dannenberg 1992), respectively.

2.2   Author's problems

Most of the existing authoring tools for multi– and hypermedia require extensive programming, or at least definition of the logical structuring of interactions with some computer–based method such as timeline or icons representing different logical structures. This limits drastically the usability of these authoring tools by non–computer–experts. The authors should not have to do any programming, since they are experts in their theme area, but probably not computer programmers. Therefore, an authoring tool should support other, visual, direct and intuitive ways of constructing hyperspaces.

The author needs to

♦ consider the best representation medium for each piece of information, together with the granularity of information

♦ design the structure of the information space; combinations of media and relations of information

♦ provide the interaction methods in the user interface

Overall, the author needs to communicate to a variety of users the contents of the application subject in a sensible order. In performing this authoring process, the author has a secondary meta–goal of attempting to communicate to the user

♦ the structure

♦ type and overview of contents

♦ how to access the info (how to use the interaction methods)

Many of the author's problems arise from not understanding the tools available for construction that often require programming. In addition to that, and as is very often the case, the author may not have skills of an "information designer" nor of a user interface designer.

3   User Interface Metaphors for Authors and Users

One prominent solution to the problems of authors and users of hypermedia systems is the application of concrete and motivating *user interface metaphors*.

Metaphors are *analogical models* to something existing outside the domain to which they are applied. Thus, knowledge in one, already familiar domain is directly applicable in another, less familiar domain. Metaphors are used in user interfaces to assure that the user can rapidly adopt a correct mental model of how the system works, thus minimizing the amount of system–specific learning that the user has to do. This suggests that metaphors are especially suitable for casual and computer–naive users. (General references for user interface metaphors can be found in (Carroll and Kellogg 1988), (Erickson 1990) and (Streitz 1988).)

User interface metaphors may cover several, partly overlapping aspects of an information system:

♦ *Presentation* – how do the objects and information spaces look, sound and feel

♦ *Structure* – what are the relationships within and between information spaces

♦ *Interactivity* – how can the user interact with the information spaces

3.1 Hypermedia Metaphor Characteristics

It is of a special interest to find appropriate metaphors that are *concrete* enough in their visual presentation, in order to let the user achieve rapid and intuitive understanding of the system functionality. Such metaphors can best be found in real–world domains. If chosen appropriately and implemented in a visually (aurally, haptically) effective way, these *real–world metaphors* can support both the users and authors in their processes of interacting with and the construction of hypermedia environments.

Hypermedia requires structural metaphors because of the inherent problem in the hyperstructures of "getting lost in the hyperspace". The structures of the metaphor will then lend themselves to impose additional structure and landmarks on the hypermedia application domain. Thus, various structures such as a group, a hierarchy or a network of the multimedia information becomes more familiar when presented as a house (Väänänen 1993), a city (Dieberger 1993) or an information landscape (Chalmers 1993).

The hypermedia metaphors will also need to embody inherent and intuitive navigation methods. These navigation methods need to be visual and presented through their natural *affordances* (Norman 1988). Thus, a door in a house represents a way to enter a information space, and an obvious way to go through the door is to knock on it. (In a more exploratory systems, though, the object presentations can also be more arbitrary. For example, a tree or an animal in a landscape, or furniture in a house may present an access point to further information.)

In addition, multimedia information systems need visual, and further, multimedia metaphors in order to match the quality and interactivity of the user interface to the quality and interactivity of the application information. Also the temporal aspects of dynamic media can be used for different effects. For example, video can be used to give an overview of the information space, and the objects on the video can act as entry points to further information (Burrill and Väänänen 1994).[1]

Spatial metaphors offer natural mapping between the hyperspace and the metaphor–based space. They may offer the user a solid cognitive model for navigation.

---

[1].   Another approach is to use virtual reality as a highly interactive and realistic user interface. See (Böhm et al. 1992) for an approach on VR user interfaces.

Such metaphors may present both 2D and 3D spaces (e.g. a book or a house, respectively).

In summary, metaphors for hypermedia need to be

♦ concrete and familiar

♦ highly and explicitly structural

♦ visual and multimedia

♦ spatial

3.2   Current Authoring Tools and their Deficiencies

Authoring tools can be classified in the following way in terms of the overall authoring style they use (Hetzner & Kummer 1992), (Nickel 1991):

♦ **Script–based systems.** The author writes short programs ("scripts") that control the interaction sequences (e.g. ToolBook, HyperCard).

♦ **Icon–based systems.** The system offers the author "icons", with which logical control structures can be defined (e.g. Authorware Professional, IconAuthor).

♦ **Time–based systems.** The author can synchronize various media and user's actions via "time lines" (e.g. Score module of MacroMind Director,Quick-Time).

Script–based methods allow a very flexible design, but the author must normally do a considerable amount of programming to achieve complex information systems. In icon–based systems authors do not need to write any program *code* as such, but they must understand and be able to construct logical flow charts with icons describing the interaction structures. Time–based systems offer advanced possibilities for the synchronization of various (esp. temporal) media, but support for the logical structuring of information and interaction is very limited.

A common deficiency of these multimedia authoring tool types is the lack of support mechanisms for design and implementation tasks of structuring information and constructing user interfaces for information spaces. More high–level methods are needed in order to avoid the extra work of the author, and in order to assure the coherency and usability of the resulting information system. For this end, metaphors are suggested as means of support for both the authors and end–users.

3.3   Use of Metaphors by Authors and Users

Various types of metaphors can be integrated within an authoring tool for multimedia environments. These metaphors are used in a similar manner by both the authors and subsequent by the users who visit the environments.

Firstly, the design of information structures may be supported by an *authoring metaphor* (such as a book, flowchart or theatre). These metaphors are used to help the author structure the information and interaction sequences but do not necessarily help the author understand the information structures and interaction possibilities from the user's point of view; these metaphors are, in fact, invisible to the users.

Secondly, the system may be supported by a *user's metaphor*. The user sees the information in a multimedia environment presented via a metaphor, and can interact with this information as if manipulating the originating objects belonging to the metaphor.

It was concluded in the previous section that the major problem with current multimedia authoring tools is in the lack of support mechanisms for design and implementation tasks for structuring information and user interfaces. The solution suggested here is that the same user interface metaphors are offered to both authors and users. This will allow authors to construct applications based on a predefined (and pretested) user interface design and without having to implement it themselves. Taken that the author chooses a sensible metaphor, the user will then be guaranteed a system that is intuitive and easy to learn and use.

The type of tool based on the concepts presented above is called a *metaphor–based authoring tool*.

4 ShareME: A Metaphor–based Authoring Tool for Multimedia Environments

ShareME – Shared Multimedia Environments – is both an authoring tool for multimedia environments and a run–time system that supports users in their task of finding information while navigating through the multimedia spaces constructed with the tool (Väänänen 1993a). ShareME uses multimedia both as information contents, and in the metaphor–based user interfaces to those environments.

4.1 ShareME Authoring Process

The ShareME tool is used without any programming. The author only has to take the following steps to construct a multimedia environment:

◆ collect and prepare the multimedia information and create links between them

◆ select a metaphor from the set of metaphors offered by the tool

◆ interactively insert the multimedia information into the structure of the metaphor; the author sees the environment through the metaphor in the same way as the end users will

Relationships between information nodes are defined either by arranging the related nodes in the same "place" or object (such as a room or a bookshelf), and by explicitly creating hyperlinks between the nodes. All this is done interactively, manipulating the objects directly.

4.2 ShareME Navigation Process

The user of a multimedia environment sees the multimedia information as being located *within* the structure of the metaphor. All interaction is performed in terms of the metaphor – it is therefore most certainly intuitive and requires only a minimal exploratory learning period.

The user typically has a goal when using a hypermedia system. An example of a *specific goal* is "I want to find a hotel in Rostock which costs less than 50 DM per night". An example of a *vague goal* is "I want to know something about churches in eastern Germany". The goal can also be just to *explore* the information environment.

Navigation is an iterative process, and be seen as follows:

♦ Developing an understanding about the facilities offered by the system.

♦ Moving around the information space using the navigation methods.

♦ Orientation and reorientation (Where am I? Where was I? Where can I go now?) (Love 1991).

♦ Reaching the goal (finding interesting information and identifying it as interesting).

The system should ideally minimise the time spent on the familiarization period of the interaction process, and allow immediate use of various intuitive navigation methods for performing the iterative steps of process.

The primary navigation method in ShareME is to move around using the *overview maps*. Overview maps show the structure and contents of the hyperspace via the metaphor–based representations of the objects and structures. The navigation is done directly by clicking on the place (represented by an icon) where one wants to go. Traversing hyperlinks between nodes takes the user to a related node or context. These "jumps" will then be reflected immediately in the overview maps.

4.3   ShareME Metaphors

One metaphor used in ShareME is that of a *house*, where the pieces of multimedia information hang as if they were pictures on the walls of the *rooms* of the house. This metaphor is represented by 2D graphical overview maps representing the various levels of the structure (see Figure 1 for metaphor–based objects of the house metaphor). The rooms may be personalized by setting different wallpapers in rooms representing different topics in the theme of the system.

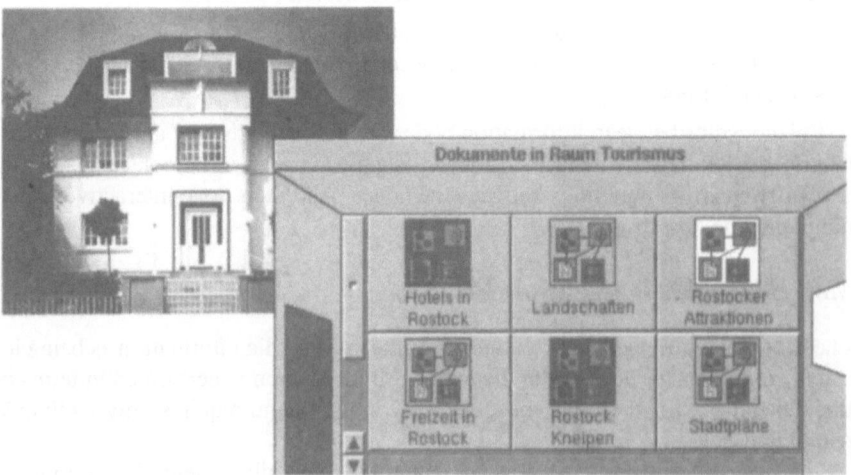

Fig. 1. The ShareME house metaphor: the house entry and the room overview map

Another metaphor implemented in ShareME is a *library* with bookshelves and books. This metaphor offers deeper hierarchy than in the house (bookshelves, shelves, books, chapters and pages). (See Figure 2. for a sample of the ShareME session with the library metaphor.) The library metaphor is more flexible than the house metaphor since the author can use just one bookshelf, or a book without chapters.

Multimedia metaphors are currently being investigated. These metaphors will use video and (later) audio as the primary interface medium. Video metaphors being designed include:

◆ a geographical landscape with towns, houses, trees, animals, people

◆ advertisement– and game–like video representations

◆ "traditional" metaphors like the house and library based on the video medium

It is estimated that a fully implemented metaphor–based authoring tool should contain a set of 20–30 different user interface metaphor alternatives (and combinations thereof). From this set the author chooses the one that best suits the structure and contents of the application information and the target users. The goal of ShareME as a metaphor testbed is to implement 5–7 metaphors. These metaphors will then be tested for their appropriateness for different application and user types.

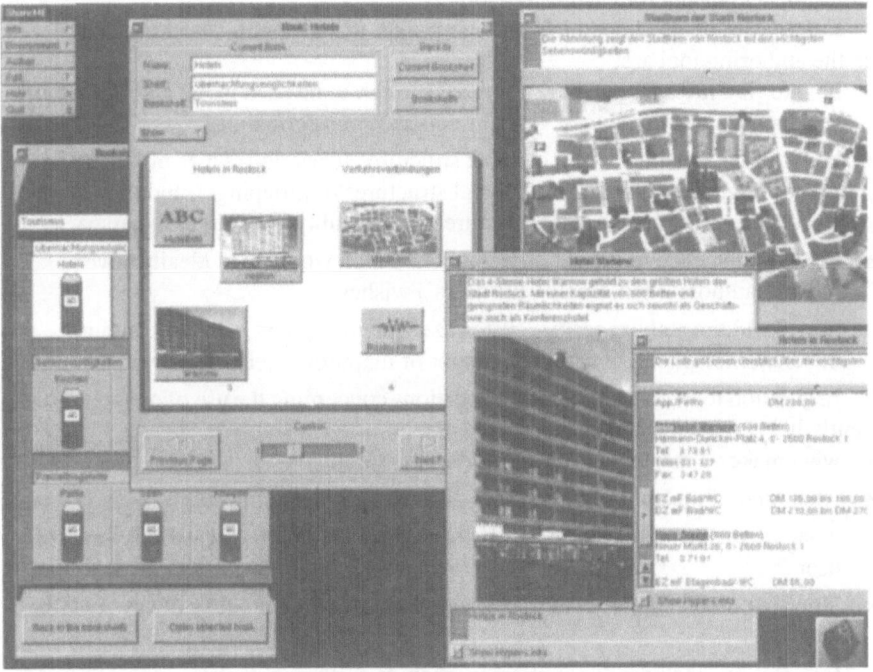

Fig. 2. The ShareME library metaphor: an example of a tourist information system

It is acknowledged that there will always be applications for which none of the metaphors offered is suitable, or which do not satisfy the author's personal taste. It is intended however to learn from experience and try to provide as representative a set of metaphors as possible, all of which can be used to construct a multimedia environment very quickly and easily. It is also an aim to test these metaphors with users to gain knowledge about the applicability of various types of metaphors.

5 Experiences and Discussion

This paper has described an approach to using various types of metaphors for interfaces to multimedia information environments. Problems of hypermedia authors and users were discussed, and it has been justified why metaphors provide a prominent solution. A system called ShareME embodying such metaphors has been presented, together with concrete examples of its user interface metaphors.

Experiences and open questions concerning the design of metaphor–based user interfaces are briefly summarized in the following.

It is not trivial to find or invent "good" or appropriate user interface metaphors. The process of designing a (real–world) metaphor–based user interface requires creative thinking and a considerable amount of "looking around" in the every day environment. In addition, the metaphor designer must decide the appropriate presentation style and media for each metaphor.

Further problems concerning the integration of metaphor–based user interfaces in the authoring tool are:

♦ how to find metaphors that are general enough to be used in the authoring tool (i.e. can be used for several types of application information)

♦ how to find metaphors with suitable structures for various types of hyperspaces (e.g. with flexible hierarchical structures or groupings), and how to effectively illustrate the total structure of a (possibly very large) hyperspace

♦ how to select a covering set of metaphors which would then ideally cover most of authors' (and, finally, the users') wishes

♦ how could the authors easily "customize" the metaphors, or even combine different metaphors, without the danger of inappropriately mixed metaphors

In addition to these design issues, questions concerning the use of metaphors currently being investigated and evaluated are:

♦ what makes a metaphor intuitive and motivating?

♦ what kind of metaphors are suitable to what kinds of applications?

♦ what are the benefits and trade–offs of various metaphors for various kinds of users?

♦ how are combined or mixed metaphors understood, or are they always confusing?

Future work includes the implementation of further metaphors in the ShareME authoring tool as described in the paper. It is of a special interest how *multimedia metaphors* support interaction in multimedia environments. Finally, user testing based on a sample set of the user interface metaphors will be performed in order to investigate which metaphors are most usable and intuitive for various kinds of applications, users and usage situations.

References

Ambron,S., Hooper,K. (1990). Learning with Interactive Multimedia: Developing and Using Multimedia Tools in Education. Microsoft Press, 1990.

Andersen,P.B. (1990). Towards an aesthetics of hypertext systems — A semiotic approach. In Rizk,A., Streitz,N., André,J. (Eds.), *Hypertext: Concepts, Systems and Applications*, Proceedings of the European Conference on Hypertext, INRIA, France, November 1990, pp. 224–237.

Blattner,M.M., Dannenberg,R.B. (Eds.) (1990). Multimedia Interface Design. ACM Press, 1992.

Böhm,K., Hübner,W., Väänänen,K. (1992). GIVEN: A 3D Toolkit for Interactions in Virtual Environments. *Proc. of Interfaces to Real and Virtual Worlds*, Montpellier, France, March 1992.

Brown,P.J. (1990). Assessing the quality of hypertext documents. In Rizk,A., Streitz,N., André,J. (Eds.), *Hypertext: Concepts, Systems and Applications*, Proceedings of the European Conference on Hypertext, INRIA, France, November 1990, pp. 1–24.

Burrill,V., Kirste.T., Weiss,J. (1993). Time–varying sensitive regions in dynamic multimedia objects: A pragmatic approach to content–based retrieval from video, *Information and Software Technology*, Butterworth–Heinemann, 1993.

Burrill,V., Väänänen,K. (1994). Books, Houses and Grazing Cows: The Evolution of Real–world User Interface Metaphors form Static to Dynamic Media. Will be submitted to *Interacting with Computers, 1994*.

Carroll,J.M. and Kellogg,W.A. (1988). Interface Metaphors. In Helander,M. (Ed.), User Interface Design Handbook, Elsevier, 1988.

Chalmers, M. (1993). Using a Landscape Metaphor to Represent a Corpus of Documents. *Proceedings of the European Conference on Spatial Information Theory*, Elba, Italy, September 1993.

Dieberger,A. (1993). The Information City — A Metaphor for Navigating Hypertexts. A research paper at *British Computer Society's HCI'93*, Loughborough, Sept. 1993.

Dyke Parunak, van,H. (1989). Hypermedia Topologies and User Navigation. *Proceedings of Hypertext'89*, Nov. 89. pp. 43–50.

Erickson,T.D. (1990).Working with Interface Metaphors. In Laurel,B. (Ed.), The Art of Human–Computer Interface Design, Apple Computer Inc., 1990.

Herzner,W., Kummer,M. (1992). MMV – Synchronizing Multimedia Documents", *Proc. of 2nd Eurographics Workshop on Multimedia*, Darmstadt, May 1992, Springer–Verlag.

Marmolin,H. (1991). Multimedia from the Perspectives of Psychology. *Proceedings of 1st Eurographics Workshop on Multimedia*, Stockholm, Sweden, Springer–Verlag, April 1991.

Nickel,T. (1991). The Developer's Dilemma. *Computer Graphics World*, Vol. 14, No. 7, July 1991, pp. 97 – 102.

Norman,D. (1988). Psychology of Everyday Things. Basic Books, 1988.

Streitz,N.A. (1988). Mental Models and Metaphors: Implications for the Design of Adaptive User–System Interfaces. In Learning Issues for Intelligent Tutoring Systems, Springer–Verlag, 1988.

Väänänen,K. (1993) Interfaces to Hypermedia: Communicating the Structure and Interaction Possibilities to the Users. *Computers & Graphics*, Vol.17, No.3, 1993.

Väänänen,K. (1993a). ShareME: A Metaphor–based Authoring Tool for Multimedia Environments. *Proceedings of to Vienna HCI'93*, Springer–Verlag, September 1993.

Love, S.J., Chapman, C.M., Connelly, T.G., Ten Haken,J.D. (1991). Design techniques for Ensuring Structure and Flexibility in a Hypermedia Environment. *Multimedia Review,* Summer 1991.

Architecture and User Interface of the IDEAS Intelligent Documentation System[*]

Andreas Birk[1], Bidjan Tschaitschian[1], Franz Schmalhofer[1],
Manfred Thüring[2], and Heiner Gertzen[3]

[1] German Research Center for Artificial Intelligence, Kaiserslautern
[2] empirica GmbH, Communications and Technology Research, Bonn
[3] Hoechst AG, Frankfurt, Germany

Abstract. In pharmaceutical industry, each new drug is tested in clinical studies before it is released on the market. Any adverse event occurring in such a study requires a difficult decision: Is the event caused by the drug under investigation or by other factors? The human decision maker trying to answer this question faces a complex problem and must consider a multitude of heterogeneous data and numerous knowledge sources. IDEAS is an intelligent documentation system (IDS) that supports this type of complex decision making. It provides (a) a model of expertise from which all relevant data and knowledge sources can be easily accessed and (b) an action event model which documents the results of the decision process. The IDEAS system is designed as a hypertext application implemented in a spreadsheet environment. The combination of the model of expertise with the 'Spreadsheet Metaphor' aims to overcome well-known problems of hypertexts, such as 'disorientation', 'cognitive overload' and 'overchoice'.

1 Introduction

Aschenbrenner et al. (1993) have recently suggested to develop an intelligent documentation system (IDS) for the explanation of adverse events in clinical studies, called the IDEAS system. An adverse event is defined as any undesirable sign, symptom or other finding occurring in subjects or patients exposed to a drug. The development of IDEAS is based on the requirements of the application domain, i.e. on requirements put forward by quality assurance in pharmaceutical industry. To satisfy these requirements, recent results from the decision sciences

---

[*] IDEAS stands for 'Intelligent Documentation for the Explanation of Adverse events in clinical Studies'. This work is financially supported by the division of clinical research and quality assurance of the Hoechst AG Frankfurt. We would like to thank K. M. Aschenbrenner, O. Kühn and J. Schmidt for their contributions. Willi Schmitz assisted in implementing the described user-interface.

(Gertzen 1990; Gertzen et al. 1993) and knowledge engineering methods
(Schmalhofer et al. 1991) are integrated into IDEAS.

Before a new drug can be released on the market, clinical studies are demanded
by law. They aim to ensure drug efficacy and drug safety with respect to potential
side effects and interactions with other substances. In the course of such a study, a
variety of adverse events may occur which must be classified and explained to
determine whether they are caused by the drug under investigation. This decision
is made by human experts, *clinical project managers* and *drug safety managers*,
using information and knowledge from numerous heterogeneous sources. The
experts must process all relevant information, generate a causal model which
explains the event, derive several judgements from the causal model and finally
document their explanation. Usually, they are overburdened with a high
proportion of routine cases, impeding application of their sophisticated medical
skills to the many exceptional cases. Therefore, the issue of how the explanation
of an adverse event can be supported by automated routines and knowledge based
methods is of crucial importance.

Typically, pharmaceutical projects proceed along the lines of well established
procedures and regulations which a drug trial must adhere to. The main steps of
these normative procedures must be properly understood and modelled to develop
a computer system which appropriately supports the human experts involved in a
pharmaceutical project. IDEAS meets this requirement by using a model of
expertise (Breuker & Wielinga 1989) which represents the required steps for
classifying and explaining adverse events in clinical studies (see figure 1).

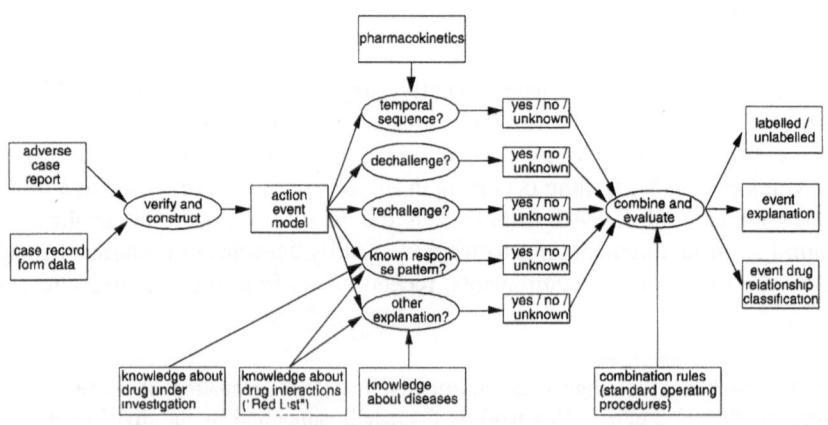

Figure 1: The IDEAS model of expertise for decision making in pharmaceutical studies
(after Aschenbrenner et al., 1993)

The model of expertise can be regarded as a certain type of task model (e.g. Kieras & Polson 1985; Gray et al. 1992) which consists of several layers and is structured in a specific way. It is incorporated into the IDEAS system and is represented as a net of :

- succeeding subtasks, called 'knowledge sources' (ellipses in figure 1),
- and knowledge or data categories, called 'metaclasses' (rectangles in figure 1).

The sequence of subtasks shown in the model constitutes the 'backbone' of decision making in a clinical study. Knowledge and data categories are used to accomplish these subtasks or are produced as output when a task is finished.

The initial input to the decision procedure consists of the case record, form data and the actual *adverse case report*, a standard form containing information in natural language (left side of figure 1). The input is transformed into the formal *action event model* representing a sequence of actions and events which are likely to have caused the adverse event. Based on standard operating procedures in pharmaceutical industries, the action event model is evaluated according to five criteria (ellipses in the middle of figure 1). The output of this evaluation is the final classification of the event and its explanation clarifying whether it was resulted from the drug under investigation or from alternative causes (right side of figure 1).

To support an expert proceeding according to the model of expertise, IDEAS is conceived as an intelligent documentation system (IDS) based on a combination of a knowledge based methods and hypertext facilities. An IDS enables its user to view the various processing components in the course of decision making and to intervene if necessary (Fischer & Reeves 1991; Schmalhofer et al. 1992). The model of expertise in figure 1 illustrates the IDS structure and serves as starting point for the interaction between user and system. Thus an intelligent documentation system can be expected to provide high transparency of the problem solving process and should be particularly useful when a task has to be accomplished in close cooperation between user and system.

According to law and the required responsibility, the review of clinical studies must be performed by a human decision maker. Therefore an IDS can not make decisions of its own. Nevertheless, it ought to be very helpful as an assistant to the decision maker. In the cooperative process between user and system, the action event model serves as the explication of the decision maker's conceptual model of the current case. It is constructed incrementally and presented as a hypertext in which the user can navigate and retrieve further information. Consequently, an intelligent documentation system in the IDEAS domain coordinates human computer interaction by two models: The overall task's model (figure 1) and the action event model specific to the particular case under investigation.

In this paper we present the general architecture and the user-interface of the IDEAS system. The requirements for intelligent documentation systems are listed in section 2 and the general architecture of IDEAS is described in section 3. In the fourth section, we introduce the 'Spreadsheet Metaphor' for designing hypertext user interfaces and then outline the IDEAS interface based on this metaphor in section 5. We finish with a summary and some conclusions in the sixth section.

2 Requirements for Intelligent Documentation Systems

The main objective of an intelligent documentation system which is employed in pharmaceutical studies is to improve the quality, turn-around time and consistency of adverse event evaluations. The result of this process is an action event model which explains the data of the event in question and provides a sound basis for taking further actions. In order to efficiently support a decision maker in the construction process of such a model, an IDS must meet the following requirements:

(a) Data and knowledge retrieval from heterogeneous sources

- An IDS must allow for retrieving data from a variety of heterogeneous sources, e.g. from the adverse case report, from medical information sources, such as the red list, and from records of previous cases. Therefore suitable interfaces to already existing databases must be built.

(b) Presentation of various types of data and knowledge

- An IDS must support data types like (formatted) natural language texts, tables, diagrams, bitmaps, etc., since several types or representations of data and knowledge are involved in the evaluation of adverse events.
- An IDS should support multiple presentations of the same data. This is especially important for the graphical presentation of data stored in tables (e.g. for laboratory values). Suitable presentations of data and knowledge are crucial for the acceptance and usefulness of an IDS.

(c) Data processing capabilities

- An IDS should be capable of numerical data manipulation (directly or at least via an interface to a conventional programming language). Especially statistical methods should be supported for the comparison and evaluation of actual data. To monitor the whole study, it should be possible to aggregate data from several adverse events. The tables which are needed for the final evaluation of the study could thus be incrementally constructed.
- An IDS should be capable of symbolic data manipulation to perform standard operating procedures on data or for (semi-) automated model construction. Based on information about similar cases and on medical and pharmaceutical knowledge, the system should generate proposals about potential relationships between data and should advice which additional data and knowledge sources should be retrieved for constructing the action event model.

- The IDS should allow for the evaluation of the final action event model by testing it against predefined criteria which ensure that the model is consistent and all relevant data and information sources have been taken into account.

(d) User-Interface

- An IDS must provide an interactive working environment in which the decision maker can easily access any data retrieved and combine them to an action event model using appropriate semantic relations, e.g. causality, temporal order, conditionality, etc. This should be realized with a graphical user-interface supporting mouse, windows, menus, dialogs, browsers, etc.
- The data and information provided by an IDS must be easy to perceive and to handle. An information presentation strategy should help to inform the users about the various building blocks of the interface.
- An IDS should be able to handle standard forms which are needed for the adverse case report as well as for the final action event model. It should give access to a documentation component which can be used by the decision maker (a) to write a report documenting his decision, (b) to aggregate all information and the action event model into a case record, and (c) to store this record in a case library.

Further requirements concerning details of the user interface are addressed in section 4.

3 The Architecture of an Intelligent Documentation System

The IDEAS architecture comprises different modules containing knowledge and data or providing system functionality. Data and knowledge modules serve as a basis for performing the intelligent documentation process or for representing its products. Functional modules manage user interaction, automated processing of routine work, retrieval and data recording. The whole system is embedded into an open environment with information sources and storage capacity distributed over a variety of different sites. Figure 2 shows the main IDEAS system modules and their interrelations in terms of control and data flow.

The basic data module is the new *adverse case report* (see section 1). It is the initial input to the system and contains information necessary for the construction of the action event model.

The *action event model* is the central part of the IDEAS system. It documents the analysis of the adverse case by reflecting the causal relationship between the drug under investigation and the adverse event. Especially the event explanation, the report procedures, and the user interaction base on the action event model.

Other relevant knowledge is embodied in the *Library of Adverse Cases* (enabling case-based reasoning) and the module of *Biomedical Knowledge*. The latter contains medical fact knowledge, such as information about the drug under study, the red list of drug side effects and interactions, knowledge about diseases and pharmacokinetics. The case library stores cases from the current study as well as from others.

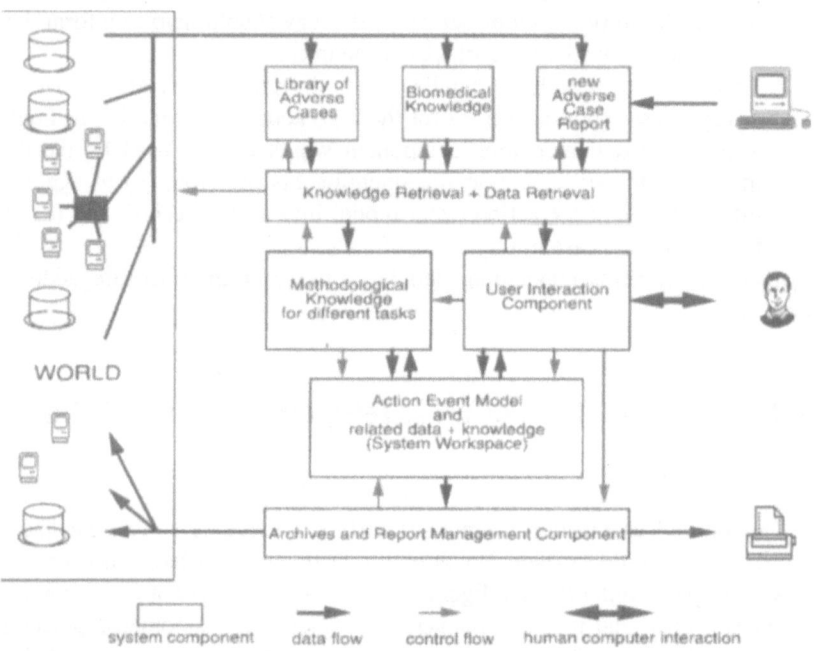

Figure 2.:The architecture of the IDEAS system

The central functional unit is the *User Interaction Component* which manages the underlying system functionality, presents data and knowledge structures, and displays retrieved data. It is designed as a hypertext system offering an intuitive link concept (see chapter 4).

Intelligent functionality is provided by the *Methodological Knowledge* unit. This component evaluates the data of the actual adverse event, relates them to those cases and biomedical knowledge sources that are relevant for explaining the event and thus generates the information base for the action event model. Moreover, there are rules for explaining and classifying the adverse case.

In an open environment *Knowledge and Data Retrieval* require a great number of different routines. They provide both retrieval and access to retrieved data and fact knowledge.

Recording of the documentation results is accomplished by the *Archives and Report Management Component*. It is also responsible for the generation of study reports.

The combination of knowledge based methods with hypertext technology (as part of the user interaction component) provides two kinds of support:

- Since IDEAS evaluates data of the adverse event, it takes over part of the expert's routine work and thus facilitates the construction of the action event model.

- Since the model of expertise specifies which information is relevant for each task, IDEAS can offer a selection of those data and knowledge sources that are relevant to accomplish the user's current task.

In the following sections, we focus on the second of these aspects by describing the user interface component of IDEAS. This component is based on the 'Spreadsheet Metaphor' and integrates hypertext facilities with spreadsheet functionalities to support decision making in clinical studies.

4 Spreadsheets as Metaphor for User Interfaces of Hypertext Systems

Common metaphors for hypertext are the 'multi-dimensional book' metaphor and the 'city map' metaphor. The former is often used for literary applications while the latter frequently serves as a basis for training and geographic information systems. In addition to these, we suggest the 'Spreadsheet Metaphor'. It provides an adequate basis for designing hypertext systems for which quick perception of information and flexible adaptation to specific user intentions are crucial requirements.

4.1 Spreadsheet Characteristics

Spreadsheets are a framework for data processing and simulation inspired by a calculation form used in book-keeping (Kay 1984). A spreadsheet consists of cells which are arranged in a two dimensional matrix. Each cell can contain a value, an instruction that determines the particular value, and a formatting instruction. Together these components specify the way in which the content of a cell is displayed on the user interface.

Originally, spreadsheets were designed to perform repeated calculations on a set of uniform economic data which could be arranged in tables. They were meant to spare the user from the necessity to manually change a complete table whenever some data had to be updated. But soon spreadsheets turned out to be more than a useful tool for easy data analysis and representation. They were discovered to represent a simulation mechanism that is both easy to understand and easy to program.

The main characteristics of a spreadsheet are its well structured presentation format and its dynamic nature: Spreadsheets display data in tables in which all cell contents are held consistent with their value specification by immediately updating the depending cell values whenever a basic value is changed. This powerful feature is implemented by separating the actual cell content from the respective calculation and formatting instructions.

Modern spreadsheet systems extend this approach in several ways and go far beyond standard table manipulation. They can handle formatted text, fill-in forms, diagrams and dialogs. Cells, regions of cells, even complete spreadsheets can be easily combined. Often interactive programming facilities and automated diagram construction are offered (Brosius 1992) thus providing a highly transparent and dynamic framework for data processing and simulation. Furthermore, spreadsheet systems provide interfaces to access and incorporate external databases, programming languages, etc.

4.2 The Spreadsheet Metaphor

The Spreadsheet Metaphor is based upon three core characteristics of spreadsheets that embody useful principles also for designing hypertext systems:

(P1) Information is presented in a well structured manner and in precise chunks with an unambiguous meaning established by the context of the particular table.

(P2) The representation of information is explicitly separated from its presentation.

(P3) The whole system is highly responsive, i.e. each change of the underlying representation dynamically leads to an immediate update of the presentation.

These three principles result in a presentation format which can be easily understood and managed. In particular, the principle of precise and well structured presentation in spreadsheets (P1) can help hypertext systems to overcome the problem of 'getting lost in hyperspace'. Instead of providing additional navigation facilities in a complex information space, complexity itself is reduced: Only those parts of the available hypertext net are presented which are relevant in a given context. For example, in the IDEAS system this context can be given by the task the user is currently working at. By selecting only those information chunks from the net that are usually needed to accomplish this task, the information space is significantly constrained and user orientation is improved.

The distinction between representation and presentation of data (P2) provides the basis for well structured and easily manageable user interfaces. In order to realize this distinction in an intelligent documentation system, the whole knowledge of the system must be separated into independent modules, i.e.:

- content information
- information appearance (formatting)
- additional filters or mappings (e.g. target group related), and
- a specification of possible contexts.

Determined by the current context, these modules can be combined to an appropriate presentation. In combination with automatic and dynamic updating (P3) whenever the basic representation has changed, the system is continuously kept consistent.

The Spreadsheet Metaphor is useful for two kinds of hypertext applications: (a) Reducing the presentation to the core information embedded into a clearly structured (table like) context is relevant for systems that have to manage huge amounts of homogeneously structured data, like the IDEAS system. (b) The Spreadsheet Metaphor is useful for systems that must flexibly adapt their presentation of information to specific user needs. An example for such an application are hypertext-based tutorial systems that have to appropriately interact with different target groups. However, the basic idea of separating presentation and representation can be regarded as an advantageous principle for any hypertext application.

5 Implementing Hypertexts by Spreadsheet Systems

Spreadsheet systems like Excel are wide-spread and well-known. Since they already have most features which are required for the implementation of an intelligent documentation system they are well suited tools for developing an IDS. Using these systems promises to yield a high user-acceptance.

An intelligent documentation system should provide both free information access and guidance to the user. To combine these superficially contradicting goals, we have chosen a particular kind of hypertext which we denote as document centered hypertext. In the IDEAS system such a hypertext is implemented with Microsoft Excel 4.0.

5.1 Document Centered Hypertext

Users of hypertexts often face a variety of problems which result from the complexity of this medium, e.g., 'lost in hyperspace', 'overchoice' and 'cognitive overload' (Horn 1989). Several approaches deal with these problems by offering models for structuring hypertexts (Garzotto, Paolini & Schwabe 1991; Thüring,

Haake, Hannemann 1991) or by designing specific interface facilities (Hannemann, Thüring & Haake 1993). They all have in common that they structure complexity, but do not reduce it (see also Conklin 1987; Horn 1989; Kuhlen 1991).

For the IDEAS system we developed a strategy which aims to minimize complexity and at the same time presents information in a way that helps the user to stay oriented: We chose an overall hierarchical structure of the presented hypertext with the model of expertise as the topmost node. The model serves as an entry point into the hypertext as well as an anchor for the user's conception of the task structure and the knowledge sources (or data) that are available. Since the model of expertise represents the relations between tasks on the one hand and useful information on the other, it tells the user what is relevant at each point of the decision process. Obviously, this approach reduces complexity. Instead of confronting a user with a mass of information, he is shown which parts of the hypertext net are currently most important. However, this is only an advice and the user is free to choose any other information. Moreover, completed subtasks are marked by the system so that the progress of the user's decision making progress becomes visible in the model of expertise. In summary, this approach yields the following advantages:

- The user gets a clear overview of the whole task structure.
- The presentation of the task structure helps the user to decide when to deal with each subtask and indicates which tasks have already been accomplished.
- The user immediately recognizes the specific knowledge sources relevant to the actual subtask he is working on.
- All subtasks, knowledge sources, databases and documents displayed in the model of expertise are directly accessible via mouse-click. Thus the model of expertise serves as graphical presentation of the decision problem as well as a main component of the IDEAS user-interface.

Furthermore, the interface integrates some features from spreadsheet systems and uses them for the layout of hypertext nodes:

- Nodes are displayed in a two dimensional area presenting those pieces of information as closely together which are likely to be subsequently accessed by the user in the context of a given task.
- The layout structure is stable and standardized, thus enabling unambiguous semantics and a uniform appearance of corresponding chunks of information.
- The presentation format of information from documents that are commonly used in clinical studies, such as the Red List, preserves the layout of the originals whenever possible. This ensures that the user is familiar with the presentation style of many knowledge sources and thus reduces the risk of misunderstandings and mistakes.

These features provide an intuitive appearance and behavior of hypertext linking functionality which facilitate information processing (Horn 1989). In addition, IDEAS employs knowledge-based techniques to filter relevant information from the various knowledge sources and to generate hypothesis in a. specific context thus reducing problems of 'overchoice' and 'cognitive overload'.

5.2 User Interaction with the IDEAS System

Figure 3 illustrates the user-interface of the IDEAS system in which the overall structure of the hypertext is represented by the model of expertise (upper right portion of figure 3).

When the user selects a metaclass box in the model the corresponding document is displayed in another window. In the example shown in figure 3, the user has selected the adverse case report (left portion of the figure) and automatically filtered entries of the 'Red List' which contains a list of drugs together with their side effects and interactions (lower right portion of figure 3). When clicking on a subtask ellipses the respective case- or rule-based inferences are activated and result in a modification of the contents of the output documents. The Red List itself is a hypertext node in which almost each statement is linked to another node. In the context of a specific adverse event, the links are filtered with respect to the concomitant drugs listed in the adverse case report. The display of additional nodes proceeds according to the IDEAS presentation principles without leaving the context of the Red List: In accordance with our principle of two dimensional layout, the list of drug/effect pairs is presented in two columns. Each new hypertext node providing detailed information on a drug or one of its effects is inserted into the Red List by horizontally expanding the list (i.e. adding a new column).

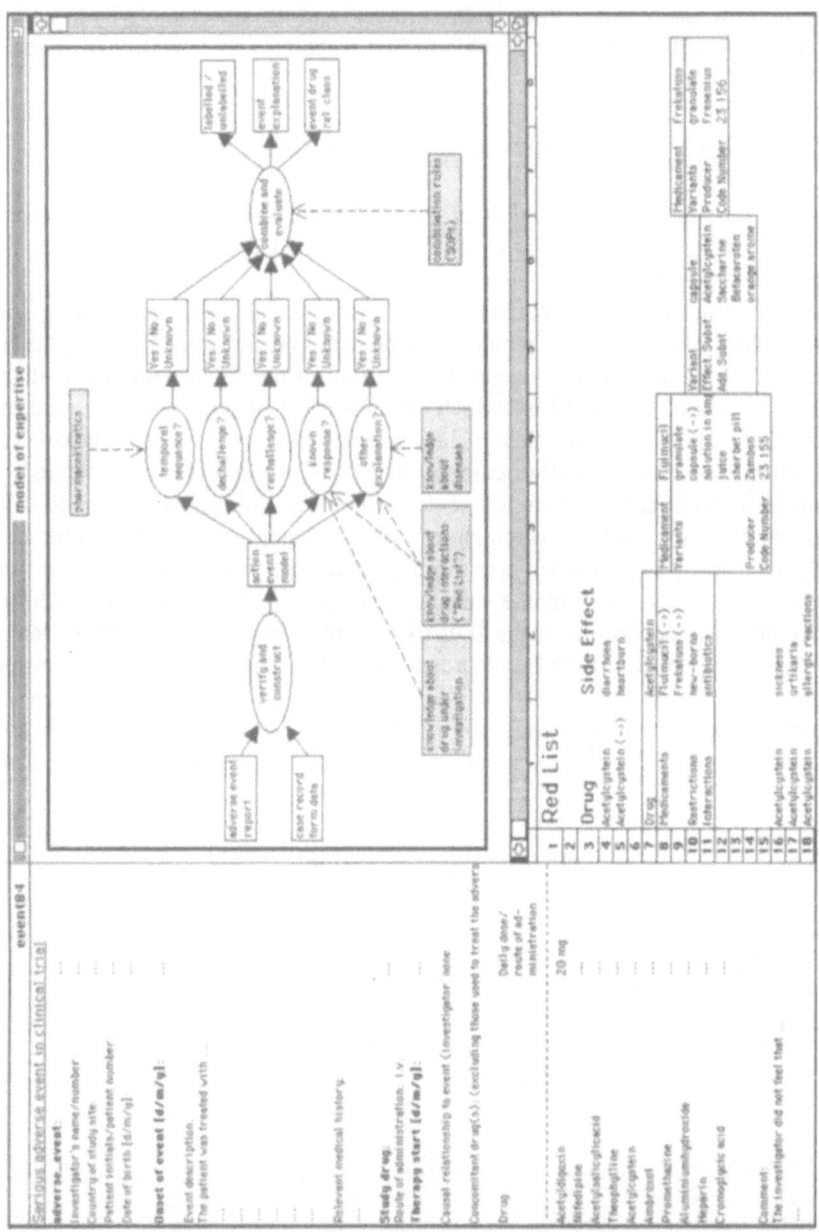

Figure 3: The IDEAS user interface for processing a hypothetical adverse event.

In the example shown in figure 3, the item selected in the list is marked by an arrow ('->') and information about the drug Acetylcystein is displayed in a new box. Subsequent selections of items by the user have opened the three boxes on the right. These were added to the table in horizontal direction, aligned at the row that contains the selected item. In the IDEAS representation of the Red List, there is a predefined set of boxes corresponding to the information types that may be required by the user. Each type of box has some fixed categories that reflect the situation specific links to further information (see also Boy 1991).

A table is the most common presentation type in spreadsheet systems. Figure 4 illustrates the use of tables and diagrams in IDEAS. Laboratory data, for instance blood pressure, are stored in tables. Diagrams can be automatically computed from the tables providing the user with an additional view on the data and helping him to check for deviations from normal.

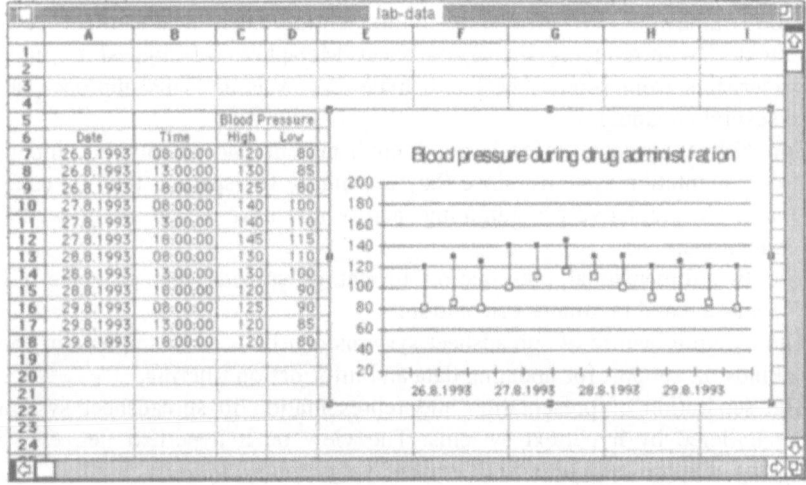

Figure 4: Laboratory data stored in a table and illustrated in a diagram.

Furthermore, the standardized data format in spreadsheets makes it possible to automatically combine data from all (or selected) patients and to compute new tables as aggregations. Such tables are required for the final evaluation of the study. Their automatic generation is extremely helpful, since a fairly large number of them are needed in each clinical study (e.g., 88 tables in the study that we analyzed). Moreover, the incremental construction of tables (i.e., their updating for each new adverse event report) ensures continuous monitoring and early evaluations. Frequently appearing abnormalities can thus be identified at an early stage. This not only decreases study time, but also reduces the risks for patients if the drug causes undesired side effects.

6 Summary and conclusions

We have pointed out how an intelligent documentation system, such as IDEAS, can be employed to support decision making in pharmaceutical industry. It aims to improve the quality, turn-around time and consistency of adverse event evaluations. This goal is addressed by providing a maximum of transparency and control facilities to the user. Two models provide the necessary support for orientation: The model of expertise monitors the overall process, while the action event model illustrates the particular case under investigation.

The basic paradigm of intelligent documentation systems is the coupling of knowledge based techniques and hypertext (Schmalhofer et al. 1992). For reasons of transparency it is necessary to avoid the problem of 'getting lost in hyperspace'. Therefore we propose the technique of document centered hypertext that provides guidance through the various information sources. We argue that spreadsheets are a good framework for efficiently implementing such a document centered hypertext. By introducing the Spreadsheet Metaphor we suggest to integrate characteristics from spreadsheets into hypertext systems. This approach should yield several advantages:

- Spreadsheet systems offer a good environment for prototyping intelligent documentation systems, since they are highly transparent, may be equipped with an interactive programming facility and have a rich set of predefined functions.
- The two dimensional presentation format of spreadsheets provides a good overview and facilitates orientation.
- The dynamic nature of spreadsheet systems can be used to implement various kinds of support for updating data and information filtering.
- The separation of presentation and representation in spreadsheet systems is paralleled by hypertext systems: The view on a hypertext net, e.g., in a graphical browser, *presents* the underlying *representation*.

These features aim to reduce common problems of hypertexts, such as disorientation, overchoice and cognitive overhead. In the IDEAS system, they are combined with knowledge-based techniques and hypertext facilities thus constituting an intelligent documentation system which is likely to efficiently support decision making and the explanation of adverse events in pharmaceutical studies. To which degree the combination of hypertext technology and knowledge-based methods will increase the quality and speed of such studies is an issue that requires future in-depth evaluation in terms of well-planned empirical investigations (see Glowalla and Hasebrook, this volume).

References

Aschenbrenner, K. M., Gertzen, H., Kühn, O., Schmalhofer, F., & Schmidt, J. (1993). *IDEAS: Unterstützung der Arzneimittelsicherheit durch eine umfassende Wissensnutzung mittels neuer Informationstechnologien.* Project Description. Hoechst AG, Frankfurt and German Research Center for Artificial Intelligence. Kaiserslautern, Germany.

Boy, G. A. (1991). Indexing hypertext documents in context. *Proceedings of the Hypertext '91 Conference, San Antonio,* Texas, December.

Breuker, J., & Wielinga, B. (1989). Models of expertise in knowledge acquisition. In G. Guida, C. Tasso (Eds.) *Topics in expert system design: Methodologies and tools,* pp. 265-295. Amsterdam: North Holland.

Brosius, G. (1992). *Excel 4.0 Professionell* (in german). Bonn: Addison-Wesley.

Conklin, J. (1987). Hypertext: An introduction and survey. *IEEE Computer,* 20 (9): 17- 41.

Fischer, G., & Reeves, B. N. (1991) Beyond intelligent interfaces: Exploring, analyzing and creating success models of cooperative problem solving. *Applied Intelligence, Special Issue Intelligent Interfaces.*

Garzotto, F., Paolini, P. & Schwabe, D. (1991). HDM - A model for the design of hypertext applications. In *Proceedings of the 3nd ACM Conference on Hypertext (Hypertext `91),* San Antonio, Texas, December 15-18, 1991, pp. 313-328.

Gertzen, H. (1990). *Entscheidungen bei sequenzierter* Informationsdarbietung *am Bildschirm.* New York: Waxmann.

Gertzen, H., Schmalhofer, F., Kühn, O., Schmidt, J., & Aschenbrenner, K. M. (1993). A decision-support system for the judgment of adverse events in clinical trials. *Paper presented at the 14th Conference on subjective probability, utility and decision making, Aix-en Provence, August 22-26.*

Gray, W. D., John, B. E., & Atwood, M. E. 1992. The precis of project Ernestine or an overview of a validation of GOMS. In *CHI '92 Conference Proceedings,* pp. 307-312. New York: ACM.

Hannemann, J., Thüring, M. & Haake, J. (1993). Hyperdocument presentation: Facing the interface. Arbeitspapiere der GMD 784. Sankt Augustin: GMD.

Horn, R. E. (1989), *Mapping hypertext: The analysis, organization, and display of knowledge for the next generation of on-line text and graphics.* Lexington, MA: The Lexington Institute.

Kay, A. (1984) Software (in german). *Spektrum der Wissenschaft,* (11).

Kieras, D., & Polson, P. G. (1985). An approach to the formal analysis of user complexity. *International Journal of Man-Machine Studies,* 22: 365-394.

Kuhlen, R. (1991). *Hypertext: A non-linear medium between book and knowledge base* (in german). Berlin: Springer-Verlag.

Musen, M. A. (1992). Dimensions of knowledge sharing and reuse. *Computers and Biomedical Research,* 25.

Schmalhofer, F., Kühn, O., & Schmidt, G. (1991). Integrated knowledge acquisition from text, previously solved cases and expert memories. *Applied Artificial Intelligence,* 5: 311-337.

Schmalhofer, F., Reinartz, T., & Tschaitschian, B. (1992). Intelligent documentation as a catalyst for developing cooperative knowledge-based systems. In Th. Wetter, K.-D. Althoff, J. Boose, B. R. Gaines, M. Linster, and F. Schmalhofer (Eds.) *Current developments in Knowledge Acquisition - EKAW '92,* pp. 406-424. Berlin: Springer.

Thüring, M., Haake, J.M. & Hannemann, J. (1991). What's ELIZA doing in the Chinese Room? Incoherent hyperdocuments - and how to avoid them. In *Proceedings of the 3nd ACM Conference on Hypertext (Hypertext `91),* San Antonio, Texas, December 15-18, 1991, pp. 161-177.

3 Evaluation and Critical Aspects of Hypermedia Design

Manfred Thüring

Hypermedia design for commercial purposes is a demanding task that frequently results in large and complex applications. In order to be marketable, such applications must be of high quality, easy to use and inexpensive to maintain. Their development must be timely and usually has to be accomplished with limited resources.

Although a number of tools and authoring systems have emerged by now that provide help for hypermedia development at a technical level, little has been done to support authors and designers in the conceptual part of their work. As a consequence, hypermedia projects are often not only unduly lengthy and hard to manage, they are also susceptible to producing systems that are difficult to handle and costly to maintain. "This is not because authors are not creative or not talented but because, in a new discipline, it is inevitable that most authors are inexperienced and the tools they are using are crude. The present state of the art of hypertext authorship can be equated to the state of programming in the fifties" (Brown 1990, p.1).

This quality assessment by Brown from 1990 is certainly still true and points to the need for methods which address the design process as well as the artefacts resulting from this process. Such methods are often the outcome of an evolutionary process that may extend over years or even decades. Obviously, the design of hypermedia cannot rely on experiences from such a long tradition. How then can we learn to optimize design procedures and to increase the quality of hypermedia applications?

The contributions by *Hofmann & Glowalla, Dillon & McKnight and Glowalla & Hasebrook* in the next three chapters provide first answers to this urgent question by focussing on the role of evaluation in hypermedia research and development. In summary, the insights resulting from their work suggest two ways for collecting information to optimize hypermedia design: Post hoc analysis should be undertaken to reveal the success factors of completed projects which have created well accepted and marketable hypermedia applications. Ad hoc studies, on the other hand, should be performed to evaluate design procedures as well as hypermedia artefacts in ongoing and future projects. While the feasibility of the former depends on a good documentation of developmental procedures and on a set of valid quality criteria for products, the latter demands the careful planning of empirical studies and their smooth integration into the software lifecycle. With these requirements in mind, let us take a closer look at the three chapters on evaluation and critical aspects of hypermedia design.

Hofmann and Glowalla investigate hypermedia design from an ad hoc perspective focussing on existing commercial applications. According to their analysis, many successful systems which incorporate hypertext functionality do not emphasize the concept of linking nor do they rely on the network metaphor for their user interfaces. Instead, commercial design focusses on the major characteristics of the application domain itself and is based on metaphors reflecting these characteristics. Hence, leaving hypertext concepts almost implicit and choosing an adequate metaphor for the application may be one of the key factors for success. Unfortunately, current tools for hypermedia development do not sufficiently support this strategy, i.e., they do not help designers to choose an appropriate metaphor, adapt it to a particular application and fill in the specific content. *Hofmann and Glowalla* regard this as an important deficit since their examination of existing application areas favors the assumption that the concept of hypertext and the related network metaphor alone are not sufficient for successful design.

From their investigation of current applications and development tools, *Hofmann and Glowalla* derive a number of recommendations. For example, hypermedia designers and authors should be supported by company and application–specific checklists and guidelines which give concrete advice and orientation. Developers of hypermedia authoring tools, on the other hand, should devise systems which support metaphor–based design, provide more sophisticated link management including consistency checks, and supply their users with more convenient facilities for structuring information. A methodology which is in line with these recommendations is highly likely to be accepted by designers since hypermedia per se is not in the centre of their activities, but the application they have in mind.

A similar emphasis on the importance of application and user–specific aspects can be found in the contribution by *Dillon and McKnight* who place the design of hypermedia applications and user interfaces into the more general context of user–centred system design. This approach advocates the involvement of users in all design phases in order develop a system that meets their requirements. In this respect, the creation of hypermedia solutions should be no different, i.e., it should rely on the close interaction between users and designers as crucial part of an iterative development process.

As a consequence, the authors argue for a data–driven approach in contrast to a purely theoretical–driven design methodology. Despite their academic success, theoretical models, such as GOMS (Card, Moran & Newell, 1983), have had little significant impact on the development of commercial applications and seem to provide no adequate guidance for design practice. Therefore, attention should be shifted to empirical design methods which explicitly address the role of the user, the characteristics of tasks and the variance of the environment in which users and tasks are situated. Within such an approach, a wide set of evaluation techniques could be employed that provide insights into the usability of hypermedia applications as well as into the efficiency of design procedures. Evaluation techniques analyzing product usability could reach from walk–throughs to experimental comparisons while methods for investigating design procedures could focus on successful hypermedia projects. With respect to the latter, *Dillon and McKnight* propose to develop a theory of design by "reverse engineering", i.e., select a well–accepted application and retrospectively investigate its design process. This data–driven approach could reveal the design rational of successful hypermedia products and finally lead to a methodology which prescribes the appropriate tools as well as the most efficient techniques for each phase of hypermedia design.

Empirical evaluation and its relation to a methodology for hypermedia design also plays a prominent role in the contribution by *Glowalla and Hasebrook*. These authors propose an evaluation model which is based on experimental techniques and relies on data collected in realistic application settings. The model emphasizes a variety of evaluation criteria, such as user acceptance, quality of performance and processing time, that should be addressed in empirical studies in order to guide the work of designers. For this purpose, it is necessary to integrate empirical evaluation techniques into the overall design process and to devise experiments which ease and support design decisions.

Experiments that are integral part of the development process should be based on factorial evaluation plans and compare different design options in order to find the most appropriate one with respect to the criteria mentioned above. Experimental evaluation models of that kind can be "local" as well as "global". While the former test different versions of the same system against each other, the latter contrast prototypes which considerably differ in their functionality, use divergent metaphors for their user interface or are even based on different technologies. Both kinds of evaluations may provide valuable insights into various aspects of hypermedia interface construction and thus support developers in selecting the most appropriate solution from a set of options. Their positive impact on design decisions is illustrated by *Glowalla and Hasebrook* in a number studies that were performed to support the creation of hypermedia teachware and the development of the hypermedia system MEM (Glowalla et al., 1993).

In summary, the three contributions in this part of the book point to various critical aspects of hypermedia design and stress the importance of empirical evaluation as integral component of the development process. Post hoc studies may reveal the success factors of well accepted hypermedia products while carefully planned ad hoc studies may support designers in finding adequate solutions that meet the requirements of users. Although thorough evaluation of products and procedures may initially entail additional costs, investments will pay off when they lead to commercial applications of higher quality and to more efficient design procedures thus increasing customer satisfaction and speed to market.

References

Brown, P. J. (1990). Assessing the Quality of Hypertext Documents. In A. Rizk, N.A. Streitz & J. Andre (Eds.), *Hypertext: Concepts, Systems and Applications*, (Proceedings of the European Conference on Hypertext, ECHT '90, Paris, France, November 1990), pages 1–12. Cambridge: University Press.

Card, S. K., Moran, T.P. & Newell, A. (1983). *The Psychology of Human–Computer Interaction*. Hillsdale NJ: Lawrence Erlbaum Associates.

Glowalla, U., Hasebrook, J., Fezzardi, G. & Haefele, G. (1993). The Hypermedia System MEM and its Application in Evaluating Learning and Relearning in Higher Education. In G. Strube & K.F. Wender (Eds.), *The Cognitive Psychology of Knowledge*. Amsterdam: Elsevier Science Publishers, pp. 367–385.

An Evaluation Model Based on Experimental Methods Applied to the Design of Hypermedia User Interfaces

Ulrich Glowalla and Joachim Hasebrook
Department of Psychology, University of Giessen, Germany

Abstract. We want to motivate an evaluation model based on the application of experimental methods. Examples from our research will illustrate how hypermedia systems and the information delivered by them can be improved systematically using this approach. User acceptance, the quality and speed of performance, the exact trace of all user-computer interactions, and finally the comparison of reasonable alternative system designs constitute the set of criteria guiding the evaluation process. Moreover, it will be shown that even informal evaluation techniques frequently used in user interface design become more powerful once they are applied within experimentally designed studies.

1   Introduction

There are many different purposes of applying systematic software design methodologies to user interfaces. In this paper we shall focus on two of them:
  (1)   The design process should lead to an increasing usability of the software system.
  (2)   The design of the software system should enable maintenance and extensions.
Determining the effectiveness of information technology and its user interface, however, is a difficult task. Many different aspects have to be evaluated: Is the software system easy to learn and simple to use? Does it provide all functions known to support the self-controlled working process? Do manuals and on-line helps comply with the cognitive principles of discourse comprehension? Are media like animation and simulation used appropriately? This list of relevant evaluation questions is already quite long, yet far from being complete.

In the past five years, we have developed an evaluation model whose key feature is the systematic use of experimental methods. In addition, we have identified a number of criteria that have proven to be very helpful in guiding our efforts to determine the effectiveness of hypermedia teachware. Several of these criteria have been used in other design models as well (cf. Greenbaum & Kyng,

1992). As far as we know, however, they have never been used in combination with each other and we hope to show that this is essential. The main purpose of this paper, then, is to propose an evaluation model which makes heavy use of empirical data collected from experimental research in realistic settings. Moreover, after motivating our approach on theoretical grounds and comparing it to other ones we shall present some examples for improvements of hypermedia teachware obtained through the application of this approach.

The design of hypermedia applications and their user interfaces are sometimes considered to be a task that calls for specialized design structures (e.g. Garzotto, Mainetti & Paolini, 1994). Other researchers argue that well-known design processes like user-centered design should be applied to hypermedia applications as well (e.g. Dillon & McKnight, 1994). We assume that these different points of view result from different research traditions: On the one hand, formal models used in software engineering lead to more or less hierarchically structured design processes which may be too rigid for hypermedia design. On the other hand, human factor experts mostly rely on user-centered design processes which may prove to be too expensive. We refer to both approaches as 'local evaluation models', because they are structuring and evaluating a single application or prototype.

In the next section we shall briefly discuss three popular local evaluation models. The principle features of global design approaches are covered in the third section. The main purpose of section four is to present some examples for improvements of hypermedia teachware resulting from the application of our evaluation approach, which is best described as a particular global design model. In the fifth section we shall explain the central characteristics of our global evaluation model, which is most importantly based on experimental research. Above all, the aforementioned evaluation criteria shall be explained and motivated in some detail. Moreover, we shall argue that the value of data gathered from more informal evaluation techniques can be improved considerably, if the data is collected during experimental studies.

2   Local evaluation models

User-centered design processes (Norman & Draper, 1986) and human activity approaches (Bødker, 1991) rely on a close cooperation of programmers, instructional experts, and computer users in realistic but limited settings. User-centered design and especially human activity approaches put analysis and design of the human activity prior to software design and place the user into the center of the design process. Both approaches help to make software engineers aware of the fact that they are constructing tools or artifacts for actual use and that user interface design is just a part of workplace and software design. Perhaps the most important contributions of user-centered design and human activity approaches are

(1) joint design of workplace and software tools, (2) continuous evaluation of usability, and (3) adaptability of the design process to different environments.

However, there are some problems with this approach. In user-centered design evaluation is often done by informal techniques like short interviews or discussions with small groups of test users. More or less informal observation of a few subjects studying with a particular system, however, is not enough. Data gathered in this way are usually not sufficient for reasonable statistical analysis (cf. Calfee, 1985). In addition, subjects participating in user-centered design studies usually possess much more expertise than the casual or novice computer user (cf. Jöns, 1992). To work with novices would not be a solution either, since they do not possess the relevant knowledge to suggest substantial improvements of the software. Finally, even experienced learners have great difficulties estimating their progress in comprehension and memory tasks (Baker, 1989).

A more formal design model is task analysis according to the GOMS model (Goals, Operators, Methods, and Selections; Card, Moran & Newell, 1983). This model allows task analysis at several technically and psychologically relevant levels reaching from the key-stroke up to the goal level. Perhaps the main advantage of the GOMS approach is its embodiment of an explicit psychological theory of human computer interaction from which predictions can be derived. Thus, it provides a framework for the use of task knowledge of well-trained users. Hence, psychological task analysis according to the GOMS model is capable of identifying inconsistent and unnecessarily complex functions of a user interface (e.g. Card, Moran & Newell, 1980).

A quote from the late author Newell, however, illustrates that GOMS is a design and not an evaluation model: 'Design is where the action is, not evaluation' (Newell & Card, 1985, p. 214). Consequently, the capability of the GOMS model to come up with proposals for software developers is limited in several ways:(1)

The model is restricted to skilled users who have their task knowledge already at hand. (2) It is not clear which specific task level should be examined in order to solve certain design problems. (3) The GOMS model analyzes software systems that already exist. Therefore, at least in early stages of system design, the approach falls back on speculations about what the new program should look like and how it could be used. (4) Some specific problems arise from simplistic assumptions made by the GOMS model: For instance, dual task capabilities (e.g. typing and reading at the same time) or dynamic models of working memory are simply ignored (cf. Bransford, Goldman & Vye, 1991). Once again and most importantly, the conclusion is that only local improvements of available systems can be achieved, since there are no mechanisms for generating and comparing alternative user interface designs (cf. Thimbleby, 1990).

A simple way to avoid all problems mentioned up to this point is not to examine but simply define what usability is. An abstract model that defines the usability of user interfaces was suggested by Dix and Runciman (1985). The PIE model (Program, Interpretation, and Effect) is a method that defines a program and its commands 'P', a set of functions to interpret user commands 'I', and consequences of these interpretations 'E'. Based on these assumptions properties of interactive systems are defined like: (1) Restartability, (2) equivalence of command sequences, (3) observability and monotony of the system and the like. Here is an example for the observability of a system: Consider two programs both providing a function *clearscreen* which blanks out the screen. While the interpretation ('I') of 'clearscreen' by the first program is simply showing a blank screen, the interpretation by the second program may be more elaborated, like for instance wiping the screen and resetting the program status. In this example, only the second program provides enough information for deciding how to continue, since a blank screen indicates consistently that the system is in one particular state.

Properties like observability can be defined for each system and thus provide a formal framework for user interface design. Some theoretical assumptions about the design of abstract functions like the 'undo' command are based on definitions of the PIE model (e.g. Thimbleby, 1990; pp. 365). Although most of the properties of the PIE model are quite plausible, there are no criteria to decide whether a property can be applied or which property should be applied: The PIE model provides an abstract description of system functions but there are no guidelines for collecting empirical evidence which may lead to substantial improvements of the evaluated software system

3   Global design approaches

In general, global design approaches rely on system analysis and models of the software life cycle. Lucas (1992) suggested a global approach to the analysis, design and implementation of information systems in three steps:

(1) Take a conceptual view using preliminary surveys and feasibility studies to identify the underlying problems and appropriate system architecture.

(2) Take a system approach to define the nature of the problem, examine the problems of users and their suggestions, document all results and test their correctness by feeding them back to the user.

(3) Select and apply tools and techniques to design and implement the information system. These tools and techniques may range from short surveys over rapid prototyping to a complete, structured system analysis and implementation cycle (for a brief overview see Hesse, 1984).

Some authors suggested that standard software development processes should be applied to hypermedia user interface design as well (Howell, 1992; pp. 31). Other authors, however, have argued that standard procedures have to be customized to the special needs of hypermedia design (Garzotto, Mainetti & Paolini, 1994). Moreover, some authors raised the issue whether general models can be applied at all. Content or domain specific approaches might have to be considered: Jonassen and Grabinger (1990), for instance, have outlined a design model for hypermedia learning environments, Hannemann and Thüring (1994) came up with an issue-based design model for hypermedia applications in general.

All these objections against standard software development in the field of hypermedia design converge to the general claim that there is an interaction between technique and context involved in the design process. And indeed, there is some evidence in favor of this position. Belotti (1990) has shown that design process and design setting are interacting on several dimensions. Therefore, it may be difficult or even impossible to select the optimal design technique for a given context.

Johnson (1992) has pointed out, however, that Belotti' s do not imply that evaluation results should simply be rejected. He argued that much more likely an evaluation process would fail to identify problems than to produce misleading results. Consequently, evaluation results should rather be regarded as "over-conservative" than "over-critical" (Johnson, 1992; p. 99). Here is an illustrative example from our own research: In order to get a wide range of evaluation data about a particular hypermedia system we decided to make use of several formal and informal evaluation techniques to assess user acceptance including ratings, direct item comparison, interviews, direct observations and anonymous comments addressing the authors of both the hyperdocument and the hypermedia system. We found that the different survey techniques provided interesting supplementary but never contradictory information.

Using evaluation results as an input for system design or design changes requires data that can be analyzed and interpreted in a reasonable way. Informal methods often fail to provide such data (cf. Mark & Greer, 1993). Moreover, experimental design and statistical analysis have been developed for careful and systematic data analysis and interpretation (e.g. Calfee, 1985; Johnson, 1992). In particular, incremental design processes based on experimental results provide insights in possible improvements and constraints of the overall system design. Experimental design may reach from simple group comparisons over multiple factorial design to cross-sectional or longitudinal studies. They all provide more valid and reliable data than informal studies. Furthermore, a wide range of systematic methods of analysis and inferential statistics are applicable exclusively for data collected in experimental studies.

Although widely accepted in many areas, experimental methods are not used very extensively in user interface design. Many objections are discussed (cf. Twidale, 1993; pp. 157):

(1) Experiments are large, slow and costly.
(2) A controlled experiment measures only one thing.
(3) Experiments produce averaged overall performance denying individual differences.
(4) Interactions of system functions cannot be examined properly.
(5) Experiments are too inflexible to support minor changes that frequently have to be made in the process of designing user interfaces.
(6) Experiments are not applicable for "real use".

(7) Experiments hamper the detection of unexpected outcomes.

We believe, however, that these objections are based on a very limited and rigid view of experimental design. In order to provide evidence for our point of view we shall review some experimental results from our own evaluation research in the next section. To help the reader to fully appreciate these examples from our findings we shall begin by providing some background information about the general framework of our research on hypermedia teachware.

4   The evaluation of hypermedia teachware

Being involved in the instruction of psychology and educational science students we decided to develop a course on human memory and information processing. To date, we conducted 15 courses with a total of more than 1,000 participants (Hasebrook, Fezzardi & Häfele, 1993). The size of the hyperdocument on human memory and information processing amounts to 60 book pages and is divided into five consecutive lessons. The document contains text, figures, several forms of exercises and questions as well as hypermedia-specific forms of information like animated overviews and recorded explanations played via headphones. Each lesson lasts approximately two hours. Two additional training lessons introduce novice users to modern computer-based learning environments (e.g. using the mouse and handling several windows) as well as the use of the hypermedia system MEM (Glowalla, Hasebrook & Häfele, 1993). These training lessons last about 30 and 15 minutes, respectively. All things considered, the hypermedia system MEM was in use for about 15,000 hours until March 1993. All aspects of the user interface of MEM relevant to our discussion will be described within this section.

4.1 Computer aided learning and relearning courses

We use MEM to conduct two different types of computer-aided courses in our hypermedia laboratory. In learning courses we present our hyperdocument on human memory to undergraduate students who have very little or no respective knowledge. In relearning courses we have former participants of our learning courses refresh their knowledge about human memory after a time interval ranging from one to six months.

A typical learning course consists of six sessions. Sessions 1 to 5 are study sessions and take place on consecutive days within the same week for instance. In the last session we administer an extensive diagnosis of the knowledge the students have acquired during the course. Among others, we investigated the following research questions in these learning courses: We compared (1) computer-aided learning to more traditional forms of learning like attending to lectures, tried to identify the principles underlying (2) the integration of knowledge from different lessons, employed (3) short summaries differing in position and contents as study aids, seeked to determine (4) the effectiveness of study techniques such as generating and answering questions, and finally measured (5) the comprehension and retention of experimental data using different forms of statistical graphs and tables to present these data (e.g. Glowalla, Rinck & Fezzardi, 1993; Glowalla, Häfele & Rinck).

A relearning course takes place on one day and lasts about 5 hours. It is divided into three parts: (1) It begins with a pretest in which we determine what the students still know about human memory. (2) The pretest is followed by the relearning period and differs depending on the recommended relearning strategy. (3) After a break, we determine what the students know about human memory for a second time in order to inquire how much knowledge they have gained from relearning. In several studies we have compared complete relearning to system-controlled selective relearning (Glowalla, Häfele, Hasebrook, Fezzardi & Rinck, 1992), system-controlled relearning to user-controlled relearning in a hypertext environment (Glowalla, Hasebrook, Häfele, Fezzardi & Rinck, 1992) and both complete, system-controlled and user-controlled relearning to mixed strategies (Glowalla & Häfele, in press).

4.2 Improving hypermedia teachware and systems

Since we have developed MEM on our own, we are in a position to improve the hyperdocument, the course design, and all system features in the course of the evaluation process. Therefore, the results obtained in each of our courses provide the opportunity to improve the teachware as well as the hypermedia system. We have thus created a setup which allows a cyclical evaluation process. In the next two sections we shall give some examples for data-guided improvements of the course design and system features.

4.2.1   Improving the course design

To give an example for the importance of measuring study times and the usefulness of comparing different course designs we want to highlight some results of our relearning courses. In two experiments we compared complete relearning to system-controlled selective relearning (Glowalla, Häfele, Hasebrook, Rinck & Fezzardi, 1992). In selective relearning, students studied just those parts of the knowledge base once again which they were no longer aware of, whereas in the complete relearning task the lessons were studied completely for the second time. The amount of relearning was similar in both conditions. Nevertheless, selective relearning was superior to complete relearning, since the same level of knowledge was acquired within only two thirds of the time required for complete relearning. Furthermore, our students preferred the selective relearning strategy as expressed by their answers to our questionnaires, because of saved time in refreshing their knowledge on the material. So in the next evaluation step we decided to use the more effective selective strategy to compare it with a strategy relying more on hypertext features.

In the third experiment we compared system-controlled selective relearning to user-controlled relearning in our hypertext environment MEM (Glowalla, Hasebrook, Häfele, Fezzardi & Rinck, 1992). Again, the amount of relearning was similar in both situations, but user-controlled relearning in the hypertext took more time. However, it was considerably faster than complete relearning. In addition, the analysis of questionnaires given to our students revealed that they liked the hypertext better than complete relearning but did not prefer it to the selective strategy. If we had compared the widely used complete relearning strategy directly to relearning within a modern hypertext environment, relearning in the hypertext would have turned out to be the recommended relearning strategy, although there is the still more effective selective strategy at hand. Therefore, in order to improve the efficiency of instructional technology in a systematic and continuous manner, it is extremely important to select promising alternatives of course designs and compare them carefully guided by appropriate empirical methods.

In the relearning courses described up to now we compared different course designs in the same setting, namely relearning. In a further experiment we compared the same set of course designs in different study settings: All students received exactly the same course materials and configuration of features of our hypermedia system MEM for both learning and relearning. The learning course consisted of five consecutive lessons giving the students the opportunity to acquire study skills like skimming and browsing. During relearning the same students were taught three different relearning strategies and practiced them. Since the course on human memory is divided into five lessons, the participants were allowed to study the first and the last lesson in any technique they liked. This resulted in a 2x2 factorial quasi-experimental design with the variables 'study setting' (learning or relearning) and practice (unskilled or skilled). Table 1 displays how the navigational and informational tools of the hypermedia system MEM were used as a function of both variables.

First of all look at the percentages of high acceptance (the numbers in brackets). At the end of the learning and the relearning course respectively, the students judged whether each tool was 'helpful', 'unnecessary' or 'disturbing'. The table shows the percentage of users that rated a tool as 'helpful'. Restricting a comparison to the acceptance ratings, it is easily concluded that there is no big difference between learning and relearning, although the students tend to favor browsing tools and the on-line glossary somewhat more during learning and the clipboard more during relearning. This is quite plausible, as the clipboard was used to look up the recent exercise or question provided by the system. This interpretation is supported by the observation that the clipboard is far more often used during relearning than learning (20% & 20% vs. 9% & 3%). Hence, in this case acceptance ratings and performance measures are supporting each other.

| Kind of tool | STUDY SETTING | | | | | |
| | LEARNING | | | RELEARNING | | |
	unskilled	skilled	(accept.)	unskilled	skilled	(accept.)
Navigation						
Paging	100%	100%	(100%)	100%	100%	(100%)
Browsing	11%	9%	(90%)	9%	20%	(77%)
Information						
Contents	49%	38%	(53%)	30%	42%	(41%)
Glossary	49%	68%	(94%)	20%	18%	(86%)
Clipboard	9%	3%	(41%)	20%	20%	(60%)
Mean			(63%)			(61%)

Table 1: Percentage of users that use a particular tool (and percentage of high (acceptance) as a function of study setting and user skills

In another case, however, the performance measures and the acceptance ratings tell quite different stories: Obviously, the percentage of students using a particular tool differed considerably as a function of both the study setting and the user skills. Whereas both experienced and inexperienced students used browsing tools almost equally frequent during learning (9% and In another case, however, the performance measures and the 11%, respectively). Relearners familiar with relearning strategies, however, used them twice as often (9% unskilled vs. 20% skilled). Nevertheless, the overall acceptance for browsing tools is even higher in the learning as compared to the relearning setting (90% vs. 77%).

In addition, informational tools such as a table of contents, an on-line glossary and a clipboard to look up questions and exercises were used in a very selective manner: Unskilled and skilled students alike made more use of information from the table of contents or the glossary during learning than during relearning. The more experienced they got the more they looked up the glossary and the less they studied the table of contents (49% vs. 38% and 49% vs. 68%, resp.). There is no such tendency during relearning (30% vs. 42% and 20% vs. 18%, resp.). This may reflect the fact that all students in the relearning setting were skilled 'learners' and therefore did not need much help from the glossary. On the other hand, a skilled 'learner' is not necessarily a skilled 'relearner'. Skilled 'relearners' used browsing tools (9% vs. 20%) and the table of contents (30% vs. 42%) more extensively. In conclusion, the significance of acceptance ratings must be evaluated on the background of appropriate performance measures: The table of contents and the glossary are rated lower in the learning setting (53% & 94% vs. 41% & 86%) and the clipboard is rated higher in the relearning setting (41% vs. 60%).

We gave a detailed presentation of this example because it illustrates two central arguments in favor of our evaluation model: (1) All data - regardless whether performance or acceptance is measured - can only be interpreted in the light of reasonable alternatives. The method to perform this kind of comparison is factorial experimental design. (2) Both acceptance and performance must be taken into account in order to evaluate the effectiveness of a hypermedia system. Moreover, we hope that the examples taken from our learning and relearning courses have shown that formal and informal evaluation techniques can be combined in a straightforward fashion within factorially designed experiments. Experimental design does by no means exclude informal evaluation techniques. Or the contrary, as we have demonstrated with practical examples from our research, these informal techniques become much more powerful once they are applied within experimentally designed studies.

4.2.2   Improving system features

The data delivered by the process protocol module of the hypermedia system MEM support not only the evaluation of the teachware but also of the hypermedia software. In one of our learning courses we investigated the efficiency of two study techniques using questions: One group of students was required to generate study questions during learning whereas the other group was asked to answer questions (Glowalla, Häfele & Rinck, in press). The second group of subjects answered just those questions generated by the first group. Other than expected we observed no significant advantage for the question asking group for those parts of the knowledge base not tested during learning. Probing information by questions, however, lead to superior retention under both experimental conditions. Content analysis of the questions generated by our students revealed that less than two thirds of them resembled study questions recommended by experts. Content analysis of the answers revealed that our students were not able to correct wrong answers without explicit feedback. Based on these and further results, we extended the questioning facilities of MEM in various ways. Now, the correct answer to a particular question can be displayed after the student has given his answer. It is even possible to arrange that students can edit their own answers at some later point in time, for instance after having studied more information relevant to the topic probed by the question. Thus, the evaluation process led to a substantial improvement of self-diagnosis facilities within our hypermedia system.

The second example for improving the user interface relates to the various ways to provide access to glossary entries (cf. Figure 1): MEM provides embedded links in the hypertext. Thus, students may consult the glossary simply by clicking on a particular concept (e.g. "long-term memory", center of Figure 1).

Students may also open an alphabetically ordered glossary index (cf. upper left of Figure 1), or inspect a list of related concepts and related topics displayed in a particular glossary entry (lower left of Figure 1). In all three cases, accessing the glossary does not result in leaving the current study focus: glossary entries are displayed in separate windows additional to the study card, which is different from most other hypertext systems. Despite this functional similarity of all three possibilities to access the glossary, our students clearly preferred the first manner, namely clicking on a concept in a study card with the mouse. In our most recent learning course, where we gave our students full access to all MEM functions, 64 out of 65 students preferred this mode.

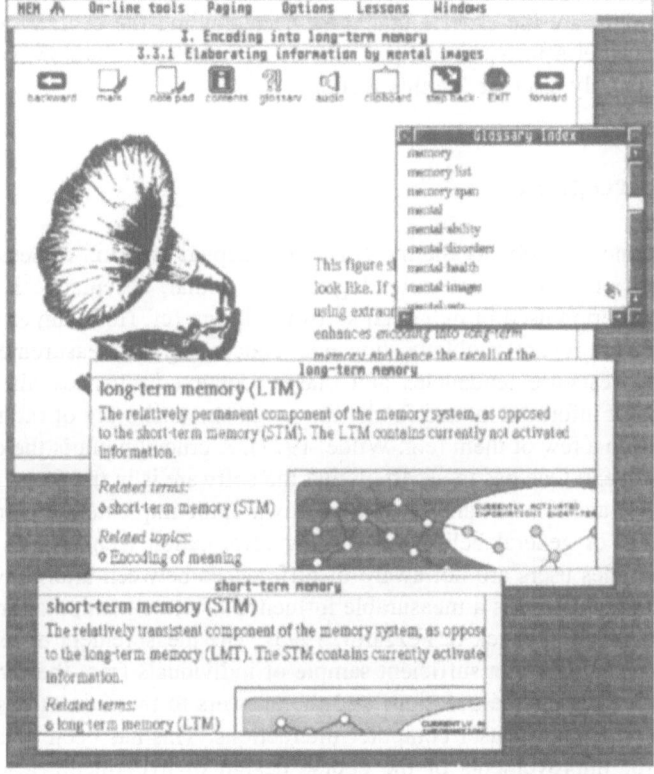

Figure 1: A study card on elaboration by mental images together with the entry for "long-term memory" from the glossary in a separate window (see center of Figure 1). The glossary entry includes cross references to related terms (see lower left of Figure 1) and related topics as well as a graphical representation. A sample section of the glossary index is shown in a separate window (see upper right of Figure 1).

5   A global evaluation model based on experimental methods

In the previous section we have presented some evidence favoring a global evaluation model based on experimental research. In particular, we have shown how the application of this model enables the discovery of both local and global improvements of the user interface and underlying systems functions of hypermedia systems. We hope that the small collection of empirical results from our evaluation research on hypermedia has convinced the reader, that Twidale's (1993) arguments against the use of experimental methods in applied research settings may not be too strong after all. What we have not covered in sufficient detail, however, are the criteria that have been guiding the evaluation process. Since these criteria form an integral part of our global evaluation model, they will be thoroughly discussed in this section.

5.1 User acceptance

User acceptance is probably the most widely accepted criterion to determine the effectiveness of instructional technology. In particular, acceptance is the most frequently criterion used in industrial software design (cf. Hofmann & Glowalla, 1994). There are several problems, however, concerning the measurement of user acceptance: Response tendencies and biases, context influences, the order of presentation of information, and finally the range and anchoring of rating scales - just to mention a few of them (e.g. Wilde, 1977). A crucial point is the context of the measurement: One has to ascertain that the software is in the focus of the decision process and not the quality of the hardware, the implementation process in the company, or general beliefs concerning information technologies. Furthermore, sometimes users are not aware of differences between alternative system designs, although there is a measurable influence of these manipulations on performance (Glowalla, Rinck & Fezzardi, 1993). The measurement of user acceptance may be helpful, if a sufficient sample of individuals from the target population answers reasonable questions and the answers to these questions are considered based on actual user computer interactions. This has been illustrated by examples for improvements of the course design of hypermedia teachware in section 4.2.1.

5.2 Quality of performance

Though desirable, high user acceptance is by no means a sufficient criterion. Information is needed about the quality of performance: We need to know, for instance, how much knowledge a student has acquired working with a particular learning system. A good way to gain information about this is to administer some kind of pretest before using the system and a posttest after having used it. The difference between these two measures indicates the increase in performance. Which aspect of performance is of special interest is determined by the task: With respect to a learning system one might focus on the amount of learning, using a technical documentation on repairing cars one might be more interested in reducing the costs of repairs.

5.3 Processing time and user computer interaction

The next criterion concerns information about the amount of function calls and time a user had to invest for solving his or her tasks and which parts of the hypertext he or she had focused on during working. As we have demonstrated with examples from our research on relearning, the effectiveness of a particular hypertext system depends on both the level of performance and the time invested by the user to acquire it. This in turn implies that we need reliable data on both aspects of performance in order to come up with a rational decision in such situations.

Moreover, this kind of data supports the purposes of formative and summative evaluation processes (e.g. Steinberg, 1991): In a formative evaluation process qualitative and quantitative data are collected in order to test whether the software is usable and the instructions are intelligible. Formative evaluation should start as soon as possible and accompany the whole software life cycle. Formative evaluation should be supplemented by two summative evaluation steps:

(1) In a first summative evaluation step the software has to be tested with the target population in the intended environment. This usually leads to a major revision of the software.

(2) In a second summative evaluation step the instructional materials and the software features have to be maintained. Please note, that the second summative evaluation step may be applied repeatedly (and we believe it should). What we presented up to this point is a rather complete evaluation model based on the measurement of user performance and acceptance. However, this model is only capable of providing local improvements. A model for global improvements has to broaden the narrow perspective of users working with a particular system.

5.4 Systematic comparison of different user interface designs

In this section we would like to argue that each new piece of hypermedia software has to be compared to other reasonable information systems. For instance, if hypermedia-based methods lead to better performance than the most effective known traditional methods, we are sure to make progress. User centered design and the human activity approach marked a shift of the focus from computer application to human activities supported by the application. What we have suggested is a model how to collect reasonable data about human activities. Systematic comparison of course designs puts the collection of data in a new context: In our view, the evaluation of all relevant aspects should be embedded into experimental studies. This broadens the approach taken in user centered design. The evaluation process is no longer a trial-and-error learning process in which programmers and users are interacting. Evaluation as experimental work amounts to the systematic variation of relevant features of the software and the user interface design. Changes in qualitative and quantitative data are measured and interpreted as a function of the efficiency differences caused by these variations (Glowalla & Schoop, 1992). Again, we refer the reader to the evidence supporting this line of reasoning in section 4.2.

In summary, factorial experimental design may be used for systematic comparison of interface designs and to identify relevant instructional variables. Collecting a wide range of acceptance and performance measures during the experimental study helps to identify parts of the hypermedia software that call for revision. Furthermore, the systematic comparison of user actions in different course designs may lead to the redesign of the software system. Ongoing performance measurements and several experimental designs can all be incorporated in a single study. Thus, most of the objections advanced by Twidale (1993) against experimental methods prove to be factually incorrect.

6   Conclusion

On a research strategic level we have tried to motivate a design approach incorporating local and global improvements of hypermedia systems and the materials delivered by those systems. Only the results of a systematic evaluation process can reveal whether a new piece of hypermedia software is better than systems currently in use. We found the set of criteria guiding our evaluation research very helpful. In particular, measuring user acceptance, the quality of performance as well as the processing time and actual user-computer interactions, and finally the systematic comparison of alternative system designs within the same evaluation process contributed to a continuous improvement of the information technology developed in our laboratory.

An optimal realization of a systematic comparison process is the use of incremental factorial designs. The cost of such formal evaluations may be reduced by combining several experiments into one study and by adding informal evaluation techniques such as surveys and interviews. In conclusion, it seems, that our approach to consider evaluation as an integral part of developing instructional technology has been quite fruitful. The approach enabled both improvements of the teachware as well as the software to deliver it.

There are all sorts of possible extensions of this approach. For instance, we are currently examining the potential benefits of multimedia: In which particular situations are expensive animations and life videos useful to support the acquisition of knowledge? Acceptance, performance and extensive process analysis are all necessary to discover the situations in which learners actually make use of multiple media illustrating a particular subject and benefit from this supply of a variety of media.

From our point of view, this work is strongly tied to the software tools in use. For instance, MEM provides automatic generation of log files, automatic adaptation to different user groups and course designs, and automatic generation of electronic bookware (cf. Glowalla, Hasebrook, Fezzardi & Häfele, 1993). Of course, the latter facility is not a necessary feature to perform data-guided design but it definitely supports the systematic design and testing of teachware prototypes.

The formative evaluation starts with the early steps of the software life cycle and accompanies the whole implementation process. It is completed by summative evaluation steps in order to revise or maintain parts of the software. Qualitative and quantitative data collected in this process may lead to new software releases and further design alternatives which subsequently can be tested in a new evaluation cycle.

In conclusion, the comparison of carefully designed variations within and between software prototypes should guide various aspects of user interface design: (1) the choice of the system metaphor (e.g. file system, book, network), (2) the overall interface design.(e.g. window-, menu-, or icon-based), (3) range and mode of system functions (e.g. how many and which methods to look for string patterns in a text), (4) the use of media (i.e. under which circumstances animation and life video should be supplied), and finally (5) the instructional materials delivered by the system (e.g. explanations of an on-line help, visualizing complex interaction sequences). Most if not all of these aspects cannot be dealt with by a single discipline but require interdisciplinary implementation and evaluation work. Expertise is needed in technical, statistical, and psychological domains and also for implementation, marketing and controlling of software production and distribution.

Acknowledgments: The research reported here was supported by grants GL 123/2-3 and GL 123/2-4 from the German Research Foundation (DFG) to the first author. We would like to thank Gudrun Häfele, Martin Hofmann, and Manfred Thüring for their comments on earlier versions of this article. We also thank Ute Schütz-Collazo for improving our English.

References

Baker, L. (1989). Metacognition, comprehension monitoring, and the adult reader. *Educational Psychology Review*, 1, 3-38.

Belotti, V.M.E (1990). A framework for a sensing applicability of HCI techniques. In D. Diaper, D. Gilmore, G. Cockton & B. Shackel (Eds.), *Human-Computer Interaction; Interact '90*. Amsterdam: North Holland/Elsevier Science Publishers.

Bødker, S. (1991). *Through the interface. A human activity approach to user interface design*. Hillsdale, NJ: Lawrence Erlbaum Associates.

Bransford, J.D. , Goldman, S.R. & Vye, N.J. (1991). Making differences in people's ability to think: Reflections on a decade of work and some hope for the future. In R.J. Sternberg & L. Okagaki (Eds.), *Influences on children*. Hillsdale, NJ: Lawrence Erlbaum Associates.

Calfee, R.C. (1985). *Experimental methods in psychology*. New York: Holt, Rinehart, and Winston.

Card, S.K., Moran, T.P., & Newell, A. (1980). Computer text editing: An information-processing analysis of a routine cognitive skill. *Cognitive Psychology*, 12, 32-74.

Card, S.K., Moran, T.P., & Newell, A. (1983). *The psychology of human-computer interaction*. Hillsdale, NJ: Lawrence Erlbaum Associates.

Dillon, A., & McKnight, C. (1994). Never mind the theory, feel the data: Observations on the methodological problems of user interface design. This volume

Dix, A.J., & Runciman, C. (1985). Abstract models for interactive systems. In P. Johnson & Cook, S. (Eds.), *Proceedings of the British computer society conference on people and computers: Designing the interface* (pp. 13-22). Cambridge: Cambridge University Press.

Garzotto, F., Mainetti, L., & Paolini, P. (1994). Hypermedia application design: a structured approach. *This volume*

Glowalla, U., & Häfele, G. (1994). Benutzer- und systemgesteuertes Wiederlernen mit Hilfe des Hypermedia-Systems MEM [User- and system-controlled relearning with the hypermedia system MEM, in German]. In preparation, University of Giessen.

Glowalla, U., Häfele. G., & Rinck, M. (in press). Studiertechniken beim Lernen aus Sachtexten: Das Stellen oder Beantworten von Verständnisfragen [Study techniques in learning from expositiory text: Generating or answering adjunct questions, in German]. *Zeitschrift für Pädadgogische Psychologie*.

Glowalla, U., Häfele, G., Hasebrook, J., Rinck, M., & Fezzardi, G. (1992). Das Wiederlernen von Wissen [Relearning of knowledge, in German]. In U. Glowalla & E. Schoop (Eds.), *Hypertext und Multimedia. Neue Wege in der computerunterstützten Aus- und Weiterbildung* (pp. 332-351). Heidelberg: Springer-Verlag.

Glowalla, U., Hasebrook, J., & Häfele, G. (1992). Evaluating computer-aided learning with the hypermedia system MEM. *Software und Ergonomie*, 17, 19-25.

Glowalla, U., Hasebrook, J., & Häfele, G. (1993). Implementation und Evaluation computer-unterstützter Aus- und Weiterbildung mit dem Hypermedia-System MEM [Implementation and evaluation of computer-supported instruction with the hypermedia system MEM, in German]. In H.P. Frei & P. Schäuble (Eds.), *Hypermedia '93* (S. 195-207). Heidelberg: Springer-Verlag.

Glowalla, U., Hasebrook, J., Fezzardi, G., & Häfele, G. (1993). The hypermedia system MEM and its application in evaluating learning and relearning in higher education. In G. Strube & K.F. Wender (Eds.), *The cognitive psychology of knowledge* (pp. 367-385). Amsterdam: Elsevier Science Publishers.

Glowalla, U., Hasebrook, J., Häfele, G., Fezzardi, G., & Rinck, M. (1992). Das gezielte Wiederlernen von Wissen mit Hilfe des Hypermedia-Systems MEM [Selective relearning of knowledge with the hypermedia system MEM, in German]. In R. Cordes & N. Streitz (Eds.), *Hypertext und Hypermedia '92. Konzepte und Anwendungen auf dem Weg in die Praxis* (pp. 45-61). Heidelberg: Springer-Verlag.

Glowalla, U., Rinck, M., & Fezzardi, G. (1993). Die Integration von Wissen über ein Sachgebiet [Integration of knowledge from expository text, in German]. *Zeitschrift für Pädagogische Psychologie*, 7(1), 11-24.

Glowalla, U., & Schoop, E. (1992). Entwicklung und Evaluation computerunterstützter Lehrsysteme [Development and evaluation of computer-supported learning environments, in German]. In U. Glowalla & E. Schoop (Eds.), *Hypertext und Multimedia. Neue Wege in der computerunterstützten Aus- und Weiterbildung* (pp. 21-36). Heidelberg: Springer-Verlag.

Greenbaum, J., & Kyng, M. (Eds.) (1992). *Design at work: Approaches to collaborative design*. Hillsdale, NJ: Lawrence Erlbaum Associates.

Hannemann, J., & Thüring, M. (1994). What matters in developing user interfaces for hyperdocument presentation? *This volume*

Hesse, W. (1984). A systematics of software engineering: Structure, terminology, and classification of techiques. In P. Pepper (Ed.), *Program transformations and programming environments*. New York, Heidelberg. Springer-Verlag.

Hofmann, M. & Glowalla, U. (1994). Design of hypermedia interfaces in commercial applications. *This volume*

Howell, G.T. (1992). *Building hypermedia applications. A software developement guide*. New York: McGraw-Hill.

Jöns, I. (1992). Möglichkeiten und Grenzen formativer Evaluation computerunterstützter Lernsysteme im Rahmen anwendungsorientierter Entwicklungsprojekte [Potentials and limitations of formative evaluation of computer-supported learning environments in the framework of developmental projects, in German]. In U. Glowalla & E. Schoop (Eds.), *Hypertext und Multimedia. Neue Wege in der computerunterstützter Aus- und Weiterbildung* (pp.279-295). Heidelberg: Springer Verlag.

Johnson, P. (1992). *Human computer interaction. Psychology, task analysis, and software engineering.* London: McGraw-Hill.

Jonassen, D.H., & Grabinger, R.S. (1990). Problems and issues in designing hypertext/hypermedia for learning. In D.H. Jonassen & H. Mandl (Eds.), *Designing hypermedia for learning* (pp. 3-25). Berlin, New York: Springer-Verlag.

Lucas, H.C. (1992). *The analysis, design, and implementation of information systems.* New York: McGraw-Hill.

Newell, A., & Card, S. (1985). The prospects for psychological science in human-computer interaction. *Human Computer Interaction,* 1, 214.

Norman, D.A., & Draper, S.W. (Eds.) (1986). *User-centered design.* Hillsdale, NJ.: Lawrence Erlbaum Associates.

Steinberg, E.S. (1991). *Computer-assisted instruction.* Hillsdale, NJ.: Lawrence Erlbaum Associates.

Thimbleby, H. (1990). *User interface design.* New York: ACM press, Addison Wesley.

Twidale, M. (1993). Redressing the balance: The advantages of informal evaluation techniques for intelligent learing environments. *Journal of Artifcial Intelligence in Education,* 4(2/3), 155-178.

In R.B. Cattell & R.M. Wilde, G.J.S. (1977). Trait descriptional measurement by personality questionnaires. Dreger (Eds.), *Handbook of modern personality questionnaires* (pp. 69-103). Washington: Hemisphere.

Never Mind The Theory, Feel The Data: Observations On The Methodological Problems Of User Interface Design

Andrew Dillon, Cliff McKnight
HUSAT Research Institute, Loughborough University of Technology,
Loughborough, UK

Keywords. User-centred design; human factors

1 Introduction

In the present paper we will seek to place the design of hypermedia-based user interfaces in the appropriate context of user-centred system design. In so doing we will outline what we believe to be the major methodological issues. As this will indicate, we view hypermedia design as essentially no different from any other kind interface design in terms of process and problem. Hence the methodological issues for hypermedia interfaces need to be seen as design problems rather than cognitive scientific ones. In this vein, we argue for a data-driven approach to design that seeks theoretical insight at the methodological and process level of design rather than the user level.

2 User-centred design and the software production process

The traditional phased or 'waterfall' model of software design is not the most appropriate for effective design of devices involving multiple and complex human interactions. Adhering rigidly to this model means that it is often too expensive to make changes late in the development process — it is too hard to push water uphill — and so cost triumphs over common sense, never mind ergonomic principles. This often leads to poor or difficult-to-use designs. Given poorly designed software, discretionary users vote with their feet and those who have no discretion over its use expend great effort learning to work around it with reciprocal effects on satisfaction (a major component of current definitions of product usability).

A significant problem for phased design processes is the adequate mapping of user requirements to interface design. Not only can this mapping prove difficult, but requirements themselves are not always simple to elicit accurately and are known to shift with time. Hence, requirements both vary in terms of accuracy and reliability across a typical design process. User-centred design has arisen as an alternative philosophy for design that advocates the use of a variety of methods aimed at the iterative development of usable technology. As the name suggests, user-centred design implies a constant focusing of efforts on usability issues and requires the involvement of users at all stages in the design process rather than simply at the later evaluation stages (as in the more traditional models). This necessarily increases some early costs of the process but, it is argued, should lead to better products which are easier to learn, use and maintain.

However, it should be noted that iron-clad evidence for the cost-benefits of user-centred design is hard to find. Chapanis (1991) presents some 'success' stories and some horror stories but his final conclusion still reads more like a statement of faith. However, analysis of well know technological disasters or near disasters such as Three Mile Island indicate that poorly designed technology can be a major cause of human error and system failure.

The human factors response to the increased awareness of the importance of ergonomic issues in software has been mixed though it is possible to distinguish several waves or movements over the last 20 years. Initially, the field of HCI expended much effort in producing guidelines for the design of user interfaces that were based on empirical comparisons of various features. Thus, a literature emerged replete with studies examining the value of say, menus over command languages, mouse input devices over function keys, and large screens over small screens. These were periodically drawn together into handbooks of design that could be used to support interface development in industry (see e.g., Smith and Mosier, 1986).

However it soon became apparent that on their own, such guidelines could be misinterpreted or be used to produce an interface that was extremely poor on usability. Such undesirable outcomes often resulted from an over-literal interpretation of guidelines and the failure to adequately address the contextual issues crucial to understanding usability.

A second wave of research tried to play down the role of empiricism in favour of more theoretical analyses of human-computer interaction. This work drew very heavily on cognitive psychology, and more recently cognitive science, to piece together models of the user or interactive process that could be employed at the earliest stages of design to test for usability without the need to run formal trials. The most successful of these is the GOMS approach of Card, Moran and Newell (1983) which postulated the existence of a model human information processor whose performance times on routine simple tasks could be accurately predicted given appropriate task analysis.

Despite impressive academic work on such models, industry has been slow to embrace them for practical use. Problems lie in their limited range of application (they tend to be useful at this time only for tasks where users exhibit routine cognitive expertise and little discretion such as text editing) and the need for some knowledge or expertise in cognition or ergonomics to utilise such formal models reliably. Recent evidence from surveys of the European software industry conducted at HUSAT (Eason *et al*, 1986; Dillon *et al*, 1993) suggest that industrial take up has remained minimal.

Current emphasis has shifted towards the context in which technology is used, explicitly embracing the determining role of user, task and environmental variance in understanding the usability of any technology. Concomitant with this has been an increased awareness of the value of field research in understanding the nature of successful technology. Shackel (1991) for example outlines an approach to usability engineering that eschews formal modeling in favour of the operationalisation of benchmarks that a design must meet. Specifying usability criteria involves not only a sound analysis of the task domain and user characteristics but also a broad knowledge of possible usability metrics. Operational definitions of usability incorporating measurable aspects of performance such as effectiveness and user satisfaction are possible and allow a practical human engineering perspective to be brought to interface design. The targets to be met are derived either by reference to standards or through negotiation between design team and intended users or clients and may even be made simply by reference to competitive systems (e.g., "new design must support at least 10% greater accuracy" or 5% less training, 20% greater satisfaction, etc.)

Giving HCI away?

Running in parallel with these developments in method and approach to user interface design has been the marked tendency for the human factors profession to market its knowledge and skills in a form transferable to the design community. The guidelines approach to design explicitly embraces this view and the modeling school certainly set out with this in mind but problems in the transfer made this more difficult. Current contextual work still has not overturned this perspective but we believe that the appropriate professionals to tackle the usability issues in the design process are human factors specialists themselves. Further, we would argue that human factors professionals should be an integral part of the design team, not simply expected to certify an interface as "user-friendly" once it has been set in the software equivalent of concrete. Current industrial practice fails to support such views and this is patently not good enough. To ensure that software design follows a user-centred course it is essential that human factors professionals become involved directly in design and do not content themselves with developing tools or methods for non-ergonomists to use or with overseeing evaluations late in the development process. The abstract and sometimes nebulous nature of human factors knowledge renders it difficult to apply without substantial experience and attempts at transferring this technology through tools rather than people is unlikely to bring much success.

3 Designing hypermedia-based user interfaces

How, then, is the design of hypertext or hypermedia different from any other interactive software application? We believe there is no inherent difference in principle and user-centred design practices are the most appropriate in this domain. However, the fact that hypermedia-based interfaces are frequently being used in novel applications renders it very difficult to perform formal task analysis, specify the context of usage, or elicit user requirements to any degree of precision. Often, users cannot conceptualise what an advanced hypertext interface will enable them to do and the quality of an interactive application is usually only appreciated with experience. Even where users are capable of conceptualising a novel application reliably, possibly with the use of good prototypes, potential problems such as navigational difficulties or loss of context may not seem likely and therefore are not appreciated until it is too late. In such cases we believe it is even more important to involve human factors specialists in the design process. Added to the novelty of applications for hypertext is the complexity of behaviours supported by modern graphical user interface (GUI) techniques. Again, it requires a thorough understanding of user characteristics and requirements to constrain the range of GUI design options.

Information usage as a psychological process

In designing hypermedia interfaces, few researchers or developers have been able to demonstrate significantly better performance for electronic information over paper documents. This, despite the much lauded arrival of hypermedia as a liberating technology, reflects a failure to understand what readers or users actually do with documents. To a large extent paper has retained its primary position in our lives due to its inherent flexibility and usability. Most people with experience of both media still prefer paper.

In order to design better information carrying media such as hypertext, designers need to understand the process of reading as a task-related information processing activity. However, current models we have of reading are limited to laboratory-derived theories of activities such as word recognition or sentence comprehension rather than ecologically-relevant representations of information usage. Similarly, ergonomists and applied psychologists have examined reading from screens by concentrating on outcome measures such as speed and accuracy at the expense of process issues (see Dillon (1992) for a review). We now know some important features in screen presentation that influence reading speed such as image polarity and resolution (Gould et al, 1987). Unfortunately, given the highly contextual nature of usability, it is unlikely that it will ever prove possible to prescribe interface design purely on a feature or attribute basis. More importantly, the process of information usage is so inherently multi-layered that other issues such as the perception of structure, navigation and location, manipulation and so forth may need to be addressed in particular ways depending on the task, the information type under consideration and the users. In other words, even meeting stringent screen ergonomic criteria will be no guarantee of success in the electronic document domain as has been reported elsewhere (Dillon *et al*, 1991).

4 The absence of applicable theory and the problems of user interface design

Currently, no relevant discipline — psychology, information science or computer science — can provide an account of the reading or information usage process adequate enough to guide design practice. As a result interactive system design often proceeds on the basis of heuristics, subjective bias or common sense assumptions about reading and information usage. These may be accurate or inaccurate but we have no way of knowing for certain until the system is actually evaluated properly.

Interestingly enough, this problem is invariant across most design domains. The literature on architectural practice, mechanical engineering and manufacturing design (see e.g., Darke, 1979; Lawson, 1980) indicate that it is in the nature of design practice that non-algorithmic procedures are followed in all designers' attempts to produce solutions. Typically, designers seek to generate a potential solution and then use this as a means of better understanding the problem. This distinction with classical scientific models of problem-solving has been well demonstrated empirically by Lawson (1980) who examined groups of scientists and architectural students tackling a constrained block-design problem. The scientists tended to proceed by logical progression, taking the problem statement and attempting to derive a step by step solution (much as one would expect scientific problem-solving to occur). Design students clearly differed in that they quickly produced potential solutions which they used to check the problem and make better progress.

The net result of this work is that contemporary cognitive theories are no guide to design practice. Yet it is precisely such cognitive theories that underlie most work on Human-Computer Interaction and therefore empirical methods must be followed. User-centred design methods are essentially predicated on empiricism as the design of even modestly successful applications such as SuperBook (Landauer *et al*, 1993) demonstrate. These developers report a series of experiments run over several years as they designed an electronic textbook to support information access. While it is common to see SuperBook cited as a hypertext success story it is important to realise that early developments of SuperBook actually led to significantly poorer performance relative to paper in certain tasks.

Although Landauer *et al.* managed to redesign the hypertext effectively they admit to being able to do so only on the basis of empirical data that had both highlighted substantial delays at certain task points due to poor system response rate and shown users to be employing sub-optimal search strategies. Even modifying the first version successfully still left room for further improvement as further evaluations indicated other sources of user difficulty.

The SuperBook project represents the classic user-centred design process but it points to several difficulties hypermedia interface designers face. First, user trials are expensive. Even where cheap prototypes can be utilised, locating and training representative users for evaluation purposes and analysing the subsequent data is not cheap and thus frequently resisted by design teams.

Second, the problems identified in the user trials were not complex (e.g., response rate, poorly formulated search criteria, etc.) With hindsight these seem obvious, yet none of this highly talented design team predicted them. This is the norm and will occur in all design processes until we have theories of the user that can predict such responses to the interface. When will we have them however? Not soon is the answer and certainly not in our lifetimes if we continue to expect cognitive psychology or information science to provide the answers. The naturally occurring variance in humans and the contextual determinism of many activities render classic theory building impossible if our goal is the establishment of a general user psychology based on small pockets of laboratory-derived knowledge.

Can such methods be made cost-effective?

Given the fact that human factors activities in the software development process costs money, it is essential to ensure that it is money well spent. This means developing cost-effective methods which provide quality data to inform the design process, reducing the development and testing time, reducing the training time, improving the maintainability or at least some combination of these benefits.

A variety of methods exist but in order for them to be cost-effective we must know when to use each. For example, modern rapid prototyping tools can be used to generate very realistic looking interfaces but there are times when paper and pencil will provide as good data. In some cases, an expert walk-through will be an appropriate way of suggesting design improvements but there comes a point when such methods can contribute no more. A properly designed experimental comparison may provide the best means of deciding between functionally equivalent versions of an interface but at some stages in the design such experiments are impractical. It may be easy to collect performance data such as time taken or errors made, but in many cases verbal protocol analysis will yield more influential data.

In 1987 Shneiderman wrote that high-level theories were 'beginning to emerge', citing such examples as his own syntactic/semantic model of user knowledge, the GOMS model of Card, Moran and Newell (1983), the four-level models of Foley and Van Dam (1982) and Norman (1984) (later to become a seven-level model) and the production rules model of Kieras and Polson (1985).

The extent to which any of these has impacted the design of real products is not clear but few examples of success are available. Hence, at this point in the development of a theory of design, a 'reverse engineering' approach may well prove instructive. That is, consider some successful or well-designed products and retrospectively study the design process through which they evolved. Some examples, such as the SuperBook project mentioned above, have been well documented and offer a rich source of information and insight but other examples need to be sought out or described. With this approach it should be possible to develop an encompassing methodology which prescribes the appropriate tools and techniques at each point in the design process.

An obvious drawback is the lack of well-documented design processes or the *post hoc* rationalisation of design decisions that can occur but this is a fact of life we must deal with appropriately. What is patently clear from the literature is that we don't need another set of design guidelines — there are too many already, and anyway designers do not use them very effectively. If the fundamental concept of user centred design is accepted, then it is appropriate for a human factors specialist to form an integral part of the design team throughout the design process. In so doing they can provide the data we need as a discipline to draw up reliable records of design rationales.

5 What hope is there for theory?

The above suggestions should lead to a more adequately specified user-centred methodology, but will it continue to be a theory-free methodology? If human factors continues to 'give itself away' (and thereby fail to influence the design process in any real sense) then the answer is almost certainly 'yes'. However, with human factors specialists involved in design, learning more about the real processes involved in design it should be possible to perform meta-analyses of the diverse experiences and thereby develop suitable theories.

Perhaps the search for theory is looking in the wrong place. Do we need a theory of the user at all? It may be that our problems are solvable methodologically at least by articulating a theory of design which provides adequate guidance on producing usable artefacts. To an extent the user-centred design approach is one such design theory (although its precise articulation and qualification for that title may be questioned). As yet however, we are only beginning to understand the cost-benefits of certain evaluation methods (Nielsen 1992) or the best means of ensuring reliable user participation (Eason 1989). These problems are tractable and would seem rich in data given the widespread occurrence of design activity. A shift of emphasis in research to address these questions would appear useful.

There is nothing special about the design of hypermedia systems which warrants their being afforded a special theory or methodology. The principles of user centred design can be applied equally to such systems and any theory which arises out of the design of products should have sufficient generality to apply to hypermedia.

References

Chapanis, A. (1991) The Business Case for Human Factors in Informatics. In B. Shackel and S. Richardson (eds.) *Human Factors for Informatics Usability.* Cambridge: Cambridge University Press. 39–71.

Card, S. K., Moran, T. P. and Newell, A., (1983) *The Psychology of Human-Computer Interaction.* Hillsdale NJ: Lawrence Erlbaum Associates.

Darke, J. (1979) The Primary Generator and the Design Process. *Design Studies,* 1, 36–44.

Dillon, A. (1992) Reading from Paper versus Screens: a Critical Review of the Empirical Literature. *Ergonomics,* 35(10), 1297–1326.

Dillon, A., Sweeney, M. and Maguire, M. (1993) Usability Engineering in the European IT Industry: Current Practices. In: J. Alty, S. Guest and D. Diaper (Eds.) *People and Computers VIII.* Cambridge: Cambridge University Press.

Dillon, A., Richardson J. and McKnight, C. (1991) Institution Alising Human Factors in the Design Process: the ADONIS Experience. In E. Lovesey (Ed.) *Contemporary Ergonomics 1991.* London: Taylor and Francis.

Eason, K. (1989) *Information Technology and Organisational Change.* London: Taylor and Francis.

Eason, K. D., Harker, S. D. P. and Poulson, D. F. (1986) Preliminary Investigations into the Use of Human Factors Data in the Design Process. HUSAT Memo Nº 377, Loughborough University of Technology.

Foley, J. and van Dam, A. (1982) *Fundamentals of Interactive Computer Graphics.* Reading, MA: Addison-Wesley.

Gould, J. D., Alfaro, L., Finn, R., Haupt, B. and Minuto, A. (1987) Reading from CRT Displays can be as fast as Reading from Paper. *Human Factors,* 29(5), 497–517.

Kieras, D. and Polson, P. (1985) An Approach to the Formal Analysis of User Complexity. *International Journal of Man-Machine Studies,* 22, 365–394.

Landauer, T., Egan, D., Remde, J., Lesk, M., Lochbaum, C. and Ketchum, D. (1993) Enhancing the Usability of Text through Computer Delivery and Formative Evaluation: The SuperBook Project. In C. McKnight, A. Dillon and J. Richardson (Eds.) *Hypertext: a Psychological Perspective*. Chichester: Ellis Horwood.

Lawson, B. R. (1980) *How Designers Think*. London: Architectural Press.

Nielsen, J. (1992) Finding Usability Problems through Heuristic Evaluation. In *Proceedings of CHI'92*. New York: ACM, 373–380.

Norman, D. (1984) Design Rules based on Analyses of Human Error. *Communications of the ACM*, 26(4), 254–258.

Shackel, B. (1991) Usability — Context, Framework, Definition, Design and Evaluation. In B. Shackel and S. Richardson (eds.) *Human Factors for Informatics Usability*. Cambridge: Cambridge University Press. 21–37.

Shneiderman, B. (1987) *Designing the User Interface: Strategies for Effective Human-Computer Interaction*. Reading, MA: Addison-Wesley.

Smith, S. L. and Mosier, J. N. (1986) *Guidelines For Designing User-Interface Software*. Report 7 MTR-10090, Esd-Tr-86-278, Mitre Corporation, Bedford, MA.

Design of Hypermedia Interfaces in Commercial Applications

Martin Hofmann[1], Ulrich Glowalla[2]
[1] SAP AG, Walldorf, Germany
[2]Justus-Liebig-Universität, Dept. of Psychology, Gießen, Germany

Abstract. Many wide-spread products in different domains of application like word-processing or multimedia authoring have been supplemented with hypermedia properties. For the development of hypertexts in these applications, it is important to consider the specific needs of each particular class of application. For the majority of applications, we doubt that there will ever be something like a generic hypertext user interface. We argue instead, that the discussion should rather be focused on the process of creating and updating hypertexts.

Keywords: Commercial Applications, Guidelines, User Interface Design, Evaluation, Hypertext Authoring

1 Hypertext as Part of Software Applications

Hypertext has become part of the common software environment. Document-processing tools like FrameMaker and Interleaf offer linking abilities (Gulbins 1992, Interleaf 1992), groupware as Lotus Notes enables the user to access other documents by links (Lotus, Iris 1993), and Microsoft's Windows Help system allows the reader to move through help texts by hypertext links (Microsoft 1993).

All these tools are relatively well-known. The Microsoft help system has even established itself as the de-facto standard for a help environment on the PC. These tools have another thing in common: Compared to research systems, they do not focus on the notion of hypertext and its links. If we take a look on hypertext solutions used in commercial environments, we can also see that they hardly ever rely on the network metaphor. Until recently, however, this metaphor has been the most popular one in hypertext research, especially in the context of the so-called *navigation problem* (Nielsen 1990a, Hofmann, Langendörfer, Laue, Lübben 1991).

In what follows we collect some hypotheses why commercial applications and tools using hypertext features do not focus on characteristics frequently found in advanced research systems. In particular, we describe various issues to be considered in current hypertext applications (section 2). On the basis of these issues, we propose some theses that focus on the main needs in commercial settings (section 3). We conclude with several suggestions towards future investigations that may prove to be fruitful (section 4).

2 Analysis of the Use of Hypermedia in Commercial Settings

2.1 Two different design factors

Like any other interactive application, the look and feel of a hypertext application is influenced by two variables:

- the design implied by the application;
- the design constrained by the abilities of the selected tool.

Many applications have a long history. User interface design has always tried to exploit well-known metaphors of these applications. For instance, forms are a popular approach of user interfaces in all areas of office-based systems (Tsichritzis 1985). The design of these forms is restricted by the existing application (i.e. existing forms, rules of business and/or government, etc.).

Hypertext adds explicit relationships between objects of a specific application. The user interface designer is required to express these links in the framework of the particular application. An example of a design rule for this requirement would then read: *"For all graphics you use add enough surrounding text so that a user, who has not read any other nodes/pages/documents, can at least understand its central contents."*

Please note that a set of such rules will make up a hypertext rhetoric. The usefulness of such a rhetoric will depend on whether its rules are adjusted to the specific requirements of the target application. Such practical guidelines for hypertext creation can be found in Landow (1987), Kahn (1989), Kahn, Peters, Landow (this volume), Brown (1990), Hofmann (1991), and Meusel, Eickemeyer (this volume).

Although the first variable may constrain the freedom of the designer in several respects, it has the potential of leading to a good user interface design based on an extension of well-established metaphors. In contrast, the second variable is usually regarded as an obstruction which unnecessarily constrains design activities. For instance, if the designer desires to work with colors to support various link types, and his or her tool does not offer coloring the anchors according to their type, he or she is forced to express the purpose of the anchors in a different way. Therefore, the function ("display link types") and its implementation on a dedicated system have to be strictly separated. Hypertext architectures like the Dexter model bear the potential for such a separation (Halasz, Schwartz 1990).

A design rule for the second factor could therefore be twofold: First, select - or, less frequently, build - a tool that enables the hypertext author to design particular applications as freely as possible. Second, a rule for the author would be to adapt the metaphor selected to the limitations of the existing tool. While the latter is definitely not a desirable solution, it is frequently found in business-oriented environments.

2.2 Hypermedia applications frequently found in industry

Today, hypermedia is used in industry mainly in the domain of *technical documentation*. Online help systems (e.g., SAP's Online help, Microsoft help, and various other products) use hypertext links as main tool for navigating through help texts. Though hypertext features are intensively used, the interfaces of these applications are rarely based on the hypertext network metaphor, which seem to be the most popular one in hypertext research. Commercial applications, however, make predominantly use of book metaphors and hierarchies, such as hypermedia teachware, (cf. Glowalla, Hasebrook, Häfele 1993).

A second area for hypertext applications is *computer-based training (CBT)*. In this context, hypertext links are used for references between related materials in order to allow the user to select among different learning paths, and to change between questions, examples, and answers (Hammond 1989). For these applications, hypertext metaphors and a special design philosophy might be appropriate; in any event, the user (the student) should be in the focus of the design approach, (cf. Glowalla, Hasebrook, this volume).

A third domain where hypertext features are widely accepted is that of (multimedia) *information systems*. Though links can be used in software products like for instance, Lotus Notes to point to documents related to the actual document presented, the basic metaphor instead is that of databases containing a set of documents, and various views on this set of documents. Other information systems are based on authoring tools such as ToolBook, etc. These tools mostly rely on the card metaphor. *World-wide public information services* such as gopher servers or the World Wide Web (WWW), offer a variety of information, but are not commercial products (Krol 1992).

Hypertext features are also part of *electronic publishing tools* (Gulbins 1992, Interleaf 1992). Applications created by tools that use these features, however, consist predominantly of technical documentation (mentioned above), catalogues, and electronic encyclopedias.

Currently, there is no application domain in which a single metaphor is used exclusively. As mentioned before, book metaphors are wide-spread in the domain of Online help, but other approaches exist as well (card-oriented, networks; for an overview, refer to Parseye et al. (1989) or Berk and Devlin (1991)). In computer-based training, tools frequently used are HyperCard by Apple or ToolBook by Asymmetrix. While the availability and the price are clear advantages of these tools, they offer no appropriate and sufficient support for sophisticated and automated user interface design. Most of the design has to be done manually. For instance, *link anchors* have to be explicitly created by the hypertext author, instead of being created as default by the system when the link itself is created. Unfortunately, this also holds for more powerful, more expensive, and more sophisticated tools like Sybase's GainMomentum (Gain 1992).

In conclusion, no tool currently available allows

  a) to choose the metaphor,

  b) to create a framework according to this metaphor automatically,

  c) to adapt simply to the application, or

  d) to update the contents easily.

In the next section, we shall deal with questions that arise from such a situation: Will new tools have a chance at the market at all? How much freedom has the user interface designer or the hypertext author to select metaphors, when he or she is already restricted by the application?

2.3 How important is hypermedia in commercial applications?

One of the main concerns of hypertext research has always been the *user inter-face*. This is no surprise, since hypertext applications are interactive applications - a fact so evident that it is sometimes simply omitted from definitions of hypermedia (cf. Nielsen 1990b, where interactivity is simply presupposed, as can be seen by his remark on "short response times", p.4). At the current state of development, we cannot discuss the design of such an interactive interface per se. Since hypertext features, especially linking, are relatively wide-spread in industry, we have to discuss this interface with respect to existing applications and their interfaces.

As already mentioned above, we believe that the area of the applications restricts the freedom of choice of the hypermedia metaphor, when developing an interface. This view is supported by a look at current software systems:

a) Properties of current systems

  • Currently, most large-scale information systems are query-, report-, or retrieval-based. It looks as if this will continue for a long time, especially in certain areas like enterprise computing (financials, materials management, etc.), and domains with a high proportion of text-based information. Please note, however, that there are noteworthy – mostly research-based – exceptions like cartography and chemical design (for an example, see Egenhofer, Frank 1988). Nevertheless, in most cases hypertext-features will only be an add-on, used in certain domains where a relativly simple structure like a hierarchy can be built and presented. So there will hardly be a *general* and typical hypermedia interface for these information systems. Linking will be possible, but the user of such applications will not think that he or she is using "hypertext".

An example is the customizing of SAP AG's client/server business software R/3. This process necessary when a new installation is tailored to the specific needs of a certain enterprise is supported by documentation. Any step of the process is linked to its respective documentation portion by hypertext links (SAP AG, 1992). The documentation portions themselves are also linked to each other. Nevertheless, customizing consultants do not focus on the hypertext notion. The reason for this could be that the customizing process itself is a rather linear task.

- Links are becoming part of the operating or database system (Pearl 1989). They are not a kind of object where a whole large information system will focus on. Even advanced commercial authoring systems like GainMomentum lack link management features that can be found in research systems such as CONCORDE (Hofmann, Laue, Lübben, Langendörfer 1990) or Sepia (Thüring, Haake, Hannemann 1991). Links seem to be a tool of secondary importance in information systems and developers will not focus on link management and anchor presentation. So it appears to be useless to develop user interface methodologies focusing exclusively on hypertext. Instead, we would like to see further work on the design of electronic (hyper-) documents in general.

- In small information systems, the stack metaphor is frequently used (HyperCard, ToolBook, etc.). However, this metaphor is only useful for rapid prototyping of small presentations, since it does not contribute to (1) fast generation, (2) updating, (3) adaptation, and (4) test on usability. One always has to go through the whole stack to do some global modifications that do not refer to the "background" (e.g. moving objects appearing on a sequence of cards from the upper right corner to the lower left corner), there is no straight-forward re-usability of code and material comparable to that of object-oriented languages, and finally consistency checks are not available.

- Large-scale applications will not focus on the notion of "hyperlinking". While current development creates graphical layers on top of SQL-interfaces, even there the links are just one minor feature of the user interface, frequently neglected by tool designers, as can be seen by the absence of link management tools.

b) The importance of hypertext in small applications

- Small information systems (kiosk systems, small CBT applications) will exploit hypermedia functionality to a larger extent. However, most of these applications are rather short-lived and marketing-oriented. In this situation, a large UIMS tool to create consistent hypertext user interfaces would only pay off, if it could be used for building many applications. Of course, this would require a very flexible (and expensive?) tool, offering easy and flexible updates.

- Other systems of a similar size that also exploit hypertext features will have a longer existence (e.g. dictionaries). But here the focus of publishers will be on fast production, straightforward and cheap updating, and simple adaptation without bothering too much on the hyperlinks. They probably disturb the updating, if there is no sophisticated hyperlink management. Here, the metaphor of the application restricts the user interface.

c) The influence of conventions in certain domains

- We also would like to point out that there are certain application domains where it is still hard to install a computer and to make this machine be used (cf. Reiter, Roller 1993 who describe an application used by blue-collar workers in the car industry). A developer has to be prepared to use metaphors common in this area. In many cases, "books" or "documents" or even "forms" will do. In general, hypertext researchers should not expect that users get excited when they get *hypermedia*. Moreover, non-linear hypertext systems may be quite confusing. The appropriateness of this point of view becomes clear, if we consider the many uses of the *book metaphor* in electronic documents. They are easy to learn, straightforward to use, and very generally applicable, not to mention the attraction of this approach for the publishing world.

- Technical documentation is an area where hypertext is already accepted. Even here we find mostly conventional metaphors: table of contents, indexes, book hierarchies, etc. Generally, computer and cognitive scientists focus their attention on the usability of the actual application, not on the "help system". Nevertheless, these help systems can be quite impressive (e.g. take a look on the help written for the spreadsheet program Lotus Improv (Lotus 1993) on NeXT machines), but they generally contain a lot of "conventional" book metaphors.

3 Recommendations

In this section, we summarize our recommendations. They are directed to hypertext editors, hypertext writers, and hypertext tool builders.

Recommendations to hypertext editors and writers:

- Design of any part of the application should be based on check-lists and *guidelines* fitting to accepted guidelines (Hofmann 1993). It is quite common in industry to use guidelines. Most companies already have styles of their own that are part of their corporate identity. An adaptation to these styles will make it easy to find acceptance for supplementary guidelines.

  At SAP, for instance, several guidelines were available for various aspects of production of conventional paper documentation. SAP implemented guidelines for hypertext creation even before hypertext became an official part of online help in the R/3 system. A typical, and quite obvious rule is: *Create only nodes with one or two pages.* The motivation for this rule was, that the first version of the hypertext software offered only a Courier-like font, rendered reading of longer texts rather tiresome as several test users criticized.

  We immediately see that guidelines have to be adjusted to further development of the tool. Consequently, this rule had to be changed after the integration of additional fonts into the hypertext viewer.

- If guidelines are developed, attention should be focused *on concrete help* for the hypertext author. Consider for instance the difference between the more generic rhetoric of Landow (1987) and the problem-oriented one proposed by Kahn (1989). While Landow (1987) states that links stress the importance of the linked information, and that their existence cannot be neglected by readers, Kahn (1989) offers guidelines for the author's daily work: e.g., that all names of nodes and links should be meaningful, and only directly related content portions should be linked.

- It is seducing to assume that to build an information system or a CBT application with a hypermedia tool results in any user having *direct access to the underlying structures of information.* Hypertext, however, does not necessarily imply "direct access to structures". According to our experience there is not much focus on the problem of linking and anchors in commercial environments. However, there should be more than currently exists. Anyway a clear structuring of the application and its user interface according to its functions will count more than sophisticated rules of what to link in which way, and how to build a metaphor around the notion of links.

Recommendations to the designers of hypertext authoring tools:

- Any particular metaphor will only fit certain applications. We have to consider whether the development of a *metaphor* top-down for a whole class of applications can be appropriate. Waterworth, Chignell, and Zhai (1993) recommend a *bottom-up approach*, which could lead to a mixture of various metaphors at the top-level of the application. Though the metaphors may not fit perfectly to each other, every metaphor itself is well understood. The potential benefits of both approaches have to be evaluated very carefully. Incidentally he bottom-up approach fits nicely with our recommendation to focus on the application and to use metaphors fitting the application.

- It should be clear by now that at least with respect to larger systems the main problem of the future will be applications that introduce links without having a *management or consistency concept*. We can observe such a situation in the domain of electronic publishing/desktop publishing, where popular tools offer linking facilities without offering management tools. This situation is unsatisfactory. Link management facilities have to be added to the average help system, word processor, or hypermedia toolbox. In order to achieve productivity, adaptability, and cost effectiveness, the ability to manage data is crucial.

- A toolbox that would allow easy, machine-supported adaptation of conventional documents to hypertext would be of great importance. Currently, many hypertexts are based on conventional ancestors. In the domain of technical documentation, for instance, we guess the ratio is ca. 100%. Tools as described by Sarre and Güntzer (1991) which support turning text into hypertext could immensely influence the acceptance of hypertext as underlying technology of information systems.

- The development of *multimedia user interfaces* should be based on evaluations of experiences with dynamic data types. Sometimes, user interface development tools may help, but are in most cases unable to model the dynamic behavior of the dialogue (Eirund, Hofmann 1993). Many times, the developer will have to program in such situations. In addition, we highly recommend the careful evaluation of the multimedia extension (Glowalla, Hasebrook, this volume). Otherwise, it will happen frequently that investments made into additional features do not pay off by better usability.

4 Conclusion

Hypertext research could probably develop a methodology for creating user interfaces specifically for hypermedia. The question is whether it really should. The reason for our doubts are, that we cannot convince developers to use these methods since the interface of most applications they are developing already have to comply with certain constraints, and the methodology to create hypertext was not developed to comply with these constraints.

Hypermedia will not be the center of their design. The application will be. Designers really need good methods for designing their dedicated applications and documents. Hypermedia interface design is only part of this process, and already is restricted by many design decisions met in the earlier stages (see e.g. Schuler, Thüring 1994). In other words, we highly recommend to develop design support of hypertext authoring, as has been done in the HYTEA project (Schröcksnadl, Meusel, Zucker, Schiff, Thüring 1992).

Many people seem to be convinced that hypermedia interfaces need a development methodology of their own. According to our view, hypertext systems are simply an additional class of information systems. The investigation of current information systems shows that their interfaces are modeled according to metaphors and applications already in use.

Based on what we stated above, we come to following quite obvious conclusion:

- Developers and designers should not concentrate on hypermedia features per se when they create new tools and applications. User interfaces have become more and more standardized. Hypermedia is not revolutionary enough to justify a total focus on its features. Instead, we recommend to concentrate our efforts on the following issues:

- Hypermedia features have to be reasonably embedded into existing user interfaces. Reasonable means, for instance, that if a link source is created by an author, a default anchor has to be created automatically.

   Hypermedia creation needs a better and more structured support; we should work on the transfer of approaches like that of Garzotto, Mainetti, Paolini (this volume) or Schuler, Thüring (1994) into industry.

- Applications and tools should be tested using reliable experimental and informal evaluation techniques (Glowalla and Hasebrook, this volume, Dillon and McKnight, this volume).

- At the same time, we need more focus on neglected aspects like updating and re-engineering of hypermedia information (Glowalla, Hasebrook, Häfele 1993). Link management and consistency seem to be underrated compared to the attention the user interface usually gets. This could be even more important in open hypertext systems (Pearl 1989).

5 References

Berk, E., Devlin, J. (1991). *Hypertext/Hypermedia Handbook*; New York: McGraw-Hill, 1991

Brown, P. (1990). Assessing the quality of hypertext documents. In A.Rizk, N.Streitz, J.André (Eds.) *Hypertext: Concepts, Systems and Applications*, Proceedings of the European Conference on Hypertext 1990 (ECHT'90), pp.1-12, Versailles. Cambridge: Cambridge University Press, November 1990

Dillon, A., McKnight, C. (this volume). *Never mind the theory, feel the data: Observations on the methodological problems of user interface design*. This Volume.

Egenhofer, M.J., Frank, A.U. (1988). Towards a Spatial Query Language: User Interface Considerations, pp.124-133. In *Proceedings of the Conference on Very Large Data Bases (VLDB'88)*, Los Angeles, September 1988

Meusel, K., Eickemeyer, K. (this volume). *Facing technical documentation with hypertext: reflections on the systematic design, construction, and presentation*. This Volume.

Eirund, H., Hofmann, M. (1993). Designing Multimedia Presentations. In H.P.Frei, P.Schäuble (Eds.) *Hypermedia*, pp.183-194, Informatik aktuell, Springer, Berlin Heidelberg, 1993

Gain Technology, a Sybase Company (1992). *Gain Extension Language (GEL)*, Vol.1, Vol.2, Technical Reference Manual. Palo Alto (CA), 1992

Garzotto, F., Mainetti, L., Paolini, P. (this volume). *Hypermedia application design: a structured approach*. This volume. 1994

Glowalla, U., Hasebrook, J. (this volume). *An evaluation model based on experimental methods applied to the design of hypermedia user interfaces*. This volume. 1994

Glowalla, U., Hasebrook, J., Häfele, G. (1993). Implementation und Evaluation computerunterstützter Aus- und Weiterbildung mit dem Hypermediasystem MEM (Implementation and Evaluation of Computer-supported Education by the Hypertext System MEM, in German). In H.P.Frei, P.Schäuble (Eds.) *Hypermedia*, pp.195-207, Informatik aktuell, Springer, Berlin Heidelberg, 1993

Gulbins, J. (1992). *Desktop Publishing mit FrameMaker* (Desktop Publishing using FrameMaker, in German). Berlin, Heidelberg: Springer, 1992

Halasz, F., Schwartz, M.D., Eds. (1990). The Dexter Hypertext Reference Model. In *Workshop Papers of the Hypertext Standardization Workshop*, Document HT-9, January 1990

Hammond, N. (1989). Hypermedia and Learning: Who Guides Whom? In *Proceedings of ICCAL'89*, pp.167-181, Dallas, LNCS, Springer, Heidelberg Berlin, May 1989

Hofmann, M. (1991). *Richtlinien zur Erstellung von Benutzerhandbüchern als Hypertexte* (Guideline for the creation of user manuals as hypertexts, in German). SAP AG, Internal Guideline, Walldorf, 1991

Hofmann, M. (1993). Richtlinien als Hilfsmittel für die Erzeugung von Hypertexten (Guidelines as Means to Support the Creation of Hypertexts; in German). In *Proceedings of tekom Online*, München, October 1993

Hofmann, M., Langendörfer, H., Laue, K., Lübben, E. (1991). The Principle of Locality Used for Hypertext Presentation: Navigation and Browsing in CONCORDE. In D.Diaper, M.Hammond (Eds.) *Human and Computers VI*, pp.419-436, Cambridge University Press, Cambridge, 1991

Interleaf Corp. (1992). *The Interleaf Hyperleaf Toolkit*. Waltham (MA), 1992

Kahn, P. (1989). Linking together books: experiments in adapting published material into Intermedia documents. *Hypermedia*, 1 (2), 1989: pp.111-145

Kahn, P., Peters, R., Landow, G.P. (this volume). *Three fundamental elements of visual rhetoric in hypertext*. This Volume.

Krol, E. (1992). *The Whole Internet*. Sebastopol (CA): O'Reilly and Associates 1992

Landow, G.P. (1987). Relationally Encoded Links and the Rhetoric of Hypertext. In *Proceedings of the ACM Workshop Hypertext'87*, pp.331-343, Chapel Hill, November 1987

Lotus Development Corp., Iris Associates, Inc. (1993). *Lotus Notes for OS/2*. Online Documentation, 1993

Lotus Development Corp. (1993). *Lotus Improv Manual*. Lotus Park, Staines, England, 1993

Microsoft Corp. (1993). *Visual C++ Documentation, Help Compiler Guide*. Redmont (WA), 1993

Nielsen, J. (1990a). The Art of Navigating through Hypertext. *Communications of the ACM*, 33 (3): pp.296-310

Nielsen, J. (1990b). *Hypertext & Hypermedia*. Boston: Academic Press, 1990

Parseye, K., Chignell, M., Khoshafian, S., Wong, H. (1989). *Intelligent Databases*. New York: John Wiley, 1989

Pearl, A. (1989). Sun's Link Service: A Protocol for Open Linking. In *Proceedings of 2nd ACM Conference on Hypertext (Hypertext'89)*, pp137-146, Pittsburgh, November 1989

Reiter, D., Roller, D. (1993). Erschließung von Information und Wissen: Verfahren zur dynamischen Aggregation von Hypertrails (Analyzing Information and Knowledge: Ways for the Dynamic Aggregation of Hypertrails; in German). H.P.Frei, P.Schäuble (Eds.) *Hypermedia*, pp.81-92, Informatik aktuell, Springer, Berlin Heidelberg, 1993

SAP AG (1992). *R/3 System - Dokumentation*. Walldorf, 1992

Sarre, F., Güntzer, U. (1991). Automatic Transformation of Linear Text into Hypertext. In *Proceedings of the International Symposium on Database Systems for Advanced Applications (DASFAA'91)*, pp.498-506, Tokyo, April 1991

Schröcksnadl, B., Meusel, K., Zucker, W., Schiff, J., Thüring, M. (1992). Hypertext Application Design Using a Model-Based Approach. In R.Cordes, N.Streitz (Eds.) *Hypertext und Hypermedia 1992*, pp.12-24, Informatik aktuell, Springer, Berlin Heidelberg, 1992

Schuler, W., Thüring, M. (1994). Pragmatical Hypertext Design (PHD). *Arbeitspapiere der GMD 813*, Gesellschaft für Mathematik und Datenverarbeitung mbH, January 1994

Thüring, M., Haake, J., Hannemann, J. (1991). What's Eliza doing in the Chinese Room? Incoherent hyperdocuments and how to avoid them. In *Proceedings of the 3rd ACM Conference on Hypertext (Hypertext'91)*, pp.161-177, San Antonio, December 1991

Tsichritzis, D. (1985). *Office Automation*. Berlin, Heidelberg: Springer, 1985.

Waterworth, J., Chignell, M., Zhai, S.Z. (1993). From icons to interface models: designing hypermedia from the bottom up. In *International Journal of Man-Machine Studies*, 39, pp.453-472, 1993

4 Detailed Design Proposals and Guidelines

Paul Kahn

The six papers that make up this section discuss a broad range of specific issues facing the designer of hypermedia systems and publications. In each case the authors are speaking from their experience. That work ranges from abstract research models to operational commercial hypermedia systems.

Kamps and Reichenberger address one of the most difficult issues in user interface design: creating effective graphical representations of interconnected networks of information. Their model builds on examples drawn from the a research prototype of the electronic Dictionary of Art, based on the printed work published by Macmillan Publishers Ltd. This is their knowledge base and the goal they are seeking is a graphical representation for information access in art history. They emphasize the need for supporting a dialog between the user and the knowledge base to provide coherence and context. The layout technique they propose identifies regularities in the relationships of each "subnet" in a query, and then presents the query results in the form of text, arrows, and rectangles coded by color. Future work will explore how well the dialog approach and the layout techniques scale up.

Neuwirth et al. discuss a topic that represents a major overlap between the research fields of hypertext and computer–supported cooperative work (CSCW): systems for recording and managing annotations. They note that textual annotations are a basic form of written communication and an oft–cited application for hypertext. However, many hypertext systems treat annotations as though they were a "free" byproduct of linking with no special requirements of their own. The authors propose a set of requirements for effective annotation that take into account features implicit in traditional written annotation systems but too often overlooked in electronic systems, such as visual context and authorial distinctions. The authors' ideas are demonstrated in the PREP Editor, which presents annotations by many authors in a visually coordinated multi–column layout.

Kahn et al. define several basic design issues related to visual representations of links in hypertext documents. They identify three elements that require visual solutions in all systems: link presence, link destination, and link mapping. Their discussion and examples focus primarily on marking links in text and between units of text in large document collections. Their examples are drawn from techniques used by the IRIS Intermedia research system and commercial systems such as Hypercard and Storyspace.

Kirste examines one of two kinds of hypermedia systems that he characterizes as general purpose hypermedia systems (GPHS). He proposes that the GPHS must be capable of capturing hypermedia structure separate from any specific application behavior. He proposes an abstract model for describing the interaction behavior of hyperstructures. The HyperPicture research system is then used to illustrate how this model can be applied.

Carey reports on an investigation of user behavior seeking information in an online documentation system. There has been a great deal of research devoted to extending information retrieval and hypertext functionality in recent years. The resulting systems, such as the product used in Carey's study, offer the user a choice of search strategies to satisfy specific information needs. In the product he examines the desired information can be found through a table of contents, a topic index (as in many printed documentation systems), or a keyword search. It is rare to find an analysis of how users respond to such choices. The author records the information–seeking strategy followed by several representative users. He presents the results in terms of two information variables: certainty of location and certainty of target. His results suggest that many users follow opportunistic rather than reflective strategies and he proposes that designers should take this factor into account.

Meusel et al. present their experiences designing a HYTEA application using Toolbook. Their applications include both an office information system and the text for an online help system. In the case of the HYTEA application, they empirically derive user interface guidelines in seven areas: usage of a grid, 3–D effects, typography, color, orientation and navigation, defining an underlying structure, and teamwork. Their recommendations concerning text for online help systems focus on structuring rules. They highlight the important differences between how text should be treated in online documentation as opposed to printed documentation.

A Dialogue Approach to Graphical Information Access

Thomas Kamps and Klaus Reichenberger
GMD-IPSI, Darmstadt, Germany

1 Introduction

The department Publication and Visualisation Environment (PaVE) at the Integrated Publication and Information Systems Institute (IPSI) is currently building a publishing environment for electronic reference works. As an example and in order to derive requirements for this publishing environment we are currently building an electronic prototype of the Dictionary of Art. Its paper version will be launched on the market place as a commercial product by Macmillan Publishers Ltd. in 1995. In addition to the extraction of facts from the texts of the Dictionary of Art and the representation of these facts in a network of information units (semantic network), one of the major tasks in building the prototype is the design of its end-user interface.

The aim of this paper is to sketch a possible user interface for an end-user of an electronic dictionary whose main goal is to retrieve information. The interface we propose consists of a browser that allows an information-seeker to access the required data graphically. A principle we follow is to formulate queries iteratively by manipulating presentation results directly.

This paper is organised as follows. First, the graphical information access is illustrated with an example session. From this example interaction requirements can be derived concerning mainly the visualisation process discussed later. Some features of an automatic visualisation component that meets these requirements are outlined. Finally, further aspects of the information access, namely data modelling in the semantic network and a model of the interaction, are discussed briefly.

2 Information access

On the one hand, somebody consulting a dictionary will normally look for a coherent and comprehensible account of some topic, unlike somebody searching a database for isolated facts. On the other hand, the Dictionary of Art contains 30,000 articles and directs itself to professional art historians, experts in their domain. Ready-made accounts will often be unsatisfactory, because they lack detail or lack some aspect or some relationship to another topic that the reader is particularly interested in. In other words, the reader may want to determine the account himself through his question, although that does not necessarily mean that his question will be well defined.

While they can be used to provide a coherent context, predefined access structures, such as the sequential order in normal text or guided tours in hypertext, cannot be adapted to the users question. Conventional information retrieval interfaces, in contrast, have the needed flexibility, but do not give coherent accounts: neither the single terms that are searched for nor the single hits resulting from the query are joined in a way so they would form a coherent whole. As this contextual information is not only relevant per se but can also serve as a corrective for the formulation of the queries, the lack of it is especially problematic for end-users who have an unprecise notion of the search topic.

Our aim is to combine the advantages of conventional information access techniques, namely the flexibility of retrieval systems, the possibility to design a coherent text (Hannemann et al., 1993) as a means to support the users comprehension and the dynamic interaction style of hypertext. Besides natural language, graphical presentations are a powerful means for flexible and coherent communication in that information meaningfully presented in a diagram can be perceived immediately and, thus may ease interpretation of complex information. In this paper, we concentrate on graphical presentations supporting information access to large networks of information units and in particular, to the electronic prototype of the Dictionary of Art.

3 Example Session

Our design study focuses on the functionality for browsing the semantic network. The browser is a framework that invokes presentation instances. Its appearance is determined by static components and by the dynamically changing output of the Automatic Visualisation Engine.

3.1 Static Browser Components

The browser shown in figure 1 consists of four static components: the action window, the object selection panel, the history panel and the clipboard. The action window is the main part of the screen, used to present the query results; it is also the central place for the user's interaction with the system. The object selection panel at the top of the window contains a number of general object types applicable as ordering criteria to the field of art history which allows the reader to determine the focus of the presentation in the action window. The history panel on the left of the window records the history of all the steps of the user-machine dialogue made during one session. It can be used for backtracking through the dialogue path or to start the exploration anew at any recorded point. The clipboard in the lower left corner is used as an intermediary storage device. A set of presentation fragments can be pasted into the clipboard. All fragments stored in the clipboard are browser status independent. However, it is possible to repaste them into the action window e.g. for the purpose of further querying.

The interface is kept fairly simple. The user interacts directly with graphical elements representing the query results that are dynamically displayed by automatic presentation processes. Each presentation is guided by the particular constellation of information units forming the query result. In this environment, specific control objects such as press buttons, menus etc. are only of secondary importance. In the example interaction we now present, the automatic layout process has been simulated manually.

3.2 Interaction

Imagine the following scenario (figure 1 to 3) illustrating the presentation interface of the Dictionary of Art. A reader, who is a professional art historian and who has to prepare a presentation, wants to have a closer look at the emergence of the Bauhaus (a German art school from the first half of the 20th century), including facts like persons founding the Bauhaus, disciplines and art movements represented in it's early stage, other institutions serving as models etc. Modern German art and architecture are not necessarily our reader's own fields of expertise and therefore he turns to the electronic Dictionary of Art as a comprehensive reference work.

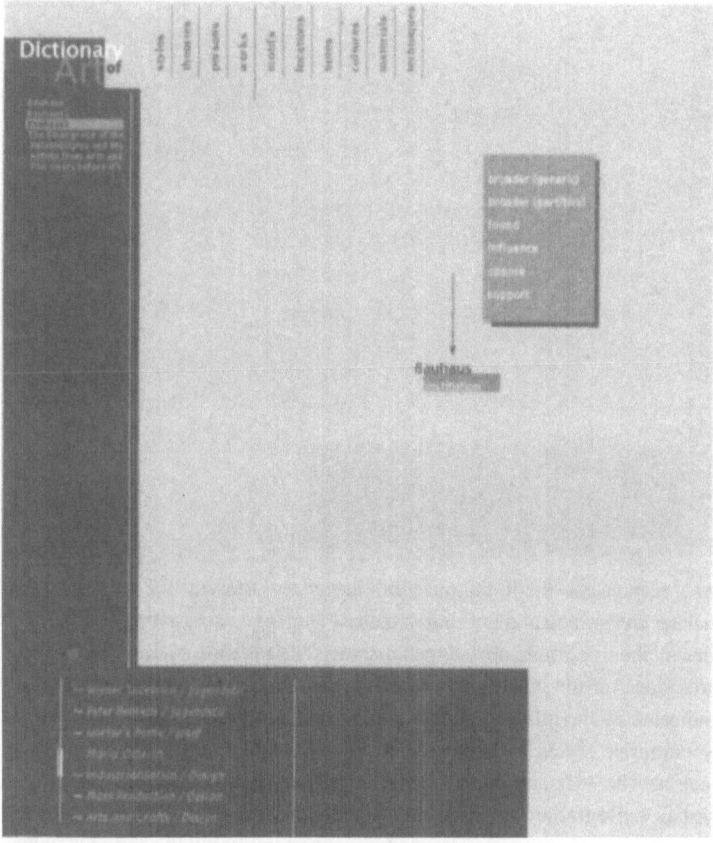

Figure 1: To begin the graphical query, the reader types in "Bauhaus" and then clicks on this string thereby asking the system to retrieve this object. The system then searches for the object within the object network. In our case, it confirms the existence of the Bauhaus as a database

object and indicates its type us ing a special colour. To look for objects related to the Bauhaus the user draws a relationship symbol. However, there are many objects and relationships of potential interest: persons founding the Bauhaus, etc. as mentioned above. Here, the user can either try to spe cify all these information interests separately or he could query the system on a, more general level by choosing one of the general relationship types at tached to the "institu- tion" type of ob ject. In this case, the "influence" relation is the one closest to his information interests, i.e. to find out about the emer gence of the Bauhaus. Thus, the reader provides the facts he knows and re quests the system to retrieve related facts, complimentary to his current knowledge.

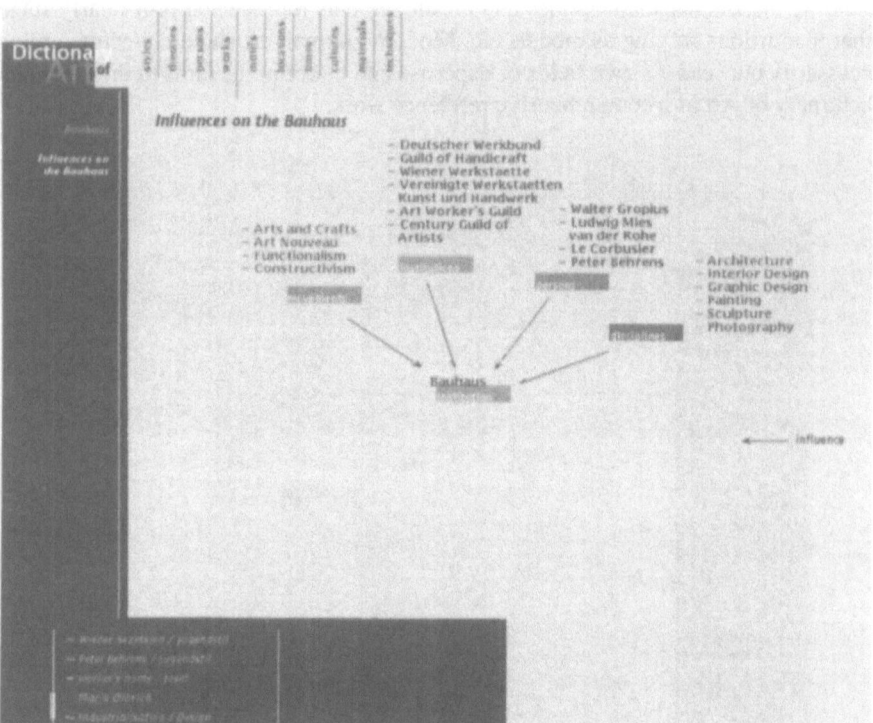

Figure2: As a response to the initial question, the system presents the answer in the follow ing way: It translates the graphical query into a natural language expression and makes "Influences on the Bauhaus" the title of the next screen display. The institu tion "Bauhaus", as the focus of interest, is dis played in the centre of the screen and all groups of objects that influ enced the Bauhaus (indicated by the influence link) are organised around it. These groups are of different types: they comprise styles and movements that had an impact on the emergence of the Bauhaus such as The Arts and Crafts Movement, 20th century functionalism in archi tecture, institu tions such as Deutscher Werkbund, outstanding personalities active in this field, and dis- ciplines the Bauhaus was active in. The reader is asked implicitly to refine his request in or der to narrow the focus of interest. He does this by selecting one or more of the groups, an operation that is facilitated by the form of the presenta tion.

Due to the vagueness of the reader's initial question there is a large number of facts that match the given graphical expression (paraphrased by "has an influence on the Bauhaus"). In order to present this large number of objects and relationships in a meaningful way, they can be grouped reducing clutter on the screen. Thus, a vague question would appropriately be answered with an overview as a help for further orientation. What the system should do concretely, in this case, would be to group the objects according to their type which is a rather simple task assuming that the type information is given by the semantic modelling of the objects. In different situations however, the objects may have to be organised by other, not quite so obvious, criteria.

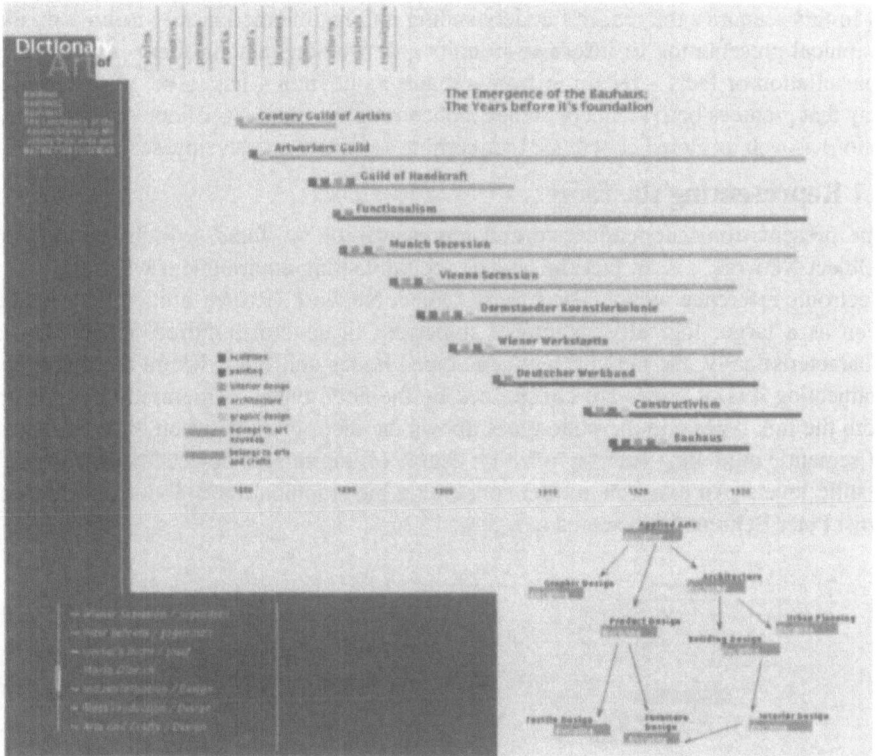

Figure 3: At a different stage of the session: Having already expressed his interest in movements that influenced the Bauhaus and their chronological sequence, the reader now also wants to see the information which movements dealt with the artistic disciplines he is interested in. The selection of the disciplines of interest is done via a thesaurus, which the reader invokes starting from a discipline he entered manually. As the selection from the thesaurus will be applied to the timeline, the thesaurus display should constitute a sub dialogue, that is, both presentations should be shown simultaneously rather than replacing the timeline presentation by the thesaurus.

4 Requirements

So far, we have presented an example of dialogue-based information access and how the interaction based on this approach might look. To offer such interactions in a hypermedia-based information system, the following prerequisites have to be satisfied:

1) The data accessed here are not just strings in a text, but facts represented formally so they can be retrieved and composed into a query result. These facts have to be represented independently of possible presentations and have to form a consistent knowledge base of the subject domain.

2) The information needs of the reader have to be derived from a graphical query.

3) In this scenario, the reader's understanding and his interaction rely heavily on the graphical presentation of information units and relations among them. An arbitrary constellation of facts – resulting from a reader's question – has to be presented in a way that grantees both local coherence (concerning the elements of one single presentation) as well as global coherence (concerning several successive presentations).

4.1 Representing the facts

The presentation-independent formal representation of facts, which we call an "Object Network", is, in fact the core of the publishing environment we propose for electronic reference works. The overall Object Network (Rostek et al. 1994) can be seen as a large, logically structured hypertext of several hundred MB, at least. Characteristically, the network contains typed nodes and links, where the link types connecting sets of nodes are constrained by the node types. A hierarchy defined on both the link types and the node types allows the distinction between different levels of semantic modelling leading to a high degree of interrelated objects on different semantic levels. An example model concerning biographical facts about the German artist Peter Behrens is presented in fig. 4.

Figure 4: Subnet of the Object Network containing biographical data

Thus, the skeleton of the knowledge base is an object network consisting of the Dictionary of Art articles and domain specific representations for styles, artists, works of art, etc. and relationships defined among these objects, describing facts like, e.g., *"Peter Behrens studied at the art school in Karlsruhe"* These facts are extracted from the articles of the Dictionary of Art. For this extraction, we use automatic text processing techniques ranging from pattern-oriented parsing to deep linguisticly oriented analysis.(Haenelt 1994, Bateman et al. 1994). An extension of the Terminology Editor, TEDI (Möhr & Rostek 1993), is the tool used to add value to the object net, e.g., to edit text, to extend the fact database manually, etc.

4.2 The graphical query

Inferring the information required by the user·actually poses two problems. One problem is to design a graphical query language that allows the user to express his information needs in an intuitive manner. A second one is to extract relevant information from the dialogue history. The grouping of the answer in fig. 2 , for example, is not only due to the very general question but also to the early stage in the dialogue. In order to make use of the dialogue history in this way, the dialogue has to be analysed in terms of a formal model. This analysis would also drive the spawning of sub-dialogues such as the additional thesaurus selection in fig. 3.

4.3 Graphical presentation

Of the three prerequisites of dialogue-based information access mentioned above, the automatic presentation of the selected information is addressed in greatest detail. The remainder of this section will illustrate the problems and an approach to their solution. The figures from the session that were designed by hand will serve as examples for the kind of presentations we want to generate automatically.

5 Explanation of the diagrams

The goal is to present graphically a set of objects and their relationships returned by the query process. A straightforward way of generating graphical presentations would be to present all objects as simple graphical elements, (e.g., as boxes labelled with the object name) and to insert additional graphical elements – like lines or arrows – between them to indicate relationships among objects. However, even in the few examples we have presented, there is much more going on than just a simple mapping of each object and relationship from the object net into a box or a line on the screen. First, the distribution of the elements is not arbitrary but requires "intelligent" layout decisions; the same is true for other attributes of the graphical elements like colour shape or size. Second, strong deviations from the default procedure of presenting objects and relationships are made.

Consider for example the graphical element presenting the "Bauhaus" object in Figure 1. It contains an additional layout component: in addition to the box and the label "Bauhaus," the "institution" label is superimposed on the box which itself is coloured yellow. Had we generated this presentation in the straightforward way mentioned above, it would show two labelled boxes and a line going from the "Bauhaus" box to the "institution" box representing the "is of type" relation. The presentation of the "institution" objects in figure 3 is another example for deviation from the default object presentation style. In this case, the bars do not have their default length, nor their default colour. Instead the length of the bars and their position indicate the duration of the institutions in time and the colour of the bars visualises the "belongs to" relationship with respect to different art styles. The "art style" and the "date" objects do not appear as independent graphical elements but only as attributes of the "institution" objects.

A different use of position can be seen in figure 2. The listed object name-strings remain the representatives of the individual object instances, but are grouped through their positions. The "class bar" and the superimposed class name as well as the arrow representing the "influence" relationship are assigned to the groups rather than to the graphical elements representing the individual object instances. If we exploded the composites we would have 21 single objects plus the arrows emanating from each object to the "Bauhaus'. Apparently, this grouping has been applied to reduce graphical complexity significantly.

In all these examples, the question arises: under which circumstances can the deviations from the default presentation style be justified? What allows us to group the objects in figure 2 and to present the objects in figure 1 and figure 3 merely as graphical attributes of other objects? We will try to answer these questions in the following section.

6 How to choose the adequate presentation-form for relationships

As we saw, there are several ways to represent relationships – and consequently objects – graphically. Since the different choices may differ significantly in their results, a major task of the layout process is to choose the adequate style for each relation.

To decide whether we can, for example, present the "is type of" relationship including the class object "institution" as an attribute of the "Bauhaus" element we have to analyse this relation. It is part of the typing of the relationships in the object network (see section "representing the facts") that the graph assigned to the relationship is always bipartite, i.e. the relationship "is of type" never relates two institutions. By definition, it relates concrete domain objects to class objects. More specifically, the relationship is a function, i.e. each domain object has one and only one class (e.g. "institution") assigned to it. Similarly, the graphical element representing "Bauhaus" can have a value assigned to one of its attributes representing its class ("institution"). Here, the chosen attribute is colour with the addition of an explanatory label.

More general, layout measurements like assignment of colours establish graphical relationships between graphical elements. The characteristics of these graphical relationship have to match the characteristics of the relationships they visualise.

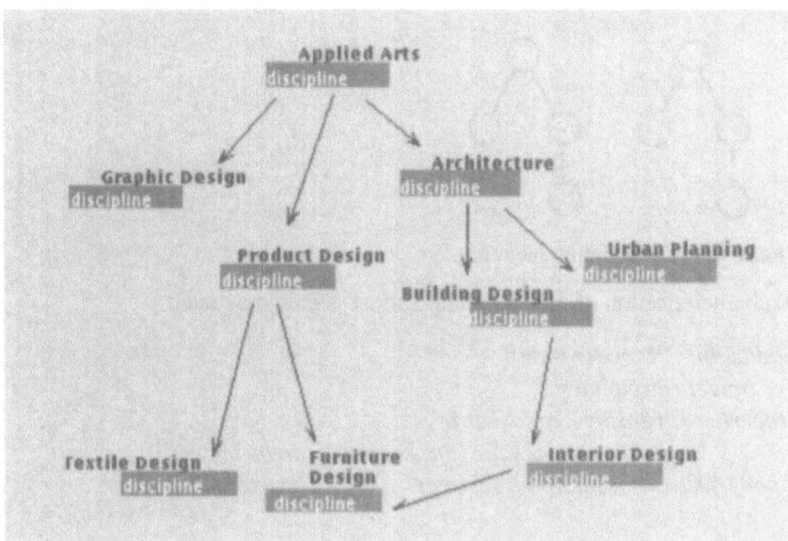

Figure 5a: Thesaurus example from figure 3

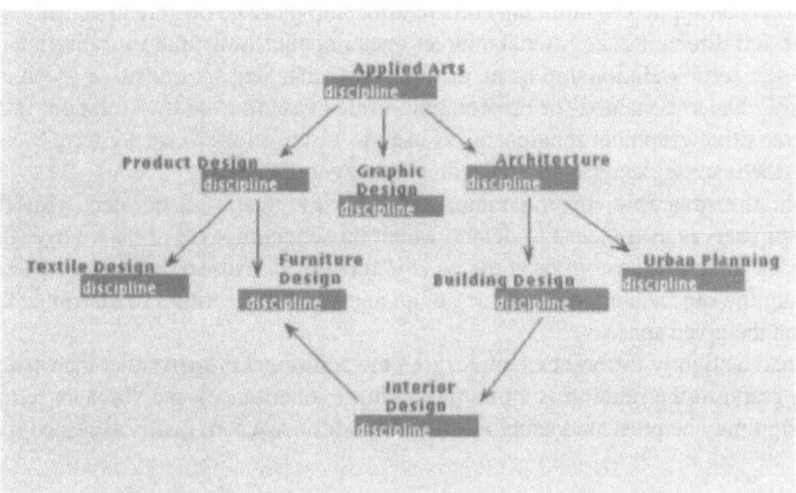

Figure 5b: The thesaurus terms might be distributed more evenly, but this would suggest a wrong interpretation of the arrow connecting "interior design" and "furniture design"

Based on that, let us have a look at the thesaurus diagram in figure 3. Here the situation is as follows: the thesaurus relationship "broader term" is defined on the domain-objects of type "discipline". The semantic modelling, i.e. the typing mentioned above, defines the relationship as transitive, asymmetric and irreflexive. From the properties "transitive" and "asymmetric" we can infer that the assigned graph is acyclic. Furthermore, the given graph contains two isomorphic subtrees starting from the source.

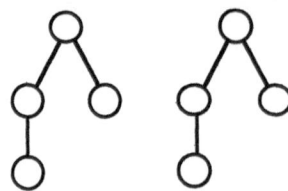

Figure 6: two isomorphic subtrees

The formal characterisation of this particular subnet is now presented.

Relationship: **"broader term"**
      range: *disciplines*
    properties: *transitive, asymmetric*
               irreflexive, acyclic (this property can be inferred)
    patterns: *two isomorphic subtrees*

We know from the above schema that the relationship forms an order which leads to a hierarchical display – further constrained by additional properties. One such property in this example is transitivity. On a transitive relation, the concepts of distance and direction can be applied to more than one relationship pair. To be able to actually see distances and directions, i.e. to make direct visual comparisons, the visualisation of the "broader term" relationship as an arrow is not sufficient. A transitive graphical relationship has to be added for presentation, in this case the "below" relation. If no strong, transitive graphical relationship is used to visualise the "broader term" relationship, the resulting diagram is misleading (see figure 5b).

Also in this example, the characterisation of the graph associated with the relationship serves as a means to decide which presentation style to take. Here, the property "is hierarchy" as opposed to, e.g., "is function," leads to the choice of lines connecting the objects and to the choice of an appropriate algorithm to distribute the objects on the given space.

If we had a slightly different example, e.g., the additional property that the corresponding graph to the relation is a tree (no multiple inheritance), the "broader term" relationship may be presented using the visual "inside" relation, that is as nested rectangles.

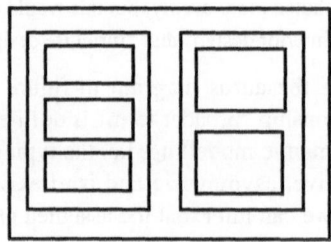

Figure 7: nested rectangle relation

Also in the example from figure 3 we can derive graphical constraints from the characterisation of the relationships involved:

> *Relationship:* **"belongs to"**
> *range:* *(institutions -->movements)*
> *properties:* *functional*
> *patterns:*
> *priority:* *3*

> *Relationship:* **"has disciplines"**
> *range:* *(institutions --> disciplines)*
> *properties:* *bipartite*
> *patterns:*
> *priority:* *4*

> *Relationship:* **"time-interval"**
> *range:* *(date --> date)*
> *properties:* *linearly ordered*
> *patterns:*
> *priority:* *1*

> *Relationship:* **"founded in"**
> *range:* *functional (institution --> date)*
> *properties:* *transitive, asymmetric,*
> *irreflexive, linear*
> *patterns:*
> *priority:* *2*

> *Relationship:* **"disbanded in"**
> *range:* *functional (institution --> date)*
> *properties:* *transitive, asymmetric,*
> *irreflexive, linear*
> *patterns:*
> *priority:* *2*

This example is comparatively more complex because the subnet consists now of three interwoven relationships where the connecting points are domain objects.

In order to continue the discussion above let us first concentrate on the "is founded in" relation. There are functional mappings from the domain-objects "institution' into a set of foundation dates. Because each institution object has exactly one foundation date, each graphical object representing an institution can be assigned a value to one of its attributes representing the institution's foundation date. The same happens with the "disbanded in" relation. However, this does not tell us *which* attributes to choose for the dates. Dates in general are linearly ordered so we would use any attribute that shows a linear graphical relationship between its values. Thus, the time events can, for example, be represented by different positions along a line or by different shades of grey but not by different colours. Out of convention we would probably prefer distribution along a horizontal line. The two remaining relationships can be explained as follows: the "belongs to" relationship maps the set of institutions uniquely onto the set of movements. We can also represent these relationships as attributes of the "institution" objects. In contrast to the dates however, there is no order defined for movements. Therefore, we have employed a colour coding for its visualisation (see figure 3). This way, each institution obtained the colour of its uniquely corresponding movement as an attribute. No functional mapping can be defined between the institutions and the disciplines. Here, it may be that an institution is linked to more than one discipline and vice versa. As we cannot assign more than one value to an attribute at a time, we assigned values (in this case colour values) to additional icons associated with the institution elements.

7 Structural regularities

Properties of relationships like transitivity and asymmetry that hold for *all* relationship pairs (links) are not the only kind of regularity that the layout process has to take into account. Others are patterns describing structural properties of the relation's assigned graph. Their scope is usually limited to substructures of the given graph. The structural regularities in the above examples can be characterised as describing repetition of a similar or even isomorphic substructure. In other words, we would not call a subtree a pattern if it occurred only once in the given data structure.

The importance of regularities, and in particular of patterns, is that they can provide an abstract description of the given graph. For example, we can produce such an abstract description by describing the thesaurus graph in figure 3 as being composed of two subtrees. Different regularities provide descriptions of the graph that are more or less compact, complete and correct. Completeness and correctness can also be expressed in terms of compactness by simply enumerating all additional facts (not covered by the regularity) and exceptions (where the regularity serves to describe a part of the given graph but only imperfectly). Therefore we can use the compactness of the description build upon a certain regularity as a measure for how well the regularity organises the given graph. Such a metric may be used to rank the regularities according to their adequacy.

Different regularities may be composed into one description – when they are either disjunct or one is completely contained in the other – or they may overlap and thus lead to competing descriptions.

An appropriate, abstract description can serve as a good starting point for drawing a graph because it allows the system to prioritise layout decisions. Thus, the more characteristic regularities and their constituent relationships consume display resources (screen space, display modalities like colour, shape etc.), thereby further constraining the less important relationships. In addition, abstract descriptions may be used more directly to reduce graphical complexity by grouping.

Taking figure 1 as an example for the role of structural regularities, we can describe the characteristics of the given subnet as follows: it contains only one relationship which is called "influenced" the assigned graph of which is acyclic. It ranges over four object types and its graph contains four similar subtrees. The following schema describes this situation formally.

> ***Relation:*** *"influence"*
>   *range:*   *movements, institutions, artists, disciplines*
> *properties:* *acyclic*
>   *patterns:* *four similar subtrees*

How do these features – particularly the similar subtrees – guide the visualisation? The abstract description of the sub graph says that it basically consists of a number of groups where each group itself consists of a set of objects of the same class – all of them related to the Bauhaus with an influence link. This does not change the choice of an arrow to visualise the "influence" relationship (this is due to the assigned graph forming a hierarchy rather than being bipartite) or the choice of colours to visualise the objects classes. What it does is that the description based on the structural regularities suggests a grouping of the elements and to associate relationships presented as colours and arrows to these groups rather than to the individual objects.

Another way of acquiring the ranking could be the use of context-information, e.g., the user's request for temporal information implies a strong constraint on the layout process. The fact that one starts a dialogue with the system and is thus interested in a particular matter, e.g., the Bauhaus, might be a hint to provide an overview presentation like in figure 2 where we used aggregation to offer the user a selection of items categorised according to domain-object classes.

8 Summary

In this paper we have present some major issues concerning automatic visualisation. A layout process that takes these issues into account is summarised below. For more details and the discussion of other approaches like, e.g., the one of Mackinlay (1986) see (Kamps & Reichenberger 1994).

The layout process starts from a given subset of the object network resulting from a query. Building upon the relational properties derived from the modelling of the relationships in the object network, additional properties are inferred. This information is used to choose appropriate graphical relations and also to help analyse further regularities on a structural level. These regularities lead to a set of – competing or complementary descriptions – that are ranked according to their importance.

The final presentation joins all the relationships together in one diagram. To distribute the limited resources of screen spaces and display modalities among the different relationships having different – and often competing – visualisation preferences corresponding to their properties is a very complex optimisation problem. Our heuristic approach towards that optimisation problem hinges on deciding first for those relationships that are engaged in the essential regularities.

9 Outlook

At the moment we are implementing the visualisation process we described as an extension of SFK. This implementation will probably raise problems we are not aware of by now. In one respect, however, our model will certainly have to be extended:

We mentioned that aspects of the dialogue situation should be reflected directly in the graphical presentation leading, e.g., to the overview presentation in Figure 1. Similarly, looking at how the different graphical presentations are related to each other – as steps in the dialogue – may lead, e.g., to the triggering of the sub dialogue in Figure 3. In general, to reflect the dialogue situation in the graphical presentation, we must be able to recognise these situation in an analysis of the dialogue. A formal description of dialogues would be very useful for that purpose.

Stein et al. (1992) proposed a conversational model for information retrieval which builds the basis of the dialogue manager of the retrieval system MERIT (Stein et al. 1992). One of the major goals described in (Maier & Sitter 1992) was to obtain dialogue coherence. (Fischer 1994) proposed a dialogue model based on COR consisting of a limited set of relationships between dialogue acts. The application of this model allows a complete description of any kind of dialogue. Analysing this description we might be able to derive the role that the coming presentation should play in the dialogue.

Global dialogue or discourse planning – as it is central to André's and Rist's (1993) approach in generating illustrated documents – is only one aspect from the domain of natural language generation that is relevant for further work on information access. Our aim is to generate multimodal presentations, that is to integrate our work with the *Komet* text generation System developed at GMD-IPSI (Bateman et al. 1991). Note for example the transformation of the graphical query into a natural language expression, mentioned in the description of figure 2. Therefore we will have to address issues like "appropriateness of the different modalities", "referencing from text to graphics" and "incorporation of graphics in text and vice versa".

Acknowledgements: We would like to thank Lynda Hardman, Gene Golovchinsky, Paul Kahn and Chris Neuwirth for their helpful comments on this paper and its earlier versions.

References

André, E. Rist, T. (1993). The design of illustrated Documents as a Planning Task, *in Intelligent Multimedia Interfaces, AAAI Press/The MIT Press, Menlo Park 1993*

Bateman, J. Maier, E. Teich, E. Wanner, L. (1991). Towards an Architecture for Situated Text Generation, *in International Conference on Current Issues in Comutational Linguistics, Penang, Malaysia, 1991.*

Bateman, J. Teich, E. Firzlaff, B. (1994). A linguistically oriented methodology for domain model constructions in knowledge-based systems, *submitted to RIAO'94 (Intelligent Multimedia Information Retrieval Systems and Management)*

Fischer, M. (1994) Weiterentwicklung und Implementierung eines Dialogmodells für Kooperative Informationssysteme, *to appear as GMD-internal Report, Sankt Augustin, GMD 1994.*

Haenelt, K. (1994) Das Textanalysesystem KONTEXT. Konzeption und Anwendungsmöglichkeiten. *In: Sprache und Datenverarbeitung. 1994*

Hannemann, J. Thüring, M. (1994) What matters in developing user interfaces for hyperdocument presentation?, *this volume.*

Kamps, T. Reichenberger, K. (1994). Automatic Layout as an Organisation Process, *Arbeitspapiere der GMD, Nr. 825, Sankt Augustin 1994.*

Mackinlay, J. Automating the Design of Graphical Presentations of Relational Information, *in ACM Transactions on Graphics, Vol. 5, No. 2, 1986.*

Maier, E. Sitter, S. (1992). An Extension of Rhetorical Structure Theory for the Treatment of Retrieval Dialogues, *in Cog. Sci'92, Proceedings of the 14th Annual Conference of the Cognitive Science Society, Indiana University, Bloomington, July 29 to August 1, 1992, Hillsdale, NJ: Erlbaum, 1992, pp. 968–973.*

Möhr, W. Rostek, L. (1993). TEDI, An Object-oriented Terminology Editor, *in TKE 93: Terminology and Knowledge Engineering, INDEKS Verlag, Frankfurt/M., 1993.*

Rostek, L. Möhr, W. Fischer, D. (1994). Weaving a Web: The Structure and Creation of an Object Network Representing an Electronic Reference Work, *Proceedings of the EP 94 Conference on Electronic Publishing, Document Manipulation and Typography, Darmstadt, April 13–15 1994, Wiley, Sussex 1994*

Stein, A. Thiel, U. Tissen, A. (1992) Knowledge Based Control Of Visual Dialogues, *in Catarci, T., Costabile, M.F. & Levialdi, S. (eds.): Proceedings of Advanced Visual Interfaces (AVI'92) Rome, Italy, May 1992, World Scientific Press, Singapore 1992, pp. 138–155.*

Annotations are not "for free": The Need for Runtime Layer Support in Hypertext Engines

Christine M. Neuwirth, Ravinder Chandhok, David S. Kaufer,
James H. Morris, Paul Erion, Dale Miller
Carnegie Mellon University, Pittsburgh, USA

1 Introduction

An important application of hypertext is the making and receiving of "annotations"--critical or explanatory notes added to a text. Rather than thinking of annotations as an application of hypertext systems, however, most hypertext system designers believe that hypertext systems are annotation systems; that is, they believe that annotations are "for free" in hypertext. After all, the reasoning runs, a hypertext system is, by definition, a system that allows users to create nodes and links between them; in particular, users can create text nodes and link those text nodes to nodes containing explanatory text; ergo, a hypertext system is an annotation system.

A cursory comparison of hypertext systems with traditional, paper-based systems of annotation, however, supports the adage, "There ain't no such thing as a 'free annotation.'" There are important gaps between the functionality of paper-based annotations and what commonly passes for annotations in hypertext. For example, in traditional, paper-based systems of annotation, creating an annotation typically requires the user to carry out one simple action to begin the task--put the pen to the page in a margin next to the place in the text the user wants to write. In many hypertext systems, the user must typically carry out four actions to accomplish the same task: create a node for the annotation, create a link, specify a "from" node and specify a "to" node--all before beginning to write. Compared to traditional paper-based systems of annotation, hypertext systems that treat annotations "for free" fail to minimize the mapping of actions to tasks, a minimization that human-computer interaction research has argued is crucial to the learnability and usability of designs (Howes & Young, 1991).

Likewise, in traditional systems of annotation, *receiving* an annotation simply requires scanning the margins of a document. In hypertext systems in which annotations are "for free," the user must "search and click," that is, the user must search a text node for each annotation and, to display it, must click on a link icon. The annotation is then often displayed out of context, usually in a separate window that may obscure the original text or appear in some arbitrary, distant place on the screen, out of alignment with the original text. While a "search and click" interface may be adequate for some tasks involving annotation (cf., Nielsen, 1989), there are others for which scanning can be predicted to be superior. For example, in the task of an author receiving comments from a reviewer, an author typically needs to scan across a set of comments rapidly in order to get an overall sense of the annotations, both to come to some understanding of the relationship among them and to make some overall plans for how to proceed with responses and revisions. Then the author can proceed with successive processing, dealing with each annotation in turn.

This paper addresses issues that application programs which wish to provide annotations raise for an underlying hypertext engine. It presents requirements for annotations and describes an application program prototype that provides one way of meeting those requirements. The paper discusses the implications of this important class of applications for the design of hypertext engines. We note that while many applications could profit from annotations, few hypertext engines provide primitives that make it easy for applications to provide them. We argue that a further specification of the runtime layer in hypertext engines is desirable in order to achieve good performance for annotations.

2 Requirements for Annnotations

The body of empirical research regarding annotations is scarce. Nielsen (1984) did a study that looked at the types of annotations students made on textbooks, but there is no empirically validated process model of making and using annotations by which to guide design. There are, however, historical systems of annotation to draw upon. These systems contain implicit process models and were evolved by their designers over time, with some developments presumably in response to "users'" problems. Among the most highly developed system was the one used for annotations of the Talmudic and Biblical texts. This is not to say that features of these systems should be carried over uncritically into electronic contexts, but that the features can be examined for their function.

We have previously analyzed the design features of twelfth century glossed bibles in Cavalier, et al. (1991). The analysis suggests the following requirements for annotations:

- *The primary text is easily distinguishable from the annotation text.* This requirement allows readers, who may not have seen either the original text or the annotations, to orient themselves to the texts quickly. In glossed bibles, this distinction was usually made by varying type size: the primary text is several points larger than text in the annotations. Of course, other typographic signals such as color could also be used.

- *The annotations are visible "at a glance" while reading the primary text.* This requirement minimizes the problems readers have in accessing annotations. Glossed bibles were usually the result of calligraphic as well as scholarly effort; the annotations were packed in an aesthetically pleasing fashion onto a page, so that all annotations, no matter how dense, are visible. As the corpus of annotations increased over time, the books were recopied with more space for annotations, preserving the easy access by expanding the leading between the lines in the primary text as needed to insure the visual alignment of all annotations.

- *The relationship between the primary text and the annotations is easy to see.* This requirement insures that readers will be able to see which annotations refer to particular portions of text. In glossed bibles, the annotations were typically aligned horizontally to the primary text, so it is possible to scan from the primary text across to the annotation rapidly. Moreover, the scope of the annotation was usually indicated by graphic symbols in the primary text.

- *Different annotators are readily distinguishable.* This requirement aids readers in interpreting annotations by different commentators. The different annotators of glossed bibles are easily distinguishable because each has his or her own column.

The result of all these features is that access to the annotations is superior to most electronic annotation systems. The reader could quickly skim the set of annotations "at a glance." For the scholar, the assignment of marginal "real estate" allowed for quick and easy annotation. A comment could be made as quickly as moving the pen to the adjacent margin. In addition, several scholars often annotated a document side by side, leading to an easy to follow parallel discussion that was the synthesis of both sets of comments.

3 A User Interface for Annotations

We have incorporated the design requirements outlined above in a prototype application that supports annotations of linear texts, the PREP Editor. The PREP Editor is a prototype intended to support aspects of collaborative writing (Neuwirth, Kaufer, Chandhok, Morris, 1990). A fundamental unit in the PREP Editor is "the column," a basic unit of exchange between collaborators. PREP columns are used for the main text of a document, a particular co-author's annotations, document "maps," and other planning representations like reader-response maps and the like. Figure 1 depicts a PREP Editor screen with three columns: a primary text, and two smaller columns to the right consisting of reviewers' annotations. Note how the primary text is easily distinguishable from the annotations: The type size, which defaults to a larger size for primary text than for annotations, and the column width, which defaults to more space allocation, both provide strong visual cues that the leftmost column is the primary one. The annotations are visible and horizontally aligned to the primary text. Finally, different annotators can be assigned different spaces.

Our derivation of requirements for annotations from paper-based systems allowed us to emphasize positive features of paper-based systems for which it is desirable to provide similar support in computer-based systems of annotations. But the PREP Editor also provides features we believe are superior to paper-based systems. For example, columns can be hidden, reordered in any fashion (e.g., an annotation column could be moved to the left of the main text), and also reformatted as a whole. These dynamic properties allow groups of authors and commenters more flexibility than groups using static, paper-based systems. Moreover, the functionality provided by an underlying hypertext mechanism supports several useful features: Annotations remain associated with the text to which they are linked, even under many editing operations;[1] and an underlying node-link architecture supports the merging of comments from multiple reviewers, allowing simultaneous display of annotations from several distributed commenters to which copies of the document were passed.

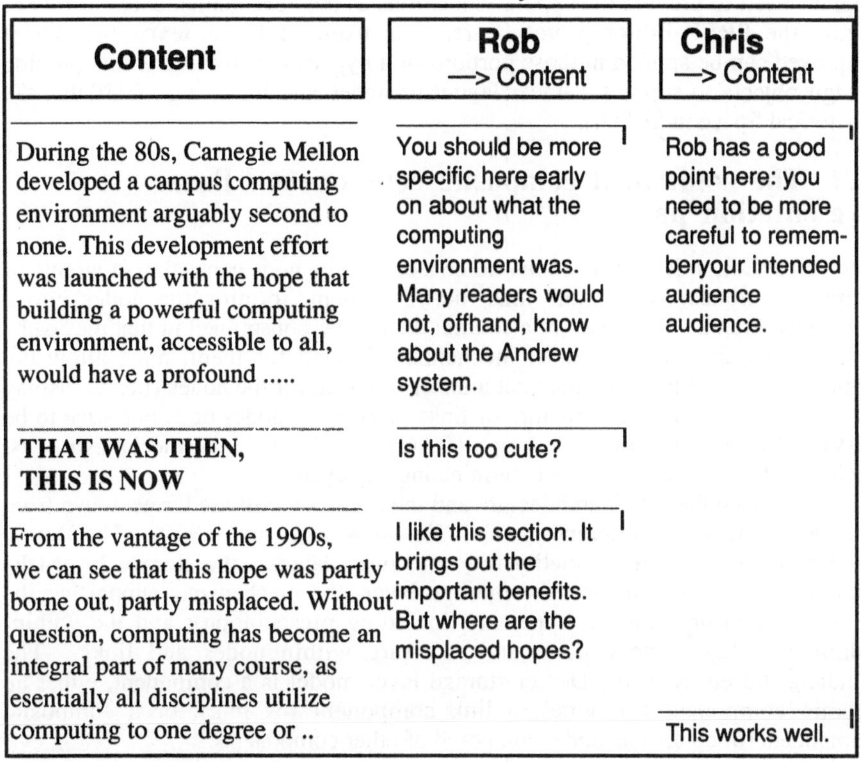

Content	Rob —> Content	Chris —> Content
During the 80s, Carnegie Mellon developed a campus computing environment arguably second to none. This development effort was launched with the hope that building a powerful computing environment, accessible to all, would have a profound	You should be more specific here early on about what the computing environment was. Many readers would not, offhand, know about the Andrew system.	Rob has a good point here: you need to be more careful to remember your intended audience audience.
THAT WAS THEN, THIS IS NOW	Is this too cute?	
From the vantage of the 1990s, we can see that this hope was partly borne out, partly misplaced. Without question, computing has become an integral part of many course, as esentially all disciplines utilize computing to one degree or ..	I like this section. It brings out the important benefits. But where are the misplaced hopes?	This works well.

Figure 1: A PREP document, with an original column and two annotation columns.

---

[1] A number of user interfaces have been designed or exploited to support glossing of electronic documents. First, there are systems that employ static glossing (Markup, 1989). These systems allow users to mark-up an electronic document as if they were marking up a printed copy of the document: Users can add text, draw arrows, and so forth, "over" the electronic document, but they cannot change the underlying document. Although we have done no formal, empirical observations of these systems, we believe that writers will experience cognitive difficulties resulting from being constrained to simply adding comments to a static page and not being able to change the document itself.   This is because a number of important problems in texts (e.g., voice, persuasiveness, organization), though easy for a skilled writer to detect, cannot be easily described.   For such problems, rewriting is often a more efficient strategy than trying to describe the problem, and skilled writers often choose this strategy when revising others' texts (Hayes, Flower, Schriver, Stratman, & Carey, 1987).   One of the design requirements we set was to try to support this revision strategy by allowing users to change the underlying document.

4 The Underlying Hypertext Mechanisms

The PREP Editor utilizes an underlying node-link architecture. This section describes those mechanisms and discusses the features that underlying hypertext engines need to provide to support annotations as they are implemented in PREP. While the PREP Editor prototype restricts itself to linear texts, the model employed can be applied in those portions of a hypertext applications that provide design objects to support a linear layout of nodes and links (e.g., GUIDE , the Rhetorical Space in SEPIA).

4.1 The column: a composite component / linear presentation pair

The PREP Editor defines a *column* to be a composite node consisting of atomic or composite nodes with "path" links between them, forming the nodes into a connected graph. The nodes of a column are further constrained in that the "path" links, together with a traversal mechanism defined for them, must allow the hypertext runtime layer to construct a linear ordering for the nodes (i.e., to display the nodes linearly). The structure of links among the nodes does not *have* to be restricted to a directed-acyclic graph (DAG), but the traversal mechanism must include a decision rule for finitely terminating any cycles.

To describe the PREP architecture and interface, we will use terms drawn from the Dexter hypertext reference model (Halasz & Schwartz, 1990). The Dexter model divides hypertext functionality into three layers: the storage layer--the node/link network structure; the runtime layer--the mechanisms supporting the user's interaction with the hypertext (including presentation); and the within-component layer--the content and structure within nodes and links. The fundamental entity in the Dexter storage layer model is a component, either an atomic component (or node), a link component (or link), or a composite component (or composite node) composed of other components.

4.2 The annotation link: a binary, directional, typed link

"Annotation links" are binary, directional, typed links from a source node to an annotation node. The PREP Editor allows users to create annotation links between columns (i.e., composite nodes).[1] For example, in Figure 1, the two columns on the right are linked to the leftmost column. Such links define a tree of linked columns (although a single PREP document can hold a forest of these trees). Links between columns allow users to create annotations rapidly: a user only has to locate *where* in the primary text to make an annotation and click next to that

---

[1]When a user creates a new column, if a column is selected, then the new column will be linked to the selected column. If no column is selected, the new column will be unlinked. To link two existing columns, a user selects the "from" column, chooses "Link" from a "Column" menu, and choose the "to" column.

location in the linked column to make both a link and new node.[1]   This user interface allows us to approximate the ease of paper-based annotating by proximal writing in a margin. However, PREP goes one step further than a paper-based metaphor in that PREP annotations remain aligned to their source even as the source text is edited.

4.3 The layout algorithm

In most hypertext systems, a link, regardless of its type, is represented in the runtime layer layout as a line connecting two squares (in a graph view), or is represented by an icon that is given a "follow it" interpretation when the user clicks on it. The links in the PREP application, however, carry different implications for the runtime/presentation layer. Path links between nodes in a column result in a linear, scrollable display of the nodes that look like an ordinary document in a word processor. Annotation links between columns result in the linked column being allocated (by default) a narrower display and smaller font; unlinked columns, which usually contain a primary text, are allocated (by default) a wider display and larger fonts. Annotation links between nodes result in the nodes being displayed in a side-by-side, horizontal alignment.

An object-oriented constraint-based layout algorithm is at the heart of determining and maintaining side-by-side layout of annotations. Whenever a user changes the screen through some operation on a column or node--creating, moving, deleting, linking, adding to and so on--constraints from the local objects on the screen whose display is affected by the change are placed in a queue. A constraint solver satisfies the constraints; their satisfaction often leads to the propagation and satisfaction of more constraints. The process of constraint maintenance and propagation continues cyclically until the display is no longer affected.

The algorithm employs two primary layout constraints: *AlignTopToTop* and *AlignTopToVirtualBottom*. *AlignTopToTop* insures that all nodes that are directly or indirectly associated with one another will have their tops horizontally aligned on the screen.[2] For example, the link between an annotation and its source imply an *AlignTopToTop* link so that the annotation is displayed aligned with its source. *AlignTopToVirtualBottom* governs the layout of a chunk's structure links (which linearly order the chunks) and unlinked chunks. It insures that the top of a chunk will align to the "virtual bottom" of the chunk immediately above it. The "virtual bottom" of a chunk is the lowest bottom of any chunk directly or indirectly associated with that chunk.

---

[1]If the user actually makes a selection in the primary text and clicks in the linked column, then the system puts a link anchor around the selection; otherwise, the system puts a zero-length link anchor in the same line as the primary text.

[2]PREP derives two basic types of associations between nodes based on their actual links and their membership in the tree of linked columns. The first type of association is direct. Direct association occurs between any nodes that are actually linked via an annotation link The second type of association is indirect. Indirect association occurs between a node A and a node C if node A is actually linked to node B and B has a direct or indirect association with node C.

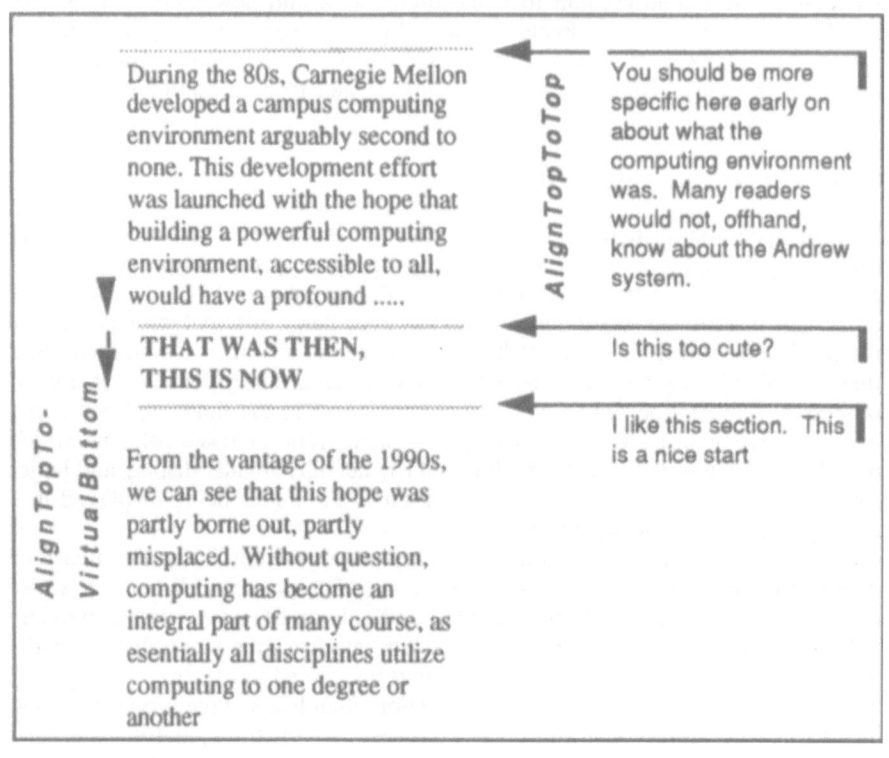

Figure 2: A view of the layout constraints in a PREP document. Note the gap inserted after the first paragraph in the leftmost column so that the annotations in the middle column do not overlap.

The *AlignTopToVirtualBottom* constraint is responsible for ensuring that the display does not contain any overlapping chunks. In other words, any particular chunk is positioned such that it is below the chunk above it, and also below any chunks associated the chunk above it. In PREP, the *AlignTopToVirtualBottom* constraint can cause the layout of the source text to contain gaps in order to preserve the at-a-glance viewing our users preferred. Figure 2 illustrates the layout constraints in the PREP Editor. PREP's use of constraints to specify the dynamic layout is not new. What is different is that PREP dynamically derives the constraints from the underlying link structure, often changing the constraint network as editing proceeds.

5 Architectual Requirements for Hypertext Engines

5.1 Defining the runtime layer

Hypermedia engines that support such concepts as the composite nodes and the typed links we used to implement annotations are common though not universal. In order to accomplish the dynamic layout just described, however, we have had to augment the information available to our runtime layer beyond that provided in standard hypertext engines. The PREP editor requires dynamic communication between the within-component layer (the content and structure within nodes and links) and the runtime-layer. In particular, the PREP editor requires *component location and size information*, and *size and location change events*. For example, a constraint such as *AlignToptoTop* requires the constraint solver to be able to query an object about its position on the screen. This, in effect, results in querying a link about the location of the component at the other end--a function not usually defined in hypermedia engines. More importantly, the designers of models for such engines have argued against providing such support. For example, in discussing the Dexter model, Halasz and Schwartz (1990) observe that "...the range of possible tools for accessing, viewing, and manipulating hypertext networks is far too broad and too diverse to allow a simple, generic model" of the runtime layer (p. 99). Thus, in the Dexter model, it is proposed that the user interface be encoded in the storage layer as *presentation specifications*, but "presentation specification" is left as a primitive in the model.

We believe, however, that it is a mistake to conclude that because the range of accessing, viewing and manipulating tools is very broad, hypertext engines should therefore provide no runtime layer facilities. There are *classes* of hypermedia usage, such as annotations, that can be and should be standardized on at the presentation level. We should not abandon standard interfaces to important (and culturally accepted) forms of hypermedia usage merely because the set of *all* applications is too diverse. Indeed, it is only possible to ignore the presentation specification because hypertext systems usually confound the data storage methodology of a loose collection of nodes and links with the presentation methodology of a loose collection of windows. It is often the case that the underlying hypertext structure is mapped one-to-one to some simple viewing structure (e.g., a window per node). We have argued that, for annotations, which depend on their linked context for meaning, the results can be less than optimal. We propose that hypertext engines should provide the following runtime layer facilities, in order to allow for interfaces such as PREP's to be constructed:

1) access to (display) attribute values (e.g., *get-location* --returns the current location, in system dependent coordinates, of a component).

2) change notification (e.g., *size-changed, location-changed*--informs any interested parties, through events or some equivalent notification mechanism, of any component movement or size change)

It is perhaps more controversial whether hypertext engines should also provide applications with support for other runtime layer concerns, such as a "presentation specification language" coupled with constraint-based layout tools. Such support would constitute a hypertext-oriented user interface toolkit. Like other work in user interface toolkits, however, it might encourage application developers to include within their programs a standard interface (which could increase the usability of hypertext applications) and it might encourage developers to include within their programs a set of support functions for important classes of applications (which could increase the usability of hypertext engines).

6 Future Work and Related Research

The extension of this work to annotating graphs (e.g., applications that implement graphical browsers for networks of hypertext nodes) remains an important open research question. One can imagine using composite nodes to define annotation "layers" rather than columns, and using color and other typographic features so that readers could distinguish annotation nodes from other nodes easily. Some of the conventions developed by graphic designers for annotating technical drawings might be adapted to solving the problems of how and where to present annotations in such graphs so that the annotations are visible "at a glance" and the relationship between the primary node and annotations are easy to see (e.g., by employing "rubber sheet" layout techniques, cf. Kaltenbach, Robillard & Frasson, 1991). Besides extension to graphs, there are research issues involving linear documents (e.g., annotating drawings; handling multiple references such as an annotation saying "move this to here"). Both lines of research require the underlying architecture of the hypertext engine to provide runtime layer support of the type we have argued for in this paper.

Only one system, PenPoint™,[1] provides the ability in an underlying hypertext engine to query links about the locations of components and to register for notification of changes that we have argued for in this paper, so it goes some way in realizing the runtime layer facilities which we have advocated.

Although the PREP Editor application is not a hypertext system, the specific work in the PREP Editor on the linear presentation of an underlying node-link structure drew upon previous work on sequencing and navigation in hypertexts (Furuta & Stotts, 1989; Marshall & Irish, 1989; Thüring, Haake & Hannemann, 1991; van Dyke Parunak, 1989; Zellweger, 1989). Our work is predicated on the notion that paths should not always be navigated, but rather should sometimes be the basis for a linear display in which the structure remains more implicit.

7 Conclusion

Note that we do not intend in this paper to completely define the presentation specifications to be used in all annotation interfaces or the entire set of runtime mechanisms that hypermedia engines should provide; instead, we have argued against the position that hypermedia engines should leave runtime layer concerns as

---

[1]PenPoint is a commercial pen-based, object oriented operating system from GO Corporation. It includes OS-level support for hypertext linking.

primitives. We have argued that good support for annotations requires that elements of a runtime layer in underlying hypermedia engines to be defined and indicated what elements are required for a particular application. The availability of such elements can significantly enhance the usability of hypermedia engines for important classes of applications.

Acknowledgements: The work reported here have been supported by the National Science Foundation (grant number IRI-8902891), by a grant from Bellcore and by a grant from External Research at Apple Computer, Inc. Thanks to Jörg Haake for his insightful comments on this paper.

References

Cavalier, T., et al. (1991). A visual design for collaborative work: Columns for commenting and annotation. In Proceedings of the HICSS-24 Hawaii International Conference on System Sciences. Jan 8-11, Kalua Kona, Hawaii.

Conklin, J. (1987). Hypertext: An introduction and survey. *IEEE Computer* 20, 17-41.

Furuta, R., and Stotts, P. D. (1989). Programmable browsing semantics in Trellis. in *Proceedings of Hypertext '89* (pp. 27-42), Nov., Pittsburgh, PA

Halasz, F. & Schwartz, D. (1990). The Dexter hypertext reference model. *NIST Hypertext Standardization Workshop*. Gaithersburg, MD.

Hayes, J. R., Flower, L., Schriver, K. A., Stratman, J., & Carey, L. (1987). Cognitive processes in revision. In S. Rosenberg (Ed.), Advances in applied psycholinguistics, Volume II: Reading writing, and language processing Cambridge, England: Cambridge University Press.

Howes, A, & Young, R. M. (1991). Predicting the learnability of task-action mappings (pp. 113-118). *CHI'91 Conference Proceedings*. Ed. Scott Robertson P., Gary M. Olson and Judith S. Olson. New Orleans, Louisiana: The Association for Computing Machinery

Kaltenbach, M, Robillard, F., & Frasson, C. (1991). Screen management in hypertext systems with rubber sheet layouts (pp. 91-105). *Proceedings of Hypertext '91*, December, San Antonio, TX.

Lesk, M. (1989). What to do when there's too much information (pp. 305-318). *Hypertext'89 Proceedings*. Pittsburgh, PA: ACM-Press

Markup. (1989). Agoura Hill, CA: Mainstay,

Marshall, C. C.& Irish, P. M. (1989). Guided tours and on-line presentations: How authors make existing hypertext intelligible for readers. *Proceedings of Hypertext '89*

Neuwirth, C. M., Kaufer, D.S., Chandhok, R., & Morris, J. H. (1990). Issues in the design of computer support for co-authoring and commenting (pp. 183-195). *Third Conference on Computer Supported Cooperative Work (CSCW'90)*. Los Angeles, CA: Association for Computing Machinery.

Nielsen, J (1984). *How readers annotate textbooks and manuals*. Computer Science Department, Aarhus University, Denmark.

Nielsen, J. (1989). The matters that really matter for hypertext usability (pp. 239-248). *Proceedings.of Hypertext' 89* . Pittsburgh, PA: ACM-Press

Thüring, M., Haake, J. M., & Hannemann, J. (1991). What´s Eliza doing in the Chinese room? Incoherent hyperdocuments -- and how to avoid them. *Proceedings of Hypertext '91.*

Van Dyke Parunak, H. (1989). Hypermedia topologies and user navigation (pp. 43-50). *Proceedings of Hypertext '89.*

Zellweger, P. T. (1989). Scripted documents: A hypermedia path mechanism (pp. 1-14). *Proceedings of Hypertext '89.*

Three Fundamental Elements of Visual Rhetoric in Hypertext

Paul Kahn, Ronnie Peters, George P. Landow
Dynamic Diagrams and IRIS, Brown University

1 Introduction

The design of information on the printed page or on the computer screen must express the overall structure of that information in order to be understood by the reader. Various conventions of typography communicate the meta-structure of a block of text such as size of type, weight of font, use of indents, initial capitals (derived from illuminated capitals in the manuscript tradition), use of bold and italic variations, and use of color. Analogous conventions exist in information graphics for communicating quantitative information, visual narrative such as instructions, and location graphics such as maps.

Hypertext adds a new element to visual communication by requiring the identification and traversal of links. This new element must either share in the established visual conventions or it must be conveyed through the creation of a new visual language. This apparent polarity is not a simple either/or proposition. In practice, the design of each hypertext system must establish the appropriate mix of convention and innovation.

There are three elements that should be communicated in any hypertext system. These three fundamental elements are:
- link presence (which must include link extent),
- link destination (which must include multiple destinations),
- link mapping (which must display link and node relationships).

This paper will briefly report the visual methods for conveying this visual rhetoric available in two hypertext systems, Intermedia and Storyspace, used for developing educational hypertext materials at Brown University. These methods will be evaluated and criticized.

2 Link Presence

Intermedia: Intermedia used a single glyph to represent the presence of a link in all types of data: text, graphics, animation, and video. This simple method was successful largely because Intermedia supported a single type of link behavior: following a link always opened the destination document window and highlighted the link extent.

Marking the link extent was supported by reusing two Macintosh conventions: highlighting text with a flashing marquee and graphics with gray "handles" (see Haan 1992 for examples). This highlighting was presented upon arrival when following a link, and when explicitly requested by the user on an anchor basis.

These design decisions were made to simplify the user interface. It was argued by the initial development team that different glyphs for different types or numbers of link destinations were unnecessary (Garrett 1986). The trade-off between supporting a complex visual code to differentiate link typing versus the simplicity of a single visual link representation is important to consider. It becomes important to distinguish among different link types only if links behave in significantly different ways or if a property of the link destination such as quality or quantity must be indicated. We have found this to be true based on our experience with systems such as HyperCard and DynaText which support a variety of link behaviors.

For example, the design of *SGML Tutorial* (van Herwijnen 1993) a DynaText version of *Practical SGML* (van Herwijnen 1990), required ten distinct icons or color treatments of text elements to distinguish a variety of link behaviors. In this hypertext following a link could perform such dissimilar events as open a graphic, run a parser on a text file, or scroll the reader's view to another location in the same book.

In addition to its simplicity, the use of a single glyph in Intermedia provided a visual "thing" with which the user could interact when editing links themselves as opposed to link content. Intermedia was a non-modal authoring and reading environment, which required the links to have a single appearance whether they were being followed, created, or modified. With the link glyph selected, the user could follow the link, add more links, push or pull data across the link, or delete the link.

However, this glyph was treated differently in different application data structures. In the graphics editor the visual connection between the glyph and the linked object or objects was entirely arbitrary, since the glyph could be moved independent of the link content. In the text editor, however, the glyph was locked in position above the first character of the link extent.

The search for the best way to represent a link marker in text is worth recounting in some detail. In Intermedia 1.0 this glyph appeared over the first character of the word being linked, often obscuring the word. Authors responded by adding a blank space at the beginning of each link in text to make room for the link marker. In Intermedia 3.0 the glyph was placed above, rather than on top of, the first character. This strategy was less destructive to legibility of the word being marked but disrupted the structure of the text itself by creating additional line spacing wherever a link occurred.

Intermedia displayed anchor extents on arrival once a link had been traversed and a new document window had been presented to the user by surrounding text with a marquee and graphic objects with gray handles, as mentioned above. The main purpose of highlighting the anchor extent was to call the user's attention to the destination of the link. An anchor's extent was not usually indicated before departure but could be displayed at the user's request. This minimized the visual disruption that displaying the marquees or handles might cause, but proved to be too subtle when links were promoted to first-class objects. As part of the development of InterNote in Intermedia 4.0, support for copying, pasting, and resizing of link extent was added (Catlin 1989). This made highlighting the anchor extent independent of link traversal more important. The interface for highlighting anchor extent was modified to support highlighting on selection of the link marker in addition to highlighting on arrival at a link destination.

Storyspace: Links in Storyspace are directional — incoming (those that point to the current space) and outgoing (those that point to other spaces). When a link is followed, the destination link extent is highlighted using the standard text highlight color. There is no visual cue to convey presence of outgoing links when a space is opened. To see these outgoing link extents, the user must hold down a two-key combination on the Macintosh keyboard (Option+Command). When these keys are depressed, a single-pixel box is drawn around the text where links originate. Links from graphics are handled in a similar manner, since graphics are treated as text "characters" in Storyspace.

This lack of a visual rhetoric to identify link presence has lead some authors to impose their own conventions, such as using bold type, to convey the presence of links in text to the reader. This design decision also requires users to operate indirectly when following links: the user must first place the cursor somewhere in the invisible link extent and then move the mouse to click on the "link follow" icon in a button matrix.

The use of a solid box to mark links decreases the legibility of type within the box. In contrast, the use of gray underlining to mark link presence in various HyperCard applications designed by The Voyager Company and Apple Computer presents a similar solution without decreasing legibility (Kahn 1993). However, Storyspace marks link presence in a transitory fashion (the box appears only when the user holds down certain keys) and so the box's effect on legibility is minimal.

In Figure 1a and 1b we enumerate various methods for marking link presence within a block of text. The variables are: use of line around text, use of background color or pattern, and use of foreground color in type. The method chosen for any specific system must balance the clarity of the marking against its effect on the legibility of the text block. The rhetorical effect of the marking system must be weighed. Methods of marking such as bolding text or reversing the space around text with strong colors will cause strong rhetorical disruptions within a block of text. Frequency of marking should also be an important consideration. If many links will appear in close proximity some forms of marking will overwhelm the content. Support for touching, nested and/or overlapping marks is also a difficult problem. While a single underscore or change of text color might suffice to mark a phrase such as "computer screen" as an anchor, the same strategies would not help the user perceive that "computer" was the anchor for one link while "screen" was the anchor for a different one. Similarly, a system which supports one link anchored to an entire paragraph while other links are anchored to words or phrases within the paragraph requires a sophisticated method for bracketing textual elements.

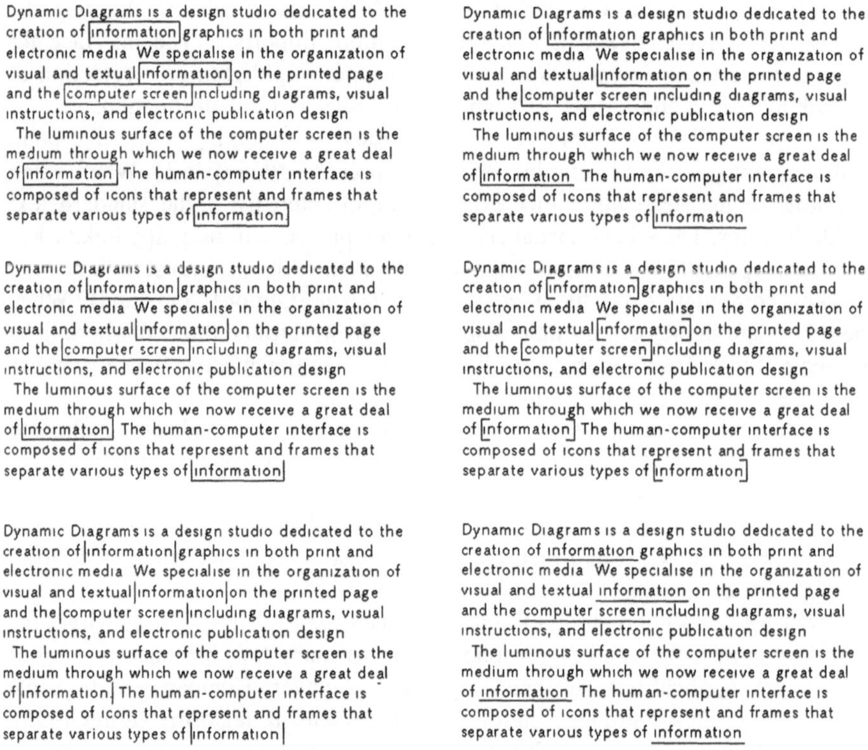

Dynamic Diagrams is a design studio dedicated to the creation of information graphics in both print and electronic media We specialise in the organization of visual and textual information on the printed page and the computer screen including diagrams, visual instructions, and electronic publication design
The luminous surface of the computer screen is the medium through which we now receive a great deal of information The human-computer interface is composed of icons that represent and frames that separate various types of information.

Dynamic Diagrams is a design studio dedicated to the creation of information graphics in both print and electronic media We specialise in the organization of visual and textual information on the printed page and the computer screen including diagrams, visual instructions, and electronic publication design
The luminous surface of the computer screen is the medium through which we now receive a great deal of information The human-computer interface is composed of icons that represent and frames that separate various types of information

Dynamic Diagrams is a design studio dedicated to the creation of information graphics in both print and electronic media We specialise in the organization of visual and textual information on the printed page and the computer screen including diagrams, visual instructions, and electronic publication design
The luminous surface of the computer screen is the medium through which we now receive a great deal of information The human-computer interface is composed of icons that represent and frames that separate various types of information

Dynamic Diagrams is a design studio dedicated to the creation of information graphics in both print and electronic media We specialise in the organization of visual and textual information on the printed page and the computer screen including diagrams, visual instructions, and electronic publication design
The luminous surface of the computer screen is the medium through which we now receive a great deal of information The human-computer interface is composed of icons that represent and frames that separate various types of information

Dynamic Diagrams is a design studio dedicated to the creation of information graphics in both print and electronic media We specialise in the organization of visual and textual information on the printed page and the computer screen including diagrams, visual instructions, and electronic publication design
The luminous surface of the computer screen is the medium through which we now receive a great deal of information The human-computer interface is composed of icons that represent and frames that separate various types of information

Dynamic Diagrams is a design studio dedicated to the creation of information graphics in both print and electronic media We specialise in the organization of visual and textual information on the printed page and the computer screen including diagrams, visual instructions, and electronic publication design
The luminous surface of the computer screen is the medium through which we now receive a great deal of information The human-computer interface is composed of icons that represent and frames that separate various types of information

Figure 1a: Variations of bracketing, underlining, boxing, and partial boxing of linked words and phrases

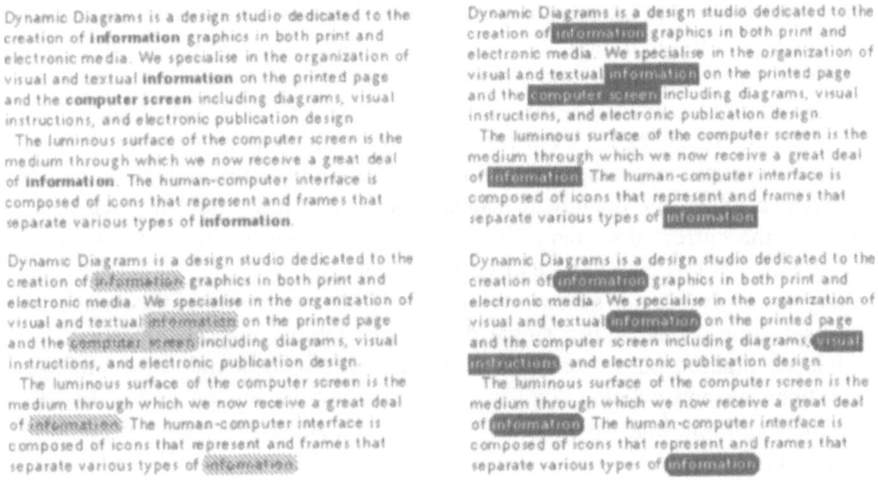

Dynamic Diagrams is a design studio dedicated to the creation of **information** graphics in both print and electronic media. We specialise in the organization of visual and textual **information** on the printed page and the **computer screen** including diagrams, visual instructions, and electronic publication design.
The luminous surface of the computer screen is the medium through which we now receive a great deal of **information**. The human-computer interface is composed of icons that represent and frames that separate various types of **information**.

Dynamic Diagrams is a design studio dedicated to the creation of **information** graphics in both print and electronic media. We specialise in the organization of visual and textual **information** on the printed page and the **computer screen** including diagrams, visual instructions, and electronic publication design.
The luminous surface of the computer screen is the medium through which we now receive a great deal of **information**. The human-computer interface is composed of icons that represent and frames that separate various types of **information**.

Dynamic Diagrams is a design studio dedicated to the creation of **information** graphics in both print and electronic media. We specialise in the organization of visual and textual **information** on the printed page and the **computer screen** including diagrams, visual instructions, and electronic publication design.
The luminous surface of the computer screen is the medium through which we now receive a great deal of **information**. The human-computer interface is composed of icons that represent and frames that separate various types of **information**.

Dynamic Diagrams is a design studio dedicated to the creation of **information** graphics in both print and electronic media. We specialise in the organization of visual and textual **information** on the printed page and the computer screen including diagrams, **visual instructions**, and electronic publication design.
The luminous surface of the computer screen is the medium through which we now receive a great deal of **information**. The human-computer interface is composed of icons that represent and frames that separate various types of **information**.

Figure 1b: Use of bold, background color, and background stripes with hard and rounded corners.

3 Link Destination

The two proto-hypertext links we are all familiar with in scholarly literature are the footnote and inline citation. Both of these conventions from print point from the text on the page to another location in the current document or in "the literature". The footnote, whether it is a superscript number or non-verbal typographic marks such as the asterisk or dagger, provides an index into a list of related information elsewhere on the page or at the end of a logical section. The inline citation provides the reader with at least an abbreviated name for the destination it points at. In either case the reader is provided with a clue as to the destination before "leaving" the narrative on the page.

The facilities for marking and previewing links in Intermedia provided some clue to the reader about a link's destination in the form of document name, document type, and anchor explainer. Selecting the marker for a link in a document would highlight the navigational possibilities from that link in the Web View's local map elsewhere on the screen. This would give the reader the document name and data type that contained possible destinations. If the link had multiple destinations, double-clicking on the marker would present a modal dialog box listing the names of documents and explainers for each destination anchor. The dialog appears in a uniform location on the screen unrelated to the link marker selected. The reader then had to choose one destination in order to continue navigation.

This Web View was intended to provide orientation and context for the reader as she navigated through the hypertext web (Utting 1989). The representation of link destinations did not indicate the place of a document in the folder hierarchy. So, for example, previewing a link and seeing in the Web View that it might lead to graphic document called "Portrait" gave no indication of who the graphic might be a portrait of, though this information might be implied in the name of the folder in which the document resided. The reader also could not see what, other than the current document, the destination document might be linked to. Other features of this map will be discussed below.

Storyspace provides a subset of this same link destination information. A reader selecting a link with a single destination gets no information about the possible destination before navigation occurs. Following a link with multiple destinations presents a dialog box listing the names of destination spaces. Figures comparing multiple link destinations in Intermedia and Storyspace are found in (Landow 1992).

We think the reader should be able to preview possible destinations before following a hypertext link. We recognize that there is sometimes a specific value to leaping blindly into hyperspace in works of hypertext fiction, but this is more the exception than the rule. We also think that this preview should appear in the context of the link source, which is to say visual related to it.

We suggest that previewing of link destination appear to the reader as a visual extension of the link presence. Selecting a link should reveal this additional information in a form that does not move the reader from his point of focus. This can be done by having a representation of the possible link destination(s) appear immediately above or below the link source. Coordinating this representation of the possible link destination with a contextual representation in a link map is an important feature discussed below.

4 Link Mapping

Much has been made of the potential dangers of a reader becoming lost when navigating in a hypertext. Conklin's oft-cited survey article (Conklin 1987) postulates this problem, though he neither proves or rigorously defines what is meant by being "lost in hyperspace".

The reader of a hypertext is often likened to a traveler through a physical landscape. A goal-oriented traveler becomes lost when she loses sight of her goal or her path to that goal. A traveler with no specific goal in mind becomes lost when he no longer perceives where he is in relation to a known landmark, such as where he came from. However, when we say a mental traveler has become "lost in thought" we mean nothing pejorative by it. Rather such a person has become completely involved or absorbed by an idea, a mental state many educators wish they could instill in their students. We have tried to take into consideration this variety of reactions to the non-linear and multi-directional nature of hypertext content in our studies of readers' reaction to educational hypertext (Kahn 1992).

A spatial representation of the connections in a hypertext is a critical support for hypertext navigation whether we want the reader to become completely absorbed or be led along a constrained path.

The shape this map can take is largely dependent on the linking model of the system. The Xerox NoteCards system could generate a binary tree graph to show links emanating from any "root" node (Halasz 1987). This map became very wide and visually difficult to manage. However, it provided the reader with both a sense of how nodes were connected and an alternate method of navigation.

The Intermedia Web View was limited to a nearest-neighbor map with no indication of directionality or hierarchy relationships between documents. In addition to the support for preview functions mentioned above, the Web View also provided navigation support. This was expected to compliment and coexist with, rather than replace, the desktop folder system which organized documents into hierarchies.

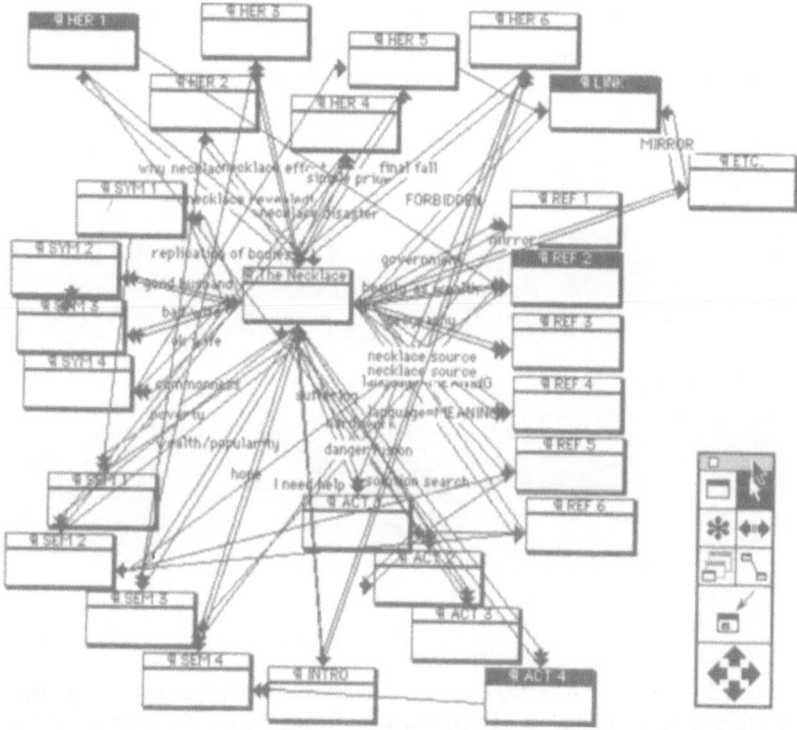

Figure 2a: A Storyspace Web representing a hypertext treatment of de Maupassant's "The Necklace," from Landow's Hypertext and Literary Theory class, Spring 1993.

Storyspace represents an entire "web" at the Macintosh desktop level as a single document. In the Storyspace view the reader gets a view of both the links and hierarchical relationships of all the spaces in the web. However, this view provides a preview of possible link destinations only between spaces within a single space (e.g. at the same level of the hierarchy).

Several students in George Landow's "Hypertext and Literary Theory" course this spring made creative use of the Storyspace view to express the connections among the spaces in the webs. They did this by making most links between spaces at a single level. When working within this constraint the results can be visual suggestive of the shape of relationships the author has in mind.

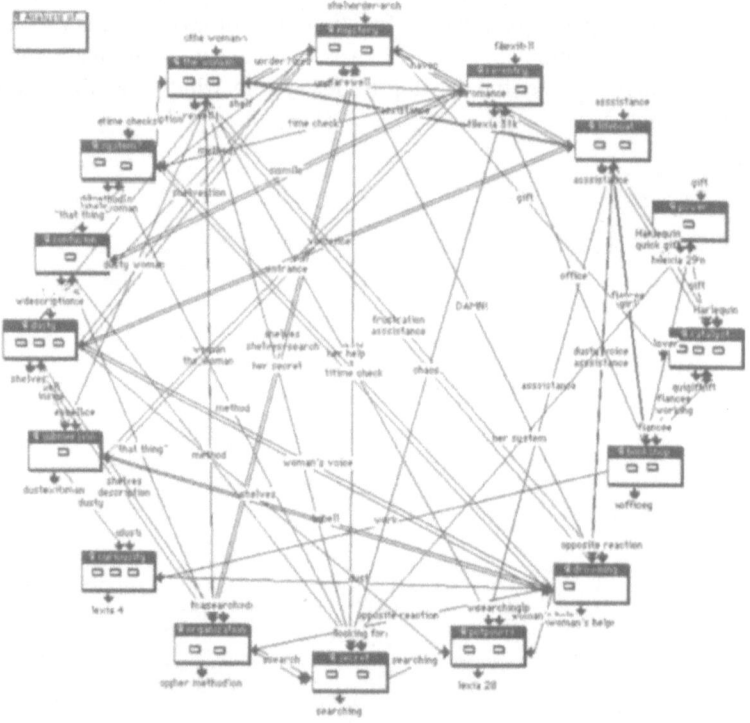

Figure 2b: A Storyspace web emphasizing the circular relationship among spaces along with crossing paths from Landow's Hypertext and Literary Theory class, Spring 1993.

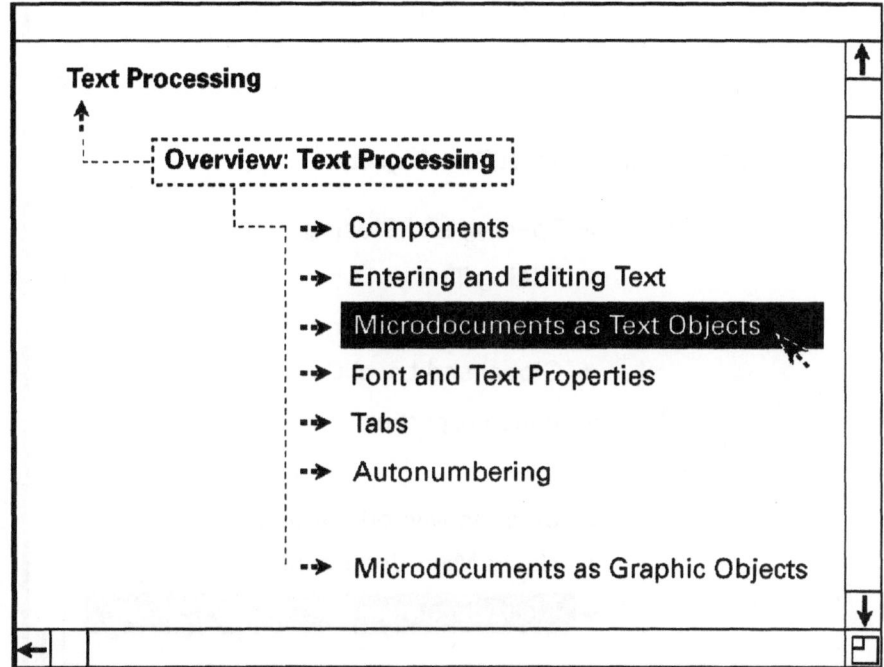

Figure 3a: Link browser for online documentation system

When working on an online documentation system, we proposed a variation of the Intermedia Web View shown in Figure 3a and 3b. The currently selected node is shown with a dotted outline. This system adds the notion of a container or parent element which appears above the currently selected node.

Linked nodes are divided into two groups, with "child" documents immediately below the selected node. "See also" or lateral links are grouped separately at the bottom of this list. This system is well suited for representing a network of links within a document hierarchy, a common situation in software and hardware documentation.

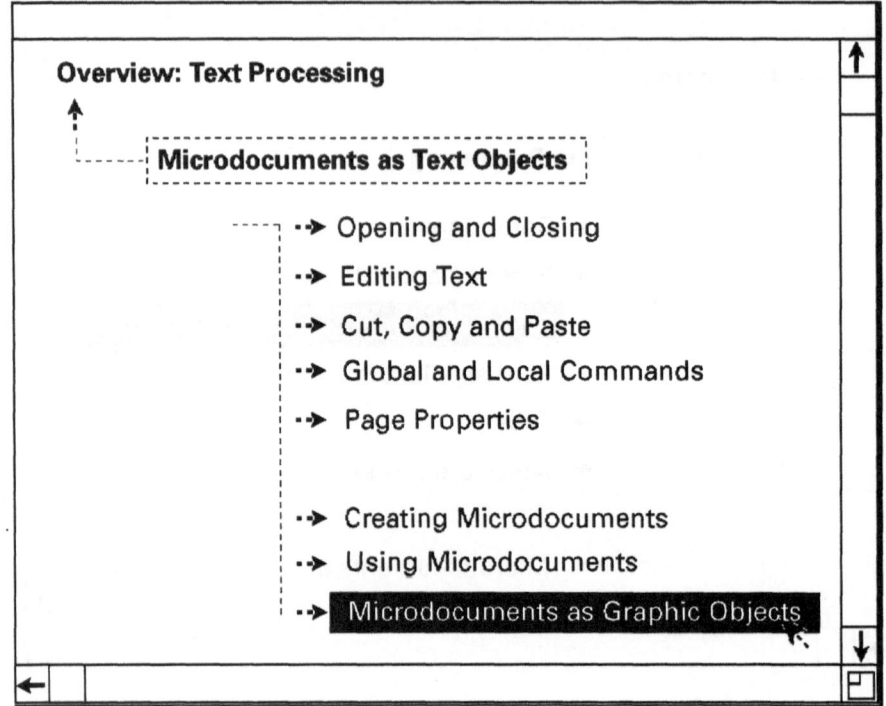

Figure 3b: Following a link to the node highlighted in Figure 3a above will redraw the view as shown here.

5 Conclusion

We have demonstrated how the three basic elements of visual rhetoric needed to support a hypertext system have been implemented in Intermedia and Storyspace, two systems used at Brown University. We have also shown several examples of alternative designs developed by Dynamic Diagrams.

Neither system is entirely successful in supporting the visual needs of a hypertext system. We have pointed out areas where improvements in future systems will help support the user's navigational needs in a clearer and more comprehensive manner.

However, both systems are noteworthy in that they do provide some support for each of the three basic elements we describe. Other systems we have used at Brown, such as Interleaf's WorldView, Apple's HyperCard, and Electronic Book Technologies' DynaText, are entirely lacking in one or more of these three basic elements.

We are reminded of a meeting in 1985 at which the representative of a major computer company explained that his company recognized how the choice of a windowing system would be a very important one for his new product. Since his company could not agree on what the best windowing system should be they had decided to bring the new product to market without one, rather than risk making the wrong choice. We hope that the developers of commercial hypertext systems do not make the same mistake a decade later. There are no clear winners in the areas of link presence, link destination, and link mapping and the problems each system must solve are varied and complex. However, the hypertext developer who avoids confronting these challenges will quickly look like a workstation without a windowing system.

References

Catlin 1989: Timothy J.O. Catlin, Paulette E. Bush, and Nicole Yankelovich, "InterNote: Extending a Hypermedia framework to support annotative collaboration," Hypertext '89 Proceedings, 1989, pp. 365-378.

Conklin 1987: Jeff Conklin, "Hypertext: An Introduction and Survey" IEEE Computer, 21(1), Jan. 1988, pp. 81-96.

Garrett 1986: L. Nancy Garrett, Karen E. Smith, and Norman K. Meyrowitz, "Intermedia: Issues, Strategies, and Tactics in the Design of a Hypermedia Document Systems," Computer-Supported Cooperative Work (CSCW '86) Proceedings, 1986, pp. 163-174,

Haan 1992: Bernard J. Haan, Paul Kahn, Victor A. Riley, James H. Coombs, and Norman K. Meyrowitz, "IRIS Hypermedia Services", Comm. of the ACM, 35(1), Jan. 1992, pp. 36-51.

Halasz 1987: Frank G. Halasz, Thomas P. Moran, and Randall H. Trigg, "NoteCards in a Nutshell," Proceedings of the CHI and GI '87 Conference on Human Factors in Computing Systems, 1987, pp. 45-52.

Kahn 1992: Paul Kahn and George Landow, "The Pleasure of Possibilities: What is Disorientation in Hypertext?" Journal of Computing in Higher Education, 4(2), Spring 1992, pp. 57-78.

Kahn 1993: Paul Kahn and Krzysztof Lenk, "Typography for the Computer Screen" Seybold Report on Desktop Publishing, July 1993.

Landow 1992: George P. Landow and Paul Kahn, "Where's the Hypertext? The Dickens Web as a System-Independent Hypertext" Proceedings of the ACM Conference on Hypertext (ECHT 92), 1992, pp. 149-160.

Utting 1989: Ken Utting and Nicole Yankelovich, "Context and orientation in Hypermedia networks" ACM Transactions on Information Systems, 7(1), Jan. 1989, pp. 58-84.

van Herwijnen 1990: Eric van Herwijnen, Practical SGML, Boston: Kluwer Academic Publishers, 1990

van Herwijnen 1993: Eric van Herwijnen, SGML Tutorial, Providence: Electronic Book Technologies, 1993.

Some issues of defining a user interface *with* general purpose hypermedia toolkits

Thomas Kirste
Computer Graphics Center (ZGDV), Darmstadt, Germany

Abstract. General purpose hypermedia systems (GPHS) facilitate the integration of heterogeneous data and applications into a homogeneous information structure. As the user accesses this structure through interactions, the issue of how this *interaction behavior* may be described becomes relevant. Current hypermedia models do not provide the descriptive potential to define the interaction behavior of hyperstructures in such a way that an easy run-time modifiability and extensibility of this behavior is possible. This, however, is a fundamental requirement for a GPHS.

This paper proposes a set of modeling primitives for describing the interaction behavior of an information structure which supports the use of external applications for object presentation and the flexible modifiability of behavior definitions.

Keywords. general purpose hypermedia systems, self describing data structures, behavior modeling

1   Introduction: General purpose hypermedia systems

Hypermedia systems can be classified into *application specific* and *general purpose* systems (Hofmann et al. 1990). Application specific systems, such as gIBIS (Conklin & Begemann 1987) or MEM (Glowalla et al. 1992) provide a data model and a system architecture tailored towards a specific application area; general purpose systems try to provide facilities for data organization – and possibly data manipulation – across a range of applications.

General purpose hypermedia systems (GPHS) may further be classified into *monolithic* and *non-monolithic* systems (Schnase 1992). Monolithic systems such as Intermedia (Yankelovich et al. 1988) implement the full system functionality from data management up to the presentation and interaction layer themselves. Non-monolithic systems allow external tools – the participating applications – to act as presentation and interaction mechanisms for individual data objects.

It is obvious that non-monolithic GPHS facilitate the *integration* of different applications into a uniform environment (Kirste & Hübner 1991, Malcolm et al. 1991).

This enables the user to pursue several tasks simultaneously – possibly using the same object in more than one task at the same time.

A central requirement for a GPHS is the removal of any content-interpretations from the definition of the system functionality, as defined by the Dexter Model (Halasz & Schwartz 1990). This is necessary in order to allow for a flexible extension of the set of content types. Interpretation of contents is only performed by the applications responsible for managing these objects. From this follows that any aspects related to content interpretation must not be defined by the GPHS. For modeling primitives whose semantics depend on content interpretation – such as anchors – GPHS and participating applications share the responsibility for implementing their respective functionality. Based on an abstract identity of these modeling primitives, the GPHS manages the content-independent static (and dynamic) aspects of an information structure, while the participating applications implement the content-specific functionalities (such as presentation of object contents, detection of interaction with parts of the contents etc.).

In this paper an abstract model for describing the interaction behavior of hyperstructures is introduced. It is based on a refinement of the "anchor" model commonly found in hypermedia data models. The goal of this model is to allow for the description of arbitrary interaction behavior of hyperstructures.

2   Behavior modeling for GPHS

The data managed by a GPHS can be regarded as an *information structure* which evolves over time (through modifications), and reacts to user interactions (e.g., by hyperlink traversal). These dynamic aspects are the structure's *behavior*. The modifiability of the information structure is a central characteristic that sets a GPHS apart from the typical 'authoring-reading'-approaches to the construction of hyperstructures: in this scenario, author and reader are the same person, even at the same time. It should be emphasized that this kind of system is not a tool for the creation of interactive multimedia presentations, but a general means for structuring and modifying multimedia data – a kind of "hyper-filesystem with intelligent desktop".

An environment for application integration should provide the user with means for extending functionality and modifying behavior in a flexible way (Encarnação & Frühauf 1993). In order to achieve this flexibility, information on the behavioral aspects of an information structure has to be kept in the structure itself rather than within the individual tools. Doing this would allow to carry out adaptions by simply changing the structure, instead of the tools operating on that structure.

As an example, consider a hyperstructure that is used for simulating a chemical process parameterized by pressure and temperature. Temperature and pressure values will be adjusted using an object which presents itself on the user interface as two scales. There is another object representing the simulation process, connected by two hyperlinks to the parameterization object. One hyperlink should be traversed if the user changes the temperature value, the other one if he changes the pressure.

In addition, the product of temperature and pressure may not exceed a certain limit. Therefore, a third hyperlink connects the parameter object to a warning message. It should be traversed, if such a situation occurs.

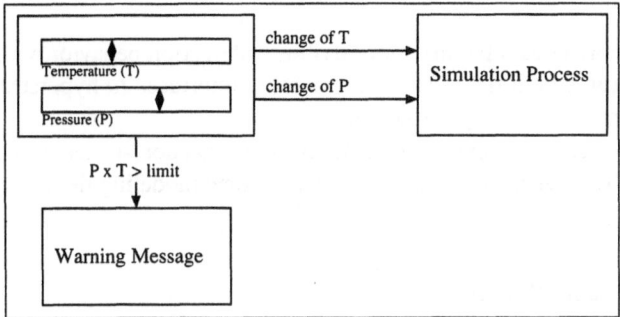

Figure 1: Example Hyperstructure

In order to reuse the scale-object in a variety of different simulations, it clearly can not be allowed to implement this navigation behavior in the presentation method. It is rather a behavioral aspect of the specific structure, the object is embedded in. Thus, the *structure* should contain this behavior information, not the tool responsible for object presentation.

Current hypermedia models do not cope well with a flexible definition of a structure's interaction behavior. Either the aspect of interacting with a structure is completely ignored, or the interaction behavior is derived from connectivity information such as "anchors". This effectively prevents the structure from containing definitions for interaction behavior *independent* of connectivity aspects. On the other hand, in design models such as HDM (Garzotto et al. 1991), the requirement for designing the "run time semantics", the interaction and navigation behavior, is well acknowledged. It thus seems obvious that a hypermedia system should provide the application designer with modeling primitives for describing this navigation behavior. This becomes even more prominent when a GPHS is considered, which – as outlined above – should be able to support a wide variety of different interaction behaviors independent of external tools.

The evolutionary nature of an information structure immediately renders all concepts of precompiled, fixed, "authored" user interfaces as inadequate, as they can not capture changes in the behavior definitions of such a structure. While the topic of capturing the evolution of the structure within the structure itself (thereby essentially defining self-applicative functions) is not discussed here[1], the description mechanisms for defining the interaction behavior will be examined further.

The GPHS setting thus introduces the following side conditions that must be considered when defining a model:

- Usability of external tools for the interaction with object contents.

---

[1] Although of high relevance for the generality of a hypermedia data model.

- No authoring/reading separation.

- Locality of interaction behavior definitions (*i.e.* object-local scope of behavior definitions and atomic modifiability of an object's behavior[2]).

It should be noted that a facility for describing interaction behavior within a hyperstructure captures both the aspects of providing interfaces *to* hyperstructures, and building interfaces *with* hyperstructures.

In the next section an extension to the classical "anchor"-concept of hypermedia is proposed that does provide the required additional modeling flexibility.

3   A sketch of a model

Interaction behavior may be defined as a function which maps an event and the current state of the user-interface to a new state and a system activity: *behavior* : *Event* $\times$ *EventState* $\rightarrow$ *EventState* $\times$ *Reaction*. This, however, is clearly much too general in order to meet the requirements given above. But it identifies the fundamental building blocks for a model:

- The model must provide the notion of *events*, which may be thought of as interesting changes in the environment.

- There must be an event-state (in order to allow a more complex behavior than a simple 1:1-mapping of events to reactions).

- There must be a function *behavior*, or rather a definition mechanism for this function, as the behavior of an information structure should be defined by the structure.

- There must be a way to specify reactions.

When looking at the semantics of anchors in hypermedia models such as the Dexter-Model, one may identify the following individual aspects which are implicitly contained in the concept of anchors:

- There exists the concept of a part of an object's content, the *extent*, which captures the structural aspects of anchors (the endpoints of hyperlinks that refer *into* an object's content).

- An anchor may define an *event* which is expected to trigger the traversal of the respective hyperlink.

---

[2]This is a prerequisite for an easy extension of the structure's behavior, such as the creation or deletion of a hyperlink.

The notion of an anchor in hypermedia has no well-defined semantics as it mixes the description of interaction behavior and structural relations[3]. However, if one separates structural and behavioral elements (as already suggested in (Kirste & Hübner 1991)), both are independently available and allow the attachment of precise interpretations.

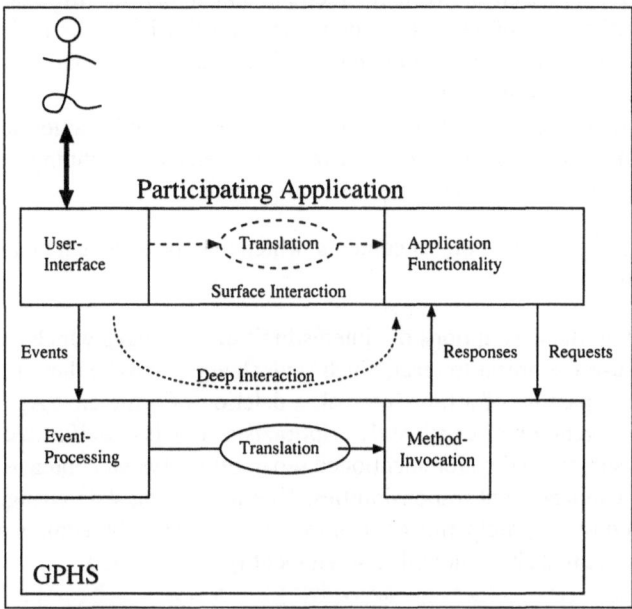

Figure 2: Communication between tools and GPHS

The second fundamental concept is the separation between *surface interaction* and *deep interaction*, as defined by (Took 1991) (see fig. 2). This directly results from the following two aspects:

- The model should allow for the use of external tools as means for presenting and interacting with individual objects.

- The model should allow the modification of object behavior without affecting external tools.

Surface interactions cause simple changes of the content presentation, such as scrolling or zooming that may be directly handled by the presentation tool. Deep interactions are sent to the underlying system, where they become translated into system activities whose results are then sent back to the presentation tools. The introduction of the deep-interaction concept is crucial for providing a tailorable object behavior.

---

[3]Due to this lack of clear semantics, the designers of the open hyperbase management system "Hyperform" have completely omitted anchors and links; here the user is responsible for implementing them (Wiil & Legget 1992).

External tools now have only to provide for the detection of atomic events. The composition of atomic into composite ones and the definition of the semantics of these composites is handled by the GPHS. Thus, the same tool may be used for different applications, where the same atomic events cause different reactions.

Furthermore, as the example above and the definition of *behavior* illustrates, a 1-to-1 correspondence between interactions and hyperlink-traversals does not necessarily exist. Therefore, a third modeling primitive is required which defines the function *behavior*. This modeling primitive ties event sequences to system activities such as hyperlink traversal.

Finally, the locality requirement calls for an object-local behavior definition, as well as for the relative independence of individual elements defining the behavior of an object. Thus, one arrives at the following model:

Extents define parts of an object contents, which may be an attachment point for a hyperlink.

Events contain the descriptions of "interesting" state changes which may potentially cause the object to react. Such state changes may be the selection of an extent, a passing of a time interval, a deletion of a file etc. As for extents, the interpretation of an event description is a content-specific aspect and therefore subject to the aforementioned separation between content-specific and content-independent responsibilities. The interesting state change has to be detected by a participating application. The GPHS only requires notification of the fact that an event with a given identity has occurred.

Rules describe composite events and map them to system activities; they are used to define the function *behavior*. A rule contains a description of the event states it is applicable to, a definition of the activity to be executed when applying this rule, and a function for updating the event state when the rule is applied.

The behavior of an object within an information structure may then be described by sets of rules and events. It may be modified by inserting or removing individual rules and events, thus allowing for a flexible adaption of the object behavior, as it is needed for modeling the creation of interactively selectable hyperlinks.

Finally, an object may be instantiated multiply (see Dexter-Model) at the same time (possibly in different tools), where each instance may have its own interaction stream – just as the same file may be displayed or edited simultaneously by different processes.

On the architectural level, the following elements have therefore to be introduced for the interaction processing by the GPHS:

- a per-instance event state is responsible for maintaining instance-local interaction streams.

- an event receiver function enters notifications sent by external tools into an instance's event state.

- a rule selection function is responsible for identifying the rule applicable to the current event state.

- a rule execution function updates the event state and hands the action-component of the rule down for execution by the underlying system.

This functionality is provided by the *session manager* of a GPHS. Event processing consists of the following steps:

1. The event receiver function enters the event into the event state of the instance, for which the event has been sent.

2. The rule selector then tries to identify the rule applicable to the current event state.

3. The applicable rule is executed by updating the instances event state according to the rule's update function, and returning the action component for further evaluation by the system.

Note that a participating application never has to operate on rules. This is the responsibility of the GPHS. All a participating application has to do is monitor user interaction with instances for occurences of atomic events. The tasks a participating application has to fulfill upon object activation (= instantiation) may be summarized as follows:

1. Obtain the list of events defined for the instance's object.

2. Monitor user interaction with the instance for the occurence of events described in the event list.

3. Upon occurence of such an event, send a notification (containing the event's identity) to the GPHS's session manager for further processing.

The model given here basically employs a production system approach for defining the interaction behavior, provided that the event state and the event-receiver function are suitably defined. Production systems have been suggested as a viable tool for specifying user interfaces (Hopgood & Duce 1979). The model thus provides the required descriptive power for the definition of arbitrary complex interaction behavior of a hyperstructure. The disadvantage of production systems, the lack of structure, is an advantage in this situation, as it is easily possible to withdraw or insert individual rules in order to tailor or extend the behavior of an object.

To subsume, the model contains the following relevant aspects of describing interaction behavior *within* a structure:

- Definition of the required descriptive elements (events and rules).

- Definition of the semantics of these elements (event receiver, rule selector and rule execution).

- Modeling of multiple instantiation (instance-local event states).

For the example given in section 2, there would be two events (one for each scale, sensitive to a value change) and three rules defined for the scale-object. The rule conditions would specify (a) legal change of temperature, (b) legal change of pressure and (c) illegal value change; the action-component of the rules would specify the traversal of the respective hyperlink.

The model introduced here defines the following extensions to the usual hyper-media concepts:

- Notion of an instance-local events state; allowing multiple interaction states for the same object.

- Separation of structural and behavioral modeling primitives.

- Support for modeling complex interaction behavior within the structure.

Especially the latter point allows now that external tools provide only primitive interaction behavior – that is, detection facilities for basic events. The session manager of the GPHS is then responsible for translating primitive events into activities, based on the rules given for the object. By changing the rules, the interaction behavior of the hyperstructure can be modified without modifying the tools – even at runtime. If, for example, the simulation is changed to give a warning if the product $P \times T$ falls *below* a give value, this can be simply realized by changing the respective rule. The structural modeling primitives as well as the presentation tools remain unaffected.

In section 6, a formal specification of this model is given.

4   Implementation aspects

4.1   The HyperPicture system

At the Computer Graphics Center, the experimental GPHS "HyperPicture" (Kirste & Hübner 1991) is being developed since the beginning of 1990. The central aspect of this development is the definition of a data model for arbitrary hypermedia structures and a runtime system for building and "executing" these structures.

4.1.1   Scope an central aspects

In scope HyperPicture is roughly comparable to open hypermedia systems such as Hyperform (Wiil & Legget 1992). However, the main research emphasis is centered around the definition of a general model for describing the connectivity between data objects, especially capturing the aspects of computational hypertext. In addition, issues of system configurability and extensibility have been a major point of interest during system development. These include the support for data manipulation by internal and external functions, flexible user- and application-specific system confi-guration and extension, and support for the integration of external data processing software.

The backbone for providing these facilities is the embedded extension language HCL (HyperPicture Command Language (Kirste 1993a)), a LISP-like language developed specifically for HyperPicture which is used to define functions for the manipulation of data objects[4], extending system functionality and configuring the system.

Objects themselves are regarded as functions that map objects ("hyperlink selectors") to other objects ("destinations"). Hyperlink traversal is thus mapped to function application. HyperPicture allows the function of an object to be described by a set of *partial* function definitions ("mappings"), which may be defined both extensionally (as a static mapping, an argument-result pair) and intensionally[5], as an algorithm written in HCL. Selecting the most specific mapping for a given argument (*i.e.*, a hyperlink selector), and applying the function defined by this mapping to the argument in order to determine the destination object, is built-in functionality of HyperPicture.

The functional object model with its extension language HCL addresses four of the well known seven issues raised by Halasz (Halasz 1988):

Issue 1: Search and Query in a Hypermedia Network

Issue 3: Virtual Structures for Dealing with Changing Information

Issue 4: Computation in (over) Hypermedia Networks

Issue 7: Extensibility and Tailorability

The interpretation of heterogeneous object contents (raster image, video, text etc.) is similar to the approach taken by several hypermedia reference models (for example (Furuta & Stotts 1990, Halasz & Schwartz 1990, Lange 1990)), based on a separation between abstract identity and concrete contents of an object. Within HyperPicture itself, abstract object identities are used as synonyms for objects, and no semantic interpretation of the *contents* of an object occurs, such that the system is open to any kind of object contents. Contents semantics (for example, the presentation and interaction mechanisms specific to video) are provided by content-specific tools on top of HyperPicture (see "PIMs" below).

Another central aspect – and the focus of this paper – is the definition of basic mechanisms which allow the abstract description of the runtime behavior of a data structure with respect to user interactions. As such, the behavior of the structure is essentially stored *within* that data structure. HyperPicture provides a subset of the model described in this paper: rules may only map a single event to a single hyperlink traversal (= function application)[6].

---

[4]Or executing queries on structures, e.g., the computation of the transitive closure of a set of objects with respect to a set of link types.

[5]"Intension": A notion taken from logic, describing the concept of identifying the elements of a set by their common properties rather than by their identity (the latter being the "extension"). For a somewhat more precise discussion see for example (Wille 1982, Woods 1975).

[6]Only a very limited flexibility is thus provided at a first glance. However, as the evaluated function may be an arbitrary HCL function, it is in effect possible to simulate actions by using functions, while

4.1.2   Architecture

The architectural concept of HyperPicture defines the following central system components:

Storage Management: This is responsible for mapping data objects to storage pools, accessing the contents of data objects, providing synchronous access to isochronal data objects and for controlling the cache.

Object Management: This is responsible for storing and accessing the abstract elements of HyperPicture; it is a hypertext abstract machine, roughly comparable in scope to machines such as HAM (Delisle & Schwartz 1986, Campbell & Goodman 1988), HB2 (Schnase 1992) or HyperBase (Schütt & Streitz 1990).

Session Management: This coordinates and synchronizes the different PIM-members of a session. It is responsible for the processing of event notifications, the selection and execution of rules and functions, and includes the HCL interpreter.

Presentation and Interaction Modules (PIMs): These components manage the type specific presentation of data objects, interpretation of event- and extent-definitions and the generation of events. In addition, they provide object-type specific mechanisms for object presentation and manipulation. This allows the creation of application specific modules which provide very specialized manipulation methods for objects. In addition, *external applications* such as a CAD-package may be used by the system as PIMs, allowing HyperPicture to operate, in effect, as an *application integrator*.

The support of external editors and data processing software makes HyperPicture an *open* Hypermedia System.

4.1.3   Additional elements of the data model

In addition to "Extents", "Events" and "Rules", the HyperPicture data model introduces the following modeling primitives:

Mappings: the partial function definitions which may be used to define the function of an object.

Information Objects: Information objects are containers for application data, such as images, text, sound and video. The structure and behavior of an information object is defined by a run-time extensible type system. For each object type, at least one content-specific tool usually exists: the Presentation and Interaction Module (PIM).

---

at the same time sacrificing the clear separation between description elements for structural and for behavioral information – a method only valid for pragmatic implementations, not for a clear abstract model.

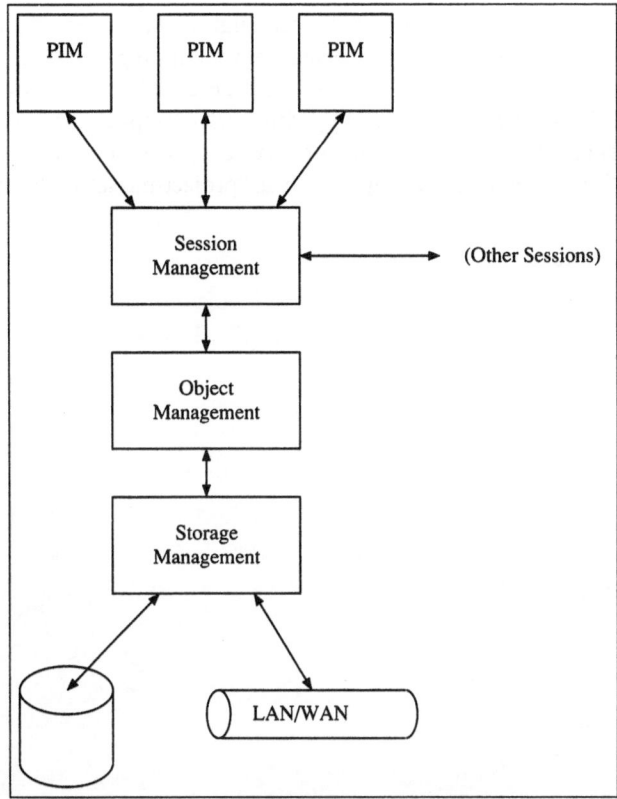

Figure 3: HyperPicture System Architecture

Furthermore, objects serve as containers for extents, events, rules, and mappings. The latter modeling primitives are only meaningful as componentens of an information object, so that the data model of HyperPicture may be termed an *extended object model*.

A complete Hyperlink in HyperPicture consists of at least three descriptive elements: an event, a rule and a mapping. Following, the notion "hyperlink" is used for simplicity as synonym for such a triple.

4.2   Applications of HyperPicture

As commercial applications, the interactive satellite image retrieval system "SpacePicture" (Kirste 1992) and the project documentation system "HYPDS" (Kirste 1993b) have been built on top of HyperPicture.

   In realizing these applications, we have used "metaphors" such as "map", "atlas" (a collection of maps) and "satellite image" in SpacePicture; "project", "project-phase", "folder" and "web" in HYPDS. Although the HyperPicture data model provides typed hyperlinks as the sole mechanism for building structures, most of the hyperlinks in both applications are hidden within these metaphors – they correspond to "structural links" in HDM. "Free" hyperlinks (*i.e.* "application links" in HDM nomenclature) are, from the users point of view, only used for structuring the data contained within a container-like object such as "project-phase" or "web".

4.2.1 SpacePicture

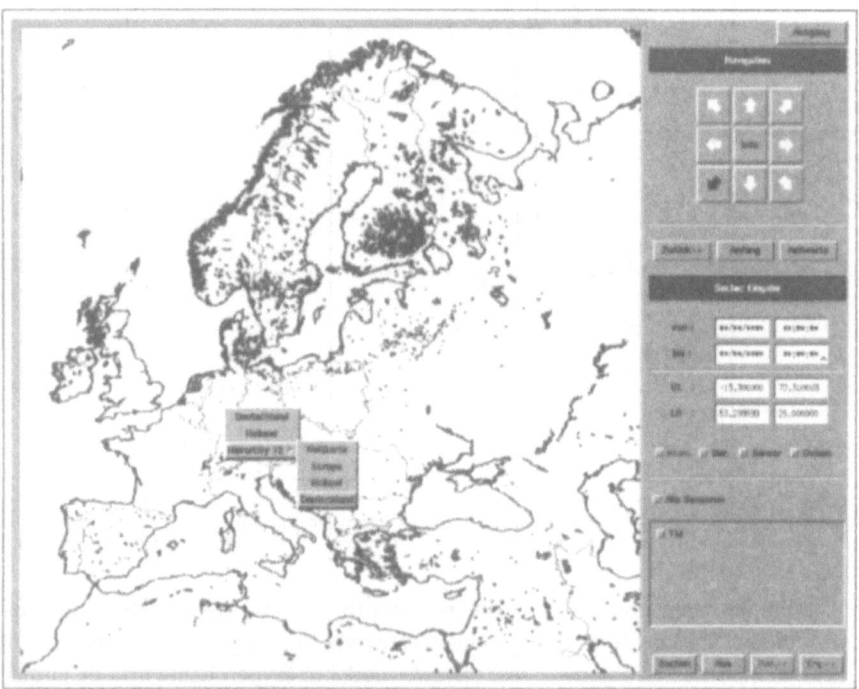

Figure 4: The Electronic Atlas of SpacePicture

Figure 4 displays the "electronic atlas" of the SpacePicture system. We have chosen the metaphor of a layered map hierarchy with different resolutions that provides a superset of the functionality of a common "paper"-atlas: navigation within one hierarchy-level is supported not only through "turning over the leaves" left and right, but to all of the eight possible neighbors of a map page. A compass-rose with eight direction buttons is used for this interaction. Zooming in and out is available through the usual "hyperjump"-metaphor of mousing the area-of-interest; multi-level jumps are possible through objects of the type "hierarchy" which behave like cascade menus on the user interface. SpacePicture uses the "event-rule-mapping" triple for representing hyperlinks. The Atlas understands two types of event definitions: One type specifies the selection of one of the compass-rose buttons, the definition of such an event simply contains a number from one to eight in addition to its type tag. The other type specifies the selection of an extent, here the definition contains the extent identity.

4.2.2   HYPDS

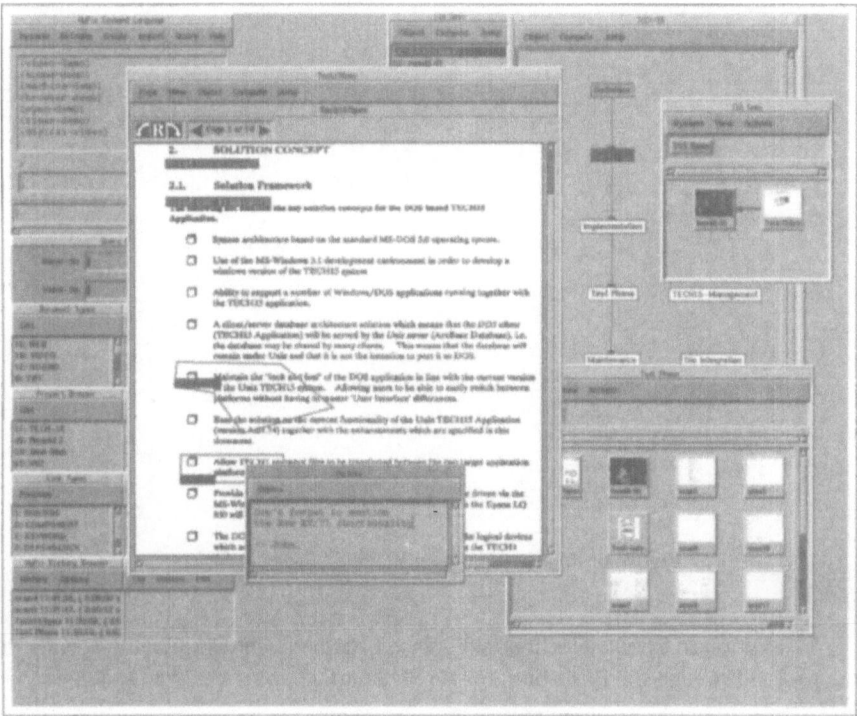

Figure 5: An HYPDS-Screen

Figure 5 shows a typical screen of the HYPDS project documentation system. Besides conventional multimedia data objects and general purpose organization metaphors such as "drawers and "webs", the object types *project* and *project phase* provide application specific support for data organization. A *project* (fig. 6) is a composite object which contains a number of *project phases*, between which time-dependencies exist. A project phase is a composite object which contains the documents related to this project phase. For the presentation of a project, the metaphor of a dependency graph has been chosen, where the individual project phases with their dependencies and a color-coding of their time state (active, overdue, fulfilled) is displayed. The project-browser understands an event definition type called "placed-button". Event specifications of this type contain the position and label of a button, which is created by the project-browser PIM when instantiating a project.

Project phases are displayed rather simple as scrollable lists.

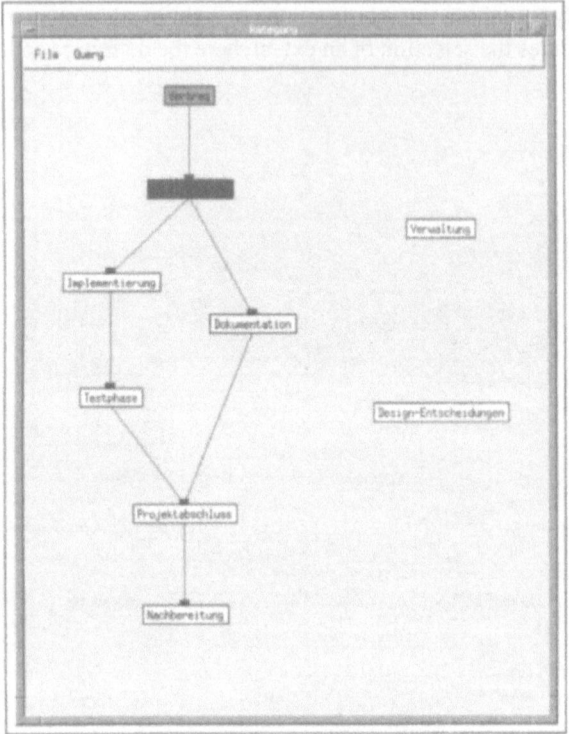

Figure 6: Presentation of an HYPDS "Project"-Object

In addition to extent selection and "placed buttons", the latter being specific to the project browser, the PIMs built for HYPDS understand such event specifications as:

- Menu item (the spec. contains menu title and item label)

- Timeout (the spec. gives the number of milliseconds)

- Object activation (needs no further spec.)

- Object deactivation (as above)

- Extent selection (the spec. contains the extent identity)

4.3   Use of the event/rule model

The separation of data model issues from concrete presentation/interaction issues and the presence of explicit modeling primitives for describing the runtime behavior of a structure, have proven to be essential for building the specialized user interfaces for these applications. SpacePicture and HYPDS both rely on the event-model of HyperPicture for introducing new event-types at the PIM-level. None of the PIMs needs to contain built-in functionality for operating on a data structure. Functions – such as hyperlink traversal or "cloning a project" (creation of a copy of a project and its phase-structure, without the documents) – are stored as rules (that is, intensional links) in the hyperbase itself. Thus a flexible extensibility of interaction behavior and functionality is guaranteed.

The implementation of metaphors (such as the "project"-metaphor) using HyperPicture is possible by using virtually only the descriptive elements of the data model. The construction of a metaphor consists of the following steps:

1. Definition of the new object and link types required for metaphor's structural aspects.

2. Definition of HCL-functions which implement the metaphor's structuring constraints (that is, assure that only metaphor instances observing the structural constraints can be created – an example is the "cloning" of projects in HYPDS).

3. Attachment of definitions for atomic events and event translation rules (which implement the metaphors interactive behavior) to the prototypes of metaphor instances (HyperPicture provides a prototyping scheme for inheriting object characteristics such as behavior).

4. If necessary, implementation of a customized PIM which realizes the metaphor's visual appearance and atomic interaction behavior. As this PIM has only to provide for atomic interactions, it may be reused for behaviorally different (but visually equivalent) metaphors.

These steps may be regarded as the process of mapping an application which has been designed using a suitable structured design methodology onto the modeling primitives of an underlying data- and interaction management system.

The most complex operation is the implementation of a PIM, which is a major counter-argument against an easy construction of metaphor-based interfaces in a GPHS-context. The model mirrors this fact by omitting any elements for describing the presentation of objects and object contents. The implementation of a PIM has, however, been simplified recently by extending HCL with the functionality of the Osf/Motif Widget set ("Widget Interpreter", see fig. 7 for a small example). The Widget-Interpreter may be regarded as a general purpose PIM with runtime programmable user interface.

5 Conclusion

A model has been sketched which allows for the flexible definition of the interaction behavior of a hyperstructure. It is claimed that this model (or a similar one) is a prerequisite for the effective definition of tailorable and extensible user interfaces to

```
(let :sequential
     ((shell (XtCreateTopLevelShell "Demo" "Xhcl" TopLevelShell))
      (label (XtCreateManagedWidget "label" XmLabel shell
               '(:backgroundPixmap (:Pixmap "slant_right")
                 :labelString     (:XmString "Hello World")
                 :fontList        (:FontList "helvb24")))))
   (XtRealizeWidget shell))
```

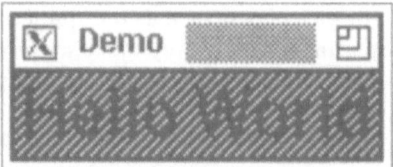

Figure 7: A Widget-Interpreter Example

hyperstructures using GPHS. By successfully implementing specialized interfaces on a subset of the model, proof has been given to that claim.

Furthermore, in the section on applications it has implicitly been suggested that the model also facilitates the definition of metaphor-based interfaces.

5.1   Open questions

One fact obviously missing is that there should be a connection between the event state kept for an instance and the state of the user interface as presented by a PIM. The HyperPicture system in fact provides this facility, as the state of the user interface may be controlled through the functionality of the Widget-Interpreter (which is part of HCL). This, however, is an ad-hoc solution, lacking the integration into the interaction model. The synchronization of event state with presentation state should not be confused with the synchronization of *object state* and presentation state. The latter is obtained through the activity tracking and change notification provided by HyperPicture.

A GPHS should be able to realize a wide variety of different applications, and even the simultaneous modeling of *several* applications. This does affect the design of hypermedia applications in two ways:

- as a GPHS is the destination system for mapping arbitrary applications onto its modeling primitives, design models for hypermedia applications should provide suitable means for supporting this mapping process. That is, their modeling elements should allow for an easy translation to the modeling primitives of the GPHS.

- the potential of application integration should be mirrored by adequate steps in the design process, where potential inter-application interfaces have to be defined, and the handling of overlapping structures managed by different applications is described.

The major impact on design methodology induced by this proposal is therefore the necessity of a methodology which explicitly supports the dynamic evolution of the design, as during the lifetime of a hyperstructure arbitrary changes in behavior (and structure) are allowed. While such flexibility clearly has to be provided by an underlying data management system, this is generally not acceptable for an application, due to higher-level integrity constraints that limit the variability of a structure stronger than the basic integrity conditions of the GPHS. Therefore, an adequate design model needs to include mechanisms for specifying the acceptable variability for a given structure – and potentially the methodology for verifying that the implementation of the design in fact guarantees this variability. It is obvious that a GPHS has to provide means for enforcing these application-specific integrity conditions, possibly using concepts such as "database rules" or "activity tracking".

5.2   Suport of metaphor-based interfaces

Metaphors – such as the desktop metaphor – are a well recognized mechanism for providing easy to use, interactive access to the complex functionalities of information systems. In the area of hypermedia systems, metaphors too are a possibility for giving the user easy access to the system potential.

The concept of "metaphors" may be subsumed in the action of identifying the task domain entities and their behavior, and implementing these using the modeling facilities of the underlying application construction toolkit. Metaphors may be abstract (such as cone-trees) or concrete (such as houses and rooms)[7]. The definability of metaphors is of a high value for the construction of usable interfaces to complex applications. Their intuitive usability allows for reducing the "semantic gap" between system and user concepts.

For a GPHS, the question is how could such a system support the use of metaphor based interfaces. Other than with application specific systems – where the set of relevant metaphors can be defined in advance (by procedures such as outlined in (Rauterberg 1993)) so that they can be custom-built –, a GPHS has to anticipate arbitrary changes in the data set and applications it has to manage, so that the set of valid metaphors may change unpredictable over time. This means, a GPHS has to be able to support arbitrary metaphors by providing a way for defining new metaphors without requiring a modification of the system itself.

From the modeling point-of-view, a "metaphor" may be assumed to consist of:

- a set of constraints which define its structuring behavior (comparable to an HDM-schema),

- a mechanism for identifying the subset of the overall structure, which defines a given metaphor instance,

---

[7](Robertson et al. 1993) and (Väänänen 1993a) discuss some aspects of using specific metaphors for visualizing information.

- a visual appearance and interaction behavior, which defines the metaphor's user-interface.

(See *e.g.* (Väänänen 1993b) for a similar definition.) Thus it can be concluded that the concept of metaphors may be adequately reflected by sets of objects with a specialized structure and a specific behavior. So it can be argued that a model containing explicit elements for describing the interaction behavior – as the one introduced above – is a prerequisite for the effective use of metaphors as means for interacting with a GPHS.

However, the claim that metaphors may be considered as object structures plus behavior information, deserves further discussion. In addition, there is a set of open questions associated with the efficient use of metaphors in a GPHS context. The most prominent are:

- What is "the" set of general purpose metaphors (corresponding to "the" set of structured data types in programming languages)? A GPHS should provide these metaphors as built-in primitives.

- Is there a general mechanism for the easy definition of "new" metaphors (i.e., a set of metaphor constructors comparable to type constructors)? Although mechanisms such as the Widget-Interpreter allow for the description of arbitrary user interfaces within a hyperstructure, this is still to be considered as a rather low-level approach which requires a substantial effort for implementing a metaphor.

6   Formal specification of the model

In this section the relevant processing and description elements required for describing the interaction behavior of a structure are formally defined; the Z-Notation (Spivey 1989) is used for formal paragraphs. It is a somewhat refined presentation of the behavioral part of the model given in (Kirste & Hübner 1991). The model is based on the following given sets:

$$[OID, IID, EID, Edef, Evalue, Estate, Act]$$

OID is the set of object identifiers, IID the set of instance identifiers and EID the set of event identifiers. $Edef$ is the set of event definitions, $Evalue$ a set of values that may be associated with an individual event occurrence, and $Estate$ the current event state of an instance. Act is the set of terms denoting system operations. Rules are elements structured according to the following schema:

$$Rule \cong [cond : \mathbb{P}\, Estate;\ upd : Estate \rightarrow Estate;\ act : Act]$$

$cond$ defines the set of matching event states for a rule, upd describes the state change when this rule gets selected. act is the system activity (such as hyperlink traversal) to be executed, if the rule gets selected. There should be a constant

$$nop : Act$$

required for describing a no-operation rule (a rule which only changes the current event state).

$$Rules == \{ \; rs : \mathbb{P} \; Rule \; | $$
$$\forall \, a, b : Rule \; | \; a \in rs \wedge b \in rs \bullet a.cond \cap b.cond \neq \varnothing \Rightarrow a = b \; \}$$

Elements of *Rules* are sets of rules, whose *cond* components are mutually disjoint (this is required for deterministic rule selection). *dummy* is a predefined dummy rule, which matches every event state and changes nothing:

$$\dummy : Rule$$

$$dummy.cond = Estate \wedge dummy.upd = \text{id} \, Estate \wedge dummy.act = nop$$

The process of receiving and processing an event is modeled by the following three functions:

$$receive : Estate \times EID \times Evalue \rightarrow Estate$$
$$select : Estate \times Rules \rightarrow Rule$$
$$fire : Estate \times Rule \rightarrow Estate \times Act$$

$$select =$$
$$\lambda \, es : Estate; \; rs : Rules \bullet$$
$$\quad \text{If } \exists \, r : rs \bullet es \in r.cond \text{ Then } r \text{ Else } dummy \text{ Fi}$$
$$fire = \lambda \, es : Estate; \; r : Rule \bullet (r.upd \; es, r.act)$$

receive maps an event state and an event id to a new event state, it models the recording of the event. *select* takes a pair of event state and rules and selects one of the rules according to event state and rule-conditions. If no rule is applicable, it returns the dummy rule. *fire* "executes" a rule by changing the event state and returning the action connected to that rule.

The schema *Structure* describes the persistent part of a hyperstructure, as far as the description of interaction behavior is concerned. It consists of two functions, mapping object id's to the set of rules resp. the events defined for the object:

$$\underline{\text{Structure}}$$
$$events : OID \nrightarrow EID \nrightarrow Edef$$
$$rules : OID \nrightarrow Rules$$

$$\text{dom } events = \text{dom } rules$$

A *Session* contains a *Structure* and two functions which map instance id's to objects id's resp. event states. Note that several instances of the same object may exist in a session, each one having its own event state.

$$\underline{\text{Session}}$$
$$Structure$$
$$iobj : IID \nrightarrow OID$$
$$evst : IID \nrightarrow EState$$

$$\text{dom } iobj = \text{dom } evst \wedge \text{dom } iobj \subseteq \text{dom } events$$

The behavior of a structure with respect to the events sent for individual instances in a given session is then described by the following function *behavior*:

$$behavior : Session \times IID \times EID \times Evalue \twoheadrightarrow Session \times Act$$

$$
\begin{aligned}
&behavior = \\
&\quad \lambda\, Session;\ i : IID;\ e : EID;\ v : Evalue \mid \\
&\qquad i \in \mathrm{dom}\, iobj \wedge e \in \mathrm{dom}\, events(iobj\ i)\ \bullet \\
&\quad (\mu\ es : Estate \mid es = receive(evst\ i, e, v)\ \bullet \\
&\qquad (\mu\ es' : Estate;\ a : Act \mid (es', a) = fire(es, select(es, rules(iobj\ i)))\ \bullet \\
&\qquad (\mu\ Session' \mid \\
&\qquad\quad \theta Structure' = \theta Structure \wedge \\
&\qquad\quad iobj' = iobj \wedge \\
&\qquad\quad evst' = evst \oplus \{i \mapsto es'\}\ \bullet \\
&\qquad\quad (\theta Session', a))))
\end{aligned}
$$

behavior uses *receive*, *select* and *fire* to process the event received. It then updates the session by entering the event state returned by *fire* into the event state table.

It is obvious that the model requires a substantial amount of detail in order to be a realistic implementation possibility. It is, after all, just a sketch. This does not only concern the definition of *Estate*, *Evalue* and *receive*, but also requires the replacement of unlimited sets and functions (*cond* and *upd* components of rules) by something efficiently representable in a finite computer store.

Acknowldegements

The author wants to thank J. Haake, P. Kahn, and W. Schuler for their valuable comments and suggestions on earlier versions of this paper. The work on Hyper-Picture has been supported by Hewlett-Packard and the Deutsche Forschungsanstalt für Luft- und Raumfahrt (DLR).

References

(CACM 1988) CACM special issue on hypertext. *Communications of the ACM*, 31(7), July 1988.

(Campbell & Goodman 1988) Campbell, B., Goodman, J.M. HAM: A general purpose hypertext abstract machine. In CACM Special Issue on Hypertext (CACM 1988), pages 856–861.

(Conklin & Begemann 1987) Conklin, J., Begemann, M.L. gIBIS: A Hypertext Tool for Team Design Deliberation. In *Proc. Hypertext '87 (November 13–15 1987, Chappel Hill, North Carolina)*, pages 247–251. The Association for Computing Machinery, 1987.

(Cordes & Streitz 1992) Cordes, R., Streitz, N.A., editors. *Hypertext und Hypermedia '92 – Konzepte und Anwendungen auf dem Weg in die Praxis*. Springer, 1992.

(Delisle & Schwartz 1986) Delisle, N., Schwartz, M. Neptune: a Hypertext System for CAD Applications. In *Proc. SIGMOD'86 (April 28–30 1986, Washington D.C.)*, pages 132–142. The Association for Computing Machinery, 1986.

(Encarnação & Frühauf 1993) Encarnação, J.L., Frühauf, M. Global Information Visualization – The Visualization Challenge for the 21st Century. In *Proc. ONR Workshop'93*, Darmstadt, Germany, July 6–8 1993.

(Furuta & Stotts 1990) Furuta, R., Stotts, P.D. The Trellis Hyperetxt Reference Model. In (NIST 1990).

(Garzotto et al. 1991) Garzotto, F., Paolini, P., Schwabe, D. HDM – A Model for the Design of Hypertext Applications. In (Hypertext 1991), pages 313–328.

(Glowalla et al. 1992) Glowalla, U., Hasebrook, J., Häfele, G., Fezzardi, G., Rinck, M. Das gezielte Wiedererlernen von Wissen mit Hilfe des Hypermedia-Systems MEM. In (Cordes & Streitz 1992), pages 45–61.

(Halasz 1988) Halasz, F.G. Reflections on notecards: Seven issues for the next generation of hypermedia systems. In CACM Special Issue on Hypertext (CACM 1988), pages 836–852.

(Halasz & Schwartz 1990) Halasz, F.G., Schwartz, M. The Dexter Hypertext Reference Model. In (NIST 1990).

(Hofmann et al. 1990) Hofmann, M., Cordes, R., Langendörfer, H., Lübben, E., Peyn, H., Süllow, K., Töpperwien, T. Vom lokalen Hypertext zum verteilten Hypermediasystem. In Gloor, P.A., Streitz, N.A., editors, *Hypertext und Hypermedia – Von theoretischen Konzepten zur praktischen Anwendung*, pages 28–42. Springer, 1990.

(Hopgood & Duce 1979) Hopgood, F.R.A., Duce, D.A. A production system approach to interactive graphic program design. In *Proc. IFIP-WG 5.2 Workshop on the methodology of interaction, Seillac 1979*, Amsterdam, 1979. North-Holland.

(Kirste 1992) Kirste, T. SpacePicture – Ein interaktives Hypermediasystem für die Archivierung und das Retrieval von hochauflösenden Satellitenbildern. In (Cordes & Streitz 1992), pages 135–147.

(Kirste 1993a) Kirste, T. HCL Language Reference Manual, Version 1.0. ZGDV-Report 68/93, Computer Graphics Center, 1993.

(Kirste 1993b) Kirste, T. HyPDS Kurzdokumentation des HyperPicture Projekt-Dokumentationssystems. ZGDV-Report 69/93, Computer Graphics Center, 1993.

(Kirste & Hübner 1991) Kirste, T., Hübner, W. An Open Hypermedia System for Multimedia Applications. In (Kjelldahl 1992), pages 225–243.

(Kjelldahl 1992) Kjelldahl, L., editor. *Multimedia: systems, interaction and applications (Proc. 1st Eurographics Workshop on Multimedia, April 18–19 1991, Stockholm, Sweden)*. Springer, 1992.

(Lange 1990) Lange, D.B. A formal model of hypertext. In (NIST 1990).

(Malcolm et al. 1991) Malcolm, K.C., Poltrock, S.E., Schuler, D. Industrial Strength Hypermedia: Requirements for a Large Engineering Enterprise. In (Hypertext 1991), pages 13–24.

(NIST 1990) National Institute for Standardisation. *Proc. NIST Hypertext Standardisation Workshop*, Gaithersburg, Maryland, January 16–17 1990.

(Hypertext 1991) *Proc. Hypertext '91 (December 15–18 1991, San Antonio, Texas)*. The Association for Computing Machinery, 1991.

(Rauterberg 1993) Rauterberg, M., Hof, M., Waldvogel, M. How to Find a Fitting Metaphor. In (Schuler & Hannemann 1993).

(Robertson et al. 1993) Robertson, G.G., Card, S.K., Mackinlay, J.D. Information Visualization using 3D Interactive Animation. *Communications of the ACM*, 36(4):47–71, April 1993.

(Schnase 1992) Schnase, J.L. *HB2: A Hyperbase Management System for Open, Distributed Hypermedia System Architectures*. PhD thesis, Texas A&M University, 1992.

(Schuler & Hannemann 1993) Schuler, W., Hannemann, J., editors. *Proc. Workshop on Methodological Issues on the Design of Hypertext-based User Interfaces (July 3–4 1993, Darmstadt, Germany)*. Springer, 1994.

(Schütt & Streitz 1990) Schütt, H.A., Streitz, N.A. Hyperbase: A hypermedia engine based on a relational database management system. In Streitz, N.A., Rizk, A., Andreé, J., editors, *Hypertext: Concepts, Systems and Applications (Proc. ECHT'90, November 27–30 1990, Versailles, France)*, pages 95–108. Cambridge University Press, 1990.

(Spivey 1989) Spivey, J.M. *The Z Notation*. Prentice Hall, 1989.

(Took 1991) Took, R.K. Out of the window: A multi-medium. In (Kjelldahl 1992), pages 70–83.

(Väänänen 1993a) Väänänen, K. Interfaces to Hypermedia: Communicating the Structure and Interaction Possibilities for the Users. *Computers & Graphics*, 17(3):219–228, 1993.

(Väänänen 1993b) Väänänen, K. Metaphor-Based User Interfaces for Hyperspaces. In (Schuler & Hannemann 1993).

(Wiil & Legget 1992) Wiil, U.K., Legget, J.J. Hyperform: Using Extensibility to Develop Dynamic Open and Distributed Hypertext Systems. In Lucarella, D., Nanard, D., Nanard, M., Paolini, P., editors, *Proc. ECHT'92 (November 30 – December 4 1992, Milano, Italy)*, pages 251–261. The Association for Computing Machinery, 1992.

(Wille 1982) Wille, R. Restructuring lattice theory: An approach based on hierarchies of concepts. In Rival, I., editor, *Ordered Sets*. Reidel, Dordrecht, Boston, 1982.

(Woods 1975) Woods, W.A. What's in a link: Foundations for semantic networks. In Bobrow, D.G., Collins, A.M., editors, *Representation and Understanding: Studies in Cognitive Science*. Academic Press, New York, 1975.

(Yankelovich et al. 1988) Yankelovich, N. et al. Intermedia: The concept and the Construction of a seamless Information Environment. *IEEE Computer*, pages 81–96, January 1988.

Analysis of Feature Usage in Access to On-line Information

Tom.T. Carey

Dept. of Computing & Information Science, University of Guelph, Canada

1 Introduction

The research reported here investigated online information seeking tasks, to understand why different users hose a particular set of access features to navigate through a space of online information. The online information was organized in book-like fashion, but the results apply equally to hypertext and hypermedia environments.

In our experiments, technical personnel obtained information from online books about how to use a computer software package, with which they had conceptual familiarity but not detailed knowledge. Given specific tasks to accomplish with the package, they accessed the information through tables of contents, indices and keyword search. All the users had substantial experience with these features. The users exhibited a wide diversity of sage patterns, which confounded the expectations of the designers of the
online access tool.

Some users clearly were able to find the required information more efficiently than others, even taking into account differences in initial knowledge. Our original mandate was to identify from the usage data the most efficient choice of features for various situations, which could then be incorporated into a "tactical" section of the online help facility to complement the existing operational help. We were also asked to consider whether some form of active help could be used to monitor people's actions and suggest more efficient tactics for hosing when to use the table of contents, index or keyword search. We determined that neither of these approaches to improving access was likely to be effective. [Carey et al, 92].

Our work revealed that the designers' conceptions of the product were centered around the task of locating information. The information seeking tasks, experienced by our users, frequently included high levels of uncertainty about the information required. The tasks should be regarded as "information discernment", because they require that users continually assess the relevancy and adequacy of the information they are encountering. This uncertainty about the appropriateness of information led to much more tentativeness for many users, and invalidated the designers' perceptions of the cost and benefit of the systems' features.

A key component of our work was to study in depth several representative users, to define why they chose a specific access feature at particular points in their tasks. Understanding the factors which determine feature choice is critical to effective design of systems with discretionary usage. In the next section we illustrate the nature of our analysis, with a description of one user's pattern of interactions. In section 3 we present general conclusions about the factors which shaped users' choices. Section 4 describes some design directions suggested by these results.

2 Analysis of discretionary usage of access features

To analyze why different users employed the access features in significantly different ways, we used a combination of observation, analysis of verbal protocols and videotape records, and post-task interviews. The analysis technique which produced the most insights was a mapping of user actions on dimensions suggested by Stevenson [88].

Figure 1 shows a first-order mapping for six tasks given one subject in the experiment. In the figure, each square represents one use of an access feature, e.g. one examination of the Table of Contents, which wastask-oriented, or one Keyword Search, or one examination of the Index. The dimension of Target Certainty indicates how sure the user is about the nature of the required information. The dimension of Location Certainty indicates how sure the user is about where in the document the required information is located. The arrows indicate the sequence of user actions.

Generally, we expect successful usage to progress towards the top and/or the right-hand side of the figure, indicating increasing focus on the required information by the user.

Comparing these maps across subjects yielded insights about differences in the regions in which the various features were used, as well as highlighting individual differences such as systematic versus intuitive searching. High-order maps were also produced to indicate the type of target information sought (i.e. information about specific objects, functions, tasks or general conceptual background), the patterns of actions within one feature use (e.g. paging through sections after using the table of contents) and switching between accessing the information and trying out a possible task solution.

N_M is action M in task N. Each action is a choice from:

Keyword search ☐   **Index** ◼   **Table of contents** ◼

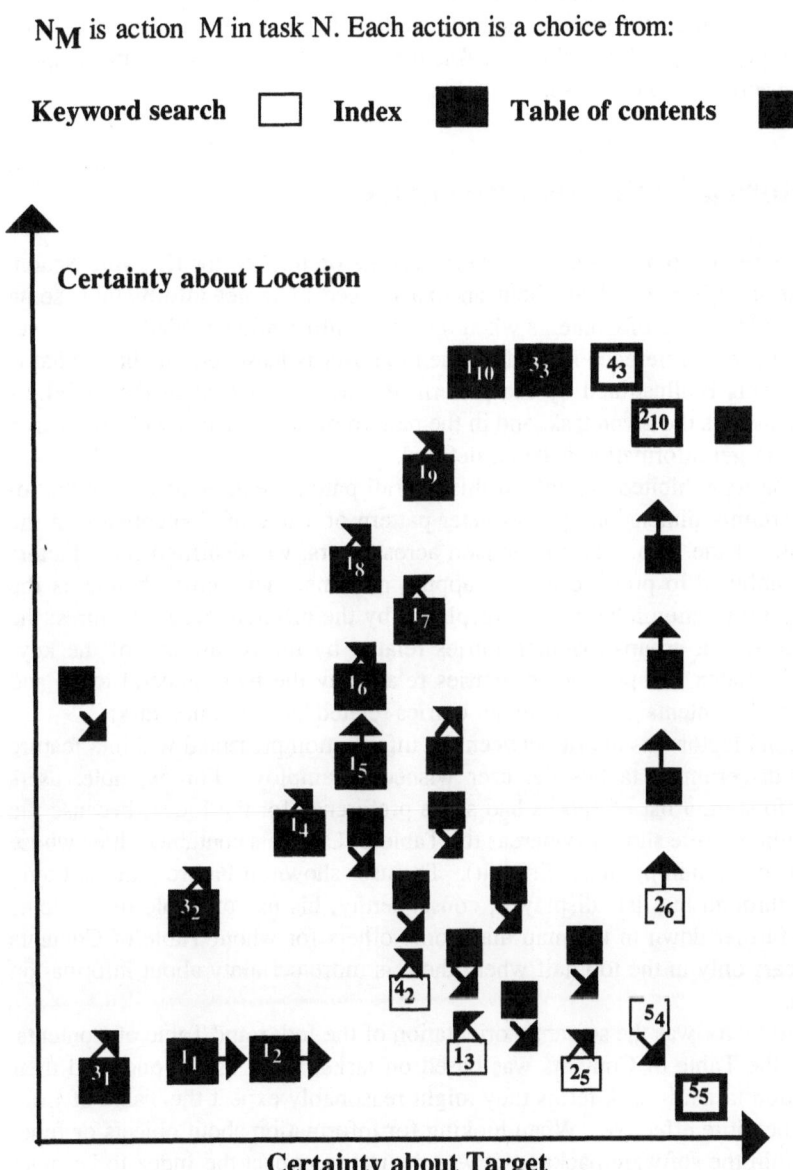

Figure 1: Access feature map for one subject

From this detailed analysis for several users, we identified six factors which determined why certain features were chosen at particular times. These will be summarized in the next section, with illustration from Figure 1. The first three factors apply to specific problem tasks; the other three factors seem to apply generally across problem tasks.

3 Factors affecting feature choice

We can observe from Figure 1 that there is some preference for Keyword Search when the user is most clear about an exact piece of target information, some preference for Table of Contents when the exact information needed is not as yet clear, and some preference for Index when the user is least certain about what is needed. This is illustrated by the pattern of features selected in the initial attempt to address the given task, and in the pattern of later use of Keyword Search when the target information is better defined.

Other users exhibited variants of this overall pattern, e.g. emphasizing the location certainty dimension by a stronger pattern of Table of Contents use in the upper half of the map. By comparison across users, we identified three factors which combined to produce these mapping patterns. The most obvious is the differing information relationships displayed by the different access features: the Keyword Search groups together entries related by the occurrence of the keywords, the Index groups together entries related by the more general term, and the Table of Contents groups together entries related by a common task.

A second factor was the fit between the information presented within a feature and the discernment tactics the user wished to employ. For example, users wishing to skim a list of entries had some preference for the Index, because the item headings were shorter (whereas the Table of Contents contained titles whose length made skimming more difficult). The user shown in Figure 1 did not tend to skim through the lists displayed; consequently, his use of Table of Contents extends further down in the map than some others for whom Table of Contents use appears only in the top half where there is more certainty about information location.

A third factor was the semantic orientation of the Index and Table of Contents. Because the Table of Contents was based on tasks, when users conceived their information target in task terms they might reasonably expect the Table of Contents to be more effective. When looking for information about objects or functions within the software package, it was natural to expect the Index to be more effective. This is illustrated in Figure 1 by the initial access choice in problem task 4, in which a Table of Contents access occurs anomalously on the left side of the map: the user was looking for background information on a specific concept, in order to better define the required target information.

There were also three more general factors which influenced feature choice. There is a tendency for momentum to prevail within a particular feature: if a particular feature is proving useful (movement within the map towards the top right corner), its use continues. This is illustrated in Figure 1 by the sequences within problem tasks 1 and 2. This phenomenon can easily have negative consequences: in problem task 5 the user continues with the Table of Contents in a region where Keyword Search would more often be selected (indeed, its eventual use led to the required information).

Another general factor was costs of use for a particular feature. The cost of use could relate to the ease of interaction with a feature, e.g. whether it was easily accessible or hidden away. But cost of use also relates to more indirect costs, such as the cognitive cost of employing a feature. Some users found Keyword Search and Index disorienting, because they could not maintain a sense of place in the document. Many users also experienced a 'commitment cost' for Keyword Search. That is, in separate test conditions in which users were restricted to a single access feature, we established that Keyword Search was the most effective feature when used in isolation (mostly because its technique for prioritizing possible entries was quite sophisticated). However, users were reluctant to use Keyword Search as a browsing device. They seemed to be uncomfortable committing to a search term when they were uncertain about the target they wanted.

A final factor distinguished various patterns of feature selection, the information processing style of individuals. Figure 1 is illustrative of a systematic style of processing, with considerable reflection about how to proceed. More intuitive users were more likely to follow hunches about the required information, less persistent with particular features, and more inclined to initially seek out examples. There were also evident differences in terms of maximal/minimal information employed and receptive/preceptive processing of the information available. [Benbasat & Taylor 82].

4 Design implications

The factors listed above represent an interpretive approach to the problem of feature choice for access to online information [Walsham 93]. Our aim was to understand the process and context of usage, to inform design. Our data indicates that users made their selection of access features in accordance with these influences, usually in an opportunistic rather than a reflective way. We do not propose that these are orthogonal factors which could be statistically separated. Rather, we believe these insights into the factors influencing user behaviour can help us improve the design of access features. We present below some of the design implications which resulted from this study. These design directions are stated in the context of online book-like information. However, similar factors influence users in access to more extensive hypermedia systems.

i) Reduce the conflicts between available information and desired tactics

Ineffective use of the access features often occurs when users must trade off one factor against another. For example, when users want to browse looking for a type of object, they have to trade off between a hierarchically browsable Table of Contents with the wrong semantic orientation and an Index with some appropriate organization (interspersed with function information) but ineffective information neighbourhoods to support browsing.

In experiments with multiple complementary tables of contents, we were able to overcome this problem by providing different semantic orientations (task, object, function, conceptual background) which all could be browsed.

We also shortened the length of each entry in the tables so that they could be skimmed more easily. The tables combined most of the benefits of traditional indices and tables of contents. Users easily employed the multiple tables in tactically effective ways and reported subjective satisfaction with their use. [Hunt, Rintjema & Carey, 93].

ii) Integrate features to lower the effects of momentum

In order to encourage users to achieve tactical advantage with opportunistic choices, the availability of different features must be perceptually salient within the range of view of displayed information. We found that listing feature choices on a menu bar at the top of a screen window was not as effective as presenting the choices within the information display itself, provided the choices could be perceived as switch settings within the current display context.

A similar integration may have contributed to the success of SuperBook [Egan et al 89]: by combining the display of keyword search and a table of contents, it is easier to use both without the perception of explicit choice between them.

iii) Anticipate differences in information processing style

For example, if users have an information processing style which leads them to seek out examples before conceptual information, they need some way to access examples easily, and then to quickly see how the example fits with other examples in an online document as a front-end to the remainder of the information. Users were able to move effectively between the examples and the surrounding information, and to discern quickly whether there was an appropriate example for their needs. [Rintjema & Carey, 93].

iv) Reduce disorientation with both conceptual and rhetorical maps

SuperBook is again a good example of increasing use of keyword search by reducing the disorientation cost through the presence of a conceptual map. But a table of contents does not always provide the necessary context. For instance, we observed users moving to and reading a section of text for which they had not seen the necessary prerequisite information one or two pages earlier. Similarly, users need to know if the example they have located is a specific illustration of a more general concept previously discussed, a counterexample to the preceding discussion or an introduction to a subsequent presentation.

We have begun to experiment with an alternative map, which includes in information displays a rhetorical map of the section in which the current information appears, and indications of prerequisite information whichprovides necessary context. This overview can be viewed as a micro-map of the surrounding rhetorical context; the cues themselves can be used as hypertext links for navigating to further information.

Acknowledgements: This research was supported by the Natural Sciences and Engineering Council of Canada, the University Research Incentive Fund of Ontario, and IBM Canada Ltd. SuperBook is a registered trademark of AT&T Bell Communications Research Inc.

References

Benbasat, I., and Taylor, R.N. *Behavioural Aspects of Information Processing for the Design of Management Information Systems.* IEEE Trans. on Systems, Man and Cybernetics, 12(4), pp 439-450. 1982.

Carey, T., R.B. Nonnecke, J. Mitterer and D. Lung., *Prospects for Active Help in OnLine Documentation.* Proceedings ACM Sigdoc Conference, October 1992, Ottawa.

Egan, D., J. Remde, T. Landauer, C. Lochbaum and L. Gome. *Behavioural Evaluation and Analysis of a Hypertext Browser.* Proceedings CHI'89, New York: ACM-Press, pp 205-210, 1989.

Hunt, W.T., L. Rintjema and T.T. Carey. *User Acceptance of Complementary Tables of Contents for Access to OnLine Information.* Interchi'93 Adjunct Proceedings, pp 181-18, 1993.

Rintjema, L. and T.T. Carey. *Example-Oriented Access to OnLine Documentation.* Technical Report CIS93-008, University of Guelph, Canada. 1993.

Stephenson, G. *Knowledge Browsing - Front ends to Statistical Databases*, IV Working Conference on Statistical and Scientific Database Management, 2, pp 55-65, 1988.

Facing Technical Documentation with Hypertext: Reflections on the Systematic Design, Construction and Presentation

Klaus Meusel, Siemens AG, Research and Development, Munich
Klaus Eickemeyer, Thomas Koslowski
Siemens-Nixdorf Informationssysteme AG, Munich, Germany

Abstract. In this paper, we propose principles and guidelines for the design, construction and presentation of hypertext in the application area of technical documentation. The issues discussed in the following chapters are based on two different approaches: First, the approach of the ESPRIT project HYTEA (ESPRIT P5252, HYperTExt Authoring), and second a pragmatic solution developed in a hypertext project at Siemens

Keywords: Model-based Hypertext, Technical Documentation, Systematic Design, Construction and Presentation, ESPRIT Project HYTEA, UNIX Desktop

1 Introduction

In HYTEA, methods and tools for the systematic design and implementation of hyperdocuments were developed. The abstract hypertext design model (HDM), the authoring environment and demonstrator applications are described in (Schröcksnadl, Meusel, Thüring 1992), (Schiff, Garzotto, Schröcksnadl, Meusel 1993), (Schröcksnadl, Meusel, Zucker, Schiff, Thüring 1992). The main goals of HYTEA were to increase productivity of the authors (Caloini 1992), (Meusel, Baltes 1993) and to improve the quality of the final hyperdocuments (Meusel, Schröcksnadl, Schiff 1993)

To meet the second goal, an extra effort was put into the professional design of the user interfaces. Chapter 2 lists some issues we discussed while designing front-ends for the target system ToolBook. The focus of this chapter is the presentation of hypertext documents.

For the application prototypes (Schröcksnadl, Meusel, Thüring 1992), (Schiff, Schröcksnadl, Meusel 1992) developed in the research environment of HYTEA, parts of existing linear documents were 'pasted' into abstract hypertext skeletons without re-writing the contents. Due to time constraints, the aspect of writing new text was not covered by HYTEA. Opposed to that, in a hypertext project at SNI the majority of the information chunks had to be re-written or even had to be written from scratch. Within the project more than ten authors from the development department contributed to the final help system. Coordination of the authors demanded a predefined, commonly agreed basis of principles and guidelines for constructing a context-sensitive hypertextual help system. They are presented in chapter 3. These guidelines are interesting for technical writers who are constructing similar help systems. On the other hand, this description of 'real-life authoring' is also important for transferring research environments as developed in HYTEA into business departments. Chapter 4 gives a Summary of this paper.

2 Presentation of HYTEA Applications

2.1 Functionality of the Hypertext Interfaces

In HYTEA, all application prototypes were structured by the hypertext design model HDM on an abstract level. For translating the abstract specifications into target systems like FrameMaker or ToolBook, we had to think about how to present the HDM skeleton to the user: Our main idea was to supply the user with additional features for orientation and navigation by visualizing hierarchies of HDM entities and components explicitly and making them mouse sensitive for link activation. Following this idea, about 40 per cent of the computer screen or the active window (depending on whether the target system is frame based or window based) has to be allocated for these structural components. Compared to many commercial hyperdocuments where only 5-10 per cent of the available space serves for structural orientation and navigation (headlines and forward/backward-buttons, for example), we had to create new visual templates, offering large navigation bars and margins, for example.

The functionality of our interfaces is described in detail in (Meusel, Schröcksnadl, Schiff 1993). For harmonizing our ideas of functionality with a good layout, we consulted F.Zebner, a professional designer. Issues discussed with him are presented in the form of guidelines in the following section. We exemplified these guidelines by creating visual templates for ToolBook applications. In the same way, they can be applied by authors working with other target systems.

2.2 Guidelines for Seven Issues on the Professional Front-End Design

Usage of a grid

The definition of a grid should be the starting point for the design of a hypertext interface. Apply the grid on all pages within an application (Meusel, Schröcksnadl, Schiff 1993). Try to use the same grid for other applications as far as possible, too. This forces you/the authors to put the same objects always on the same place, which is important for readers. Otherwise, the readers are disturbed by 'flipping' buttons or icons while browsing through an application or they have to understand different layouts each time they start a new application.

Snap all objects to that grid on pixel-level. Otherwise, tiny little inconsistencies are caused, which also burden an extra cognitive load onto the reader.

3-D-effects

Try to avoid different light- and shadow-effects. Don't use 3-D-buttons and several layers of dialog boxes and function bars. A 14" screen is small, and these features waste a lot of space by additional lines indicating shadows. Again, a side effect is the extra load on the user which he has to carry by understanding the different layers of objects. And from the artist's-point-of-view, the change of light sources that takes place when buttons are pressed is confusing/inconsistent, anyway!

Besides these technical arguments, you should also think about the corporate identity (CI) of your company (Pogarell 1993). The style of your hyperdocuments should be similar to other products in your spectrum, like software manuals, for example. Don't just copy the CI of other vendors of hyperdocuments/GUI's. Their success mostly is related to marketing strategies, not to the use of 'buttons'.

Following this guideline, we created a plain 2-D-design, with a few thin lines indicating areas with different functionalities.

Typography

Use one or two font styles, not more ('fontitis'!). Avoid visual rivers (Kahn 1992) by using 'align left' instead of 'justified' when formatting your paragraphs. Snap the text-portions to the grid, and use margins and white spaces to improve readability. Use specific fonts for the screen: Arial or Helvetica, for example. Don't use fonts like Times Roman. They are nice to read on paper, but the readability is bad on the screen. Remember: You're designing information for the computer screen (Kahn, Lenk 1992). Also: Good hardware support does not imply good typography, or, in other words, you can prepare good typography even for a Hercules card!

Colors

Use a few colors only! Also, make sure that objects with the same color have the same function or semantics. Plain white pages can be more attracting than fancy colors. Use ideas from color theory for defining good contrasts and avoiding disharmony. Remember: Apple Macintosh systems mostly use black-and-white interfaces, which can be much more professional and readable than badly-designed color applications.

Also be aware of technical problems: Colors used by application software like ToolBook will look different on different displays. For example, we experienced that 'petrol' defined on a PC changed to 'light blue' on a notebook.

Orientation and Navigation

Allocate big parts of the screen for orientation bars (headlines, names of structural elements) and navigation facilities (Meusel, Schröcksnadl, Schiff 1993). Good ideas for 'navigation' concepts are offered by Smalltalk class hierarchy browsers and by the Norton Commander. Combine these concepts with the common 'hotword' approach. Hotwords can be activated fast, typically by a single mouse click. But sometimes the link anchored in a hotword doesn't take the reader to the expected place, because of bad wording, for example. Therefore, we recommend the additional use of a navigation bar. See (Meusel, Schröcksnadl, Schiff 1993) for detailed discussion.

Figure 1. Layout example for navigation and orientation bars, contents part and a margin containing link anchors. All objects are snapped to an invisible grid. Text that is bold faced indicates link presence.

Structured skeleton beyond the visual interface

If you dive beyond the interface, a clear structure should become visible. A professional visual design is useless without a good 'engine' (HDM (Garzotto, Paolini, Schwabe 1991), for example). Figure 1 shows the combination of the last two issues. In an electronic service manual, two main information types are defined ('facts' for look-up and 'procedures' for performing service tasks), which are offered in the navigation bar. By selecting one of them, the next level of the hierarchy becomes visible. To improve readability and usability of the hyperdocument, hotwords are offered in a margin and the information type of the link destination is always added to the hotword. This is also a simple way of visualizing link types that are defined on conceptual level.

Teamwork

Last but not least we think that it requires a team of multiple experts with strongly varying backgrounds for designing the interface of a technical hypertext. For example, we have discussed the need of a professional designer for the general layout, for good typography, color design and so on in the above listed issues. Below, we will see that domain experts (for example: implementors of software) and technical writers should also be members of the interface development team, because of their deep understanding of the domain, and also computer scientists for efficient implementation and users for evaluating the hypertext interface.

A project where a designer, several computer scientists and technical writers were involved is described in (Zeis, Meusel 1993).

3 Constructing a Context-Sensitive Hypertextual Help System

The following principles and guidelines are proposed for constructing a system of linked help texts forming a hypertext. They were developed in a hypertext project at Siemens Nixdorf and served as a common denominator of the authors writing help texts for the UNIX desktop SINIX/windows User Environment. They concentrate on the needs of an on-line technical documentation being an integral part of the software and being primarily accessed asking for context-sensitive help on a visible software component. They address the issue of constructing a structured skeleton beyond the visual interface from the perspective of a pragmatic solution.

3.1 Principles for Structuring a System of linked Help Texts

The following principles are proposed for designing the structure of the hypertextual help system. Primarily they are principles valid as a starting point for the coordination of authors and making decisions in the large and only secondarily apply for writers dealing with detailed problems. The principles closely relate to the principles for the design of the X Window System as found in the book "X Window System" by Robert W. Scheifler and James Gettys, 1990.

- It is as important to decide what a system is not, as to decide what it is. Do not serve all the world's needs; rather, make the system of help texts extensible so that additional needs can be met in an upwardly compatible fashion.
- Isolate complexity as much as possible.
- The only thing worse than generalizing a design from one example is generalizing from no examples at all.
- If a design problem for the system of help texts is not completely understood, it is probably best to provide no design solution at all.
- If you can get 90 percent of the desired effect for 10 percent of the work, use the simpler solution.
- Provide global structure rather than local structure and wording. In particular, place local structure and wording in the writer's hands.
- Do not add any new link type, or help texts of a new information type unless a reader cannot complete a real task without it.

3.2′   Guidelines for Writing a System of Linked Help Texts

The following guidelines are for writing the help-system contents, that is, writing texts and linking texts to one another. Note that the first two guidelines already mentioned as principles are mentioned again because of their importance for both activities, structuring and writing.

- If you can get 90 percent of the desired effect for 10 percent of the work, use the simpler solution.
- Keep the structure of the system of help texts simple.

Guidelines related to Information Types

- Differentiate between two information types in the system of help texts:
  usage-oriented information: that is, information on style-guide conformant
      general usage of a style-guide conformant general controls. Information
      on the usage of file-selection boxes, dialog boxes, radio buttons, scroll
      bars are examples of usage-oriented information.
  task-oriented information: that is, information on work items whereby the user
      can manage his or her tasks. That might be an overview for each
      window, desktool, or similarly complex interface component - giving an
      application-specific outlook to the tasks the user can accomplish by using
      that interface component. Or it might be context-sensitive help for the
      specific button, menu entry, or similarly simple interface component -
      giving a precise and very narrow application-specific help on the actions
      the user can perform using that component in that context. If well-
      designed and well-written, you can reuse the help texts giving the

detailed description of the tasks mentioned in the overviews for context-sensitive help.
- Keep conceptual descriptions as short as possible. Provide the writer of the manual with information on your needs for conceptual descriptions.

Guidelines related to Help Text Contents

- Keep help texts short - preferably a single, visible help screen.
- Keep help texts self-contained.
- Balance between self-containment and shortness of help texts.
- Provide referenciable help texts on topics that are foreseeable common to a group of help texts.
- Be aware of reusability issues: Do not use application-specific wording if wording of a higher-level abstraction suffices.
- Be specific: Inform the user about the tasks he or she can manage using the active component of the user interface he or she requested help for. Do not tell him or her about the tasks he or she could do if he or she activated another component.
- Ensure that the points of entrance to the system of help texts are well-designed.
- Concentrate on the writing of a help text more whenever the user is more likely to use it.
- Whenever possible use the heading "Using <a control>" for help texts providing usage-oriented information, e.g., "Using a File-Selection Box". Do not use that heading for help texts providing task-oriented information.
- Whenever possible use the heading "<Working on> <an Object>" for help texts providing task-oriented information, e.g. "Opening a File" or "Deleting a File". Ideally "<Working on>" is a precise verbal phrase for an action the user can perform on the object. Do not use that heading for help texts providing usage-oriented information.

Guidelines related to Links between Help Texts

- Provide the user with links that are meaningful to him or her in the situation he or she is currently in when reading the help text.
- Be aware of the tendency that meaningfulness of links in a help text is greatly influenced by the overall number of links provided.
- Provide the user with an orientation on the structure of the system of help texts. For example, table of contents, overviews, a consistent usage of paths, and the like.
- Provide the user with a recognizable path from task-oriented information to usage-oriented information.
- Do not provide a link from a help text providing usage-oriented information to a help text providing task-oriented information.
- Be consistent in your usage of links giving access to general purpose features of the system of help texts. For example, links to glossary entries, to the table of contents, or links from help texts providing task-oriented to help texts on usage-oriented information. In particular, pay attention to the following three guidelines.
- Only use links of a predefined set of types.
- Try to visualize the type of a link.
- Always visualize the links of one type in the same way, concerning representation and placement within a help text.

3.3 The First Steps to Construct a Context-Sensitive Hypertextual Help System

This part proposes a procedure for the steps one could take to write a system of linked help texts forming a hypertext that is primarily accessed by asking for context-sensitive help from within a software module.

1. Identify the points of entrance to the system of help texts: a help menu in windows, a help button in dialog boxes and context-sensitive help for every user identifiable component (or group of components) of the user interface telling the user what he or she can accomplish by using the component.
2. Identify the topics to cover.
3. Match the points of entrance with the topics. Identify additional topics resulting from unmatched points of entrance.
4. Decide on the global structure of the hypertext (the books and chapters to use the book metaphor). The global structure is determined by hypertext subnets, each corresponding to one topic.
5. Try to reuse help texts.
6. Try to figure out the necessary number of help texts for each topic. Balance between completeness (of information) and time (necessary to read the information). You might want to split a topic into several topics if you get more than 10 help texts out of it.

7. Organize the system of help texts for each topic in a hierarchical tree-like way just as you do it in a technical text using decimal classification (chapter 1.1.1.1).
8. Decide on the number of tree levels.
9. Decide on the help texts for each topic (the paragraphs to stick to the book metaphor).
10. Decide on the way the user gets full information.
11. Decide on the way the user gets an overview on the information available.
12. Decide on the source structure of your system of help texts.
13. Write the help texts, include keywords, links, and the like. When writing the help texts, be aware of the seven issues mentioned in the second chapter of this paper.

4 Summary

In this paper, we proposed principles and guidelines for the design and presentation of hypertext in the application area of technical documentation. Although coming from different approaches - one concentrating on stand-alone hypertext applications, one concentrating on the integration of hypertext features in a software-integrated context-sensitive help system - the principles and guidelines proposed complement each other in a natural way. We first gave a survey on issues related to the presentation of the hypertext structure, thereby addressing the interface the reader of a hypertext encounters. Thereafter, we presented a pragmatic solution how to provide a structured skeleton beyond the visual interface, thereby addressing the interface the author of a hypertext deals with.

Acknowledgments. We want to express our gratitude to Frank Zebner for all the fruitful discussions on our hypertext interfaces. Due to his improvements, we could give successful presentations on conferences in Milano, Zürich and Seattle. We also want to thank the members of our groups and our students for their contributions to the ideas presented in this paper.

5 References

Caloini, A. (1992). 'Matching Hypertext Models to Hypertext systems: a Compilative Approach'; Proceedings of the 4th ACM Conference on Hypertext, p. 91-101, ACM Press, Milano - Italy, November 30 - December 4, 1992

Eickemeyer, K. (1992). 'Vom Buch zur Online-Hilfe, Links inklusive'; Vortrag auf der Hypertext/Hypermedia'92 / München, in: Cordes/Streitz, Informatik Aktuell, Springer-Verlag, September 1992

Glowalla, U., Hasebrook, J., Häfele, G. (1993). 'Implementation und Evaluation computerunterstützter Aus- und Weiterbildung mit dem Hypermedia-System MEM'; in: Frei, Schäuble (Hrsg.): "Hypermedia", 1993, Springer-Verlag

Garzotto, F., Paolini,P., Schwabe, D. (1991). `HDM - A model for the design of hypertext applications', Proceedings of the 3rd ACM Conference on Hypertext, pp. 313-328, San Antonio, Texas, December 1991

Hofmann, M. (1993). 'Richtlinien als Hilfsmittel für die Erzeugung von Hypertexten'; Proceedings tekom Online'93, München, Oktober 1993

Hofmann, M., Glowalla, U. (1993). 'Hypermedia Interfaces for Commercial Applications'; Position Paper, Workshop on Methodological Issues of the Design of Hypertext-based User Interfaces, GMD-IPSI, Darmstadt, July 13 - 14, 1993

Kahn, P. (1992). 'Visual Logic - User Interface Guidelines for Language Software Products', Houghton Mifflin Company / Software Division, IRIS / Brown University, Dynamic Diagrams, Houghton Mifflin Company 1992

Kahn, P., Lenk, K. (1992). 'Designing Information for the Computer Screen' (Tutorial T11) and 'Hypertext Readability' (Panel), ECHT '92, Milano, Italy, December 1992

Meusel, K., Baltes, H. (1993). 'Online-Dokumentation mit strukturiertem Hypertext: Wirtschaftlichkeit und Richtlinien zur Gestaltung des Front-Ends'; Tekom Online 1993

Meusel, K., Schröcksnadl, B., Schiff, J. (1993). 'Orientierung und Navigation in strukturierten Hyperdokumenten', Tagungsband der Hypermedia'93 / Zürich, Informatik Aktuell, Springer-Verlag, März 1993

Pogarell, R. (1993). 'Corporate Identity in der Sprache technischer Dokumente'; tekom Nachrichten 2.93, München/Stuttgart, Juni 1993

Reiter, D., Roller, D. (1993). 'Erschließung von Information und Wissen: Verfahren zur dynamischen Aggregation von Hypertrails'; in: Frei, Schäuble (Hrsg.): "Hypermedia", 1993, Springer-Verlag

Rockley, A. (1992). 'Designing Online Documentation with the Aid of Hypertext'; Tutorial, ECHT '92, Mailand

Scheifler, R. W., Gettys, J. (1990). 'X Window System'; Digital Press, 1990

Schiff, J., Meusel, K. (1992). 'Informationszugriff in strukturierten Hyperdokumenten'; GI Ergonomie und Informatik, Themenheft Multimedia, Stuttgart, November 1992

Schiff, J., Schröcksnadl, B., Meusel, K. (1992). 'Anwendungsmodellierung auf der Basis eines Hypertext Design Modells'; 2.Tagung Technische Dokumentation: Anforderungen, Technologien, Werkzeuge, Lösungen; Siemens, Nbg-M, Februar 1992

Schiff, J., Garzotto, F., Schröcksnadl, B., Meusel, K. (1993). 'Experiences and Results from Esprit Project HYTEA (HYperTExt Authoring)'; Proceedings of 18th Annual International Conference with Summer School: IT and Programming, Sofia, Bulgaria, 27.06-04.07.1993

Schmitz, L., Meusel, K. (1991). 'SmallCard - ein Hypertext-System zur Erstellung rechnergestützter Lerneinheiten', Hypertext/Hypermedia'91 / Graz, Informatik-Fachberichte 276, Seite 266 ff., Mai '91

Schröcksnadl, B., Meusel, K. (1992). 'Benutzerdokumentation von Anwender-Software mit strukturiertem Hypertext', 3.Tekom Fachtagung für Online-Dokumentation in Stuttgart/Böblingen, Nov. 1992

Schröcksnadl, B., Meusel, K., Thüring, M. (1992). *'HYTEA Technical Documentation: Application requirements; User manual of the forms processing system SIFORM'*, Esprit Project 5252, Deliverable D4.1, February 1992

Schröcksnadl, B., Meusel, K., Zucker, W., Schiff, J., Thüring, M. (1992). *'Hypertext Application Design using a Model-Based Approach'*, Kurzvortrag und Systemvorführung auf der Hypertext/Hypermedia'92 / München, Informatik Aktuell, Springer-Verlag, September 1992

Zeis, P., Meusel, K. (1993). *'Werkzeug für Informationsstrukturierung und optimale Hypertext-Navigation in mit ToolBook erzeugten Katalogen'*, 3.Tagung Technische Dokumentation, Siemens, Mch-P, 22. und 23.März 1993

HIFI - Hypertext interface to external databases

Umberto Cavallaro
Systems & Management S.p.A., Turin, Italy

1 Introduction

HIFI is the ESPRIT Project within the IPSS area (Information-Processing Systems and Software) that organised the Workshop on "Methodological issues of the Design of Hypertext-based User Interfaces"; from that Workshop held in Darmstadt (Germany) on July 13-14th, 1993, the current book has been originated.

The purpose of HIFI is to provide a hypertext-based navigational front-end to external heterogeneous, possibly pre-existing, databases managed by conventional DBMSs [Cav93a, Cav93b].

Information systems currently found are based on a variety of tools and often use database technology; They usually have no mechanism to support a hypertext-like navigational style of accessing the information: they are rather based on predefined access paradigms, like queries (relational databases) or pointers (object-oriented databases).

Hypertext tools, on the other hand, provide interactive navigation to access heterogeneous bodies of information. The intuitiveness of their approach is one of the key factors for the success of these tools which are becoming quite popular in business, education and entertainment applications. On the negative side they are usually conceived as managing their own internal information base and often they lack the efficiency and robustness of the database systems.

HIFI's goal is to combine these two technologies.

Few existing tools already allow a hypertext-like access to SQL database. The main problem with this approach is that the resulting hypertext application has the same structure as the underlying database's schema, without the possibility of adapting it to reader needs. This implies that, in general, the resulting application is difficult to be used or to be navigated through. As a further limitation, different multimedia databases cannot be accessed, unless specific ad-hoc programs are developed.

HIFI provides instead an environment where the hypertext interface has its own conceptual and visual structure, defined according to the reader needs, rather than determined by the structure of the pre-existing databases. In addition both relational and multimedia databases, are accessible via the same Hypertext interface.

The front-end interface is logically independent of the external databases' structure and implementation. It is described in terms of the high level primitives of HDM -- Hypertext Design Model [Sch92, Gar93] -- which was defined as an outcome of the Esprit Project 5252 HYTEA. One of the results of the HIFI project has been to produce HDM+ [HIFI93a], as an extension of the original HDM primitives, in order to meet the requirements of innovative applications that manage in a hypertext style both formatted and non-formatted data.

2 HIFI Architecture

One of the purposes of the HIFI tools is to provide a generic technology [HIFI93b] allowing to access external information systems (either consisting of formatted data or multimedia) from an hypertext interface designed according to the HDM+ model.

We assume that the external information system and the structure of the underlying database do pre-exist, and have a structure that cannot be modified. This does not exclude that, since the external information system is a living application, data are frequently updated, implemented and modified, using the usual database management facilities in their "native" environment.

In the current version, HIFI assumes that formatted data are managed with the relational technology, which has the largest share of the market[1]. It is less obvious to find the equivalent of relational databases for multimedia data, since there is no universally acknowledged standard in this area. For the time being, HIFI assumes, as multimedia data manager, OVM [Chr92] developed by one of the partners of the consortium.

For flexibility and portability reasons, currently available GUI tools will be also used as to manage the hypertext interface.

The core of the technical approach is to define a set of application-independent mappings between HDM+ primitives and database primitives. These mappings are used in different ways: to materialize hypertext objects, i.e. to provide the actual contents and connections of the hypertext network, and to interpret the hypertext operations of navigation and query in terms of database operations.

---

[1]Extensions to include O-O database technology have been investigated. The implementation has not been scheduled since, for the time being, OODB represent only a negligeable fraction of the market.

HIFI architecture is based upon two distinct levels: the Definition Level and the Execution Level. The Definition Level is used off-line by the application designer while the Execution Level is used on-line by the reader.

2.1 The Definition Environment

The Definition Environment provides a set of tools to define the HDM+ specifications of the hypertext interface.

An HIFI application requires a number of different definitions, which can be classified in different categories:
- Interface Definitions, describing how the application will be "perceived" by the reader
- General Mapping Definitions, describing the global features of the mapping between the hypertext interface and the databases
- Data Application Definitions, describing the Relational DB's schema
- Multimedia Application Definitions, describing the multimedia database.

During the definition phase all these definitions are inserted in the HIFI repository. In the subsequent configuration phase, such definitions are "downloaded" from the repository, and made available to the different execution tools, in the proper format.

2.2 The Execution Environment

The reader accesses an HIFI application through the Interface Manager (IM) which provides the basic mechanism for processing and executing a user request. In order to satisfy the user-request, the IM may need database information; if this is the case, the IM sends a request to the underlying modules. A communication protocol -- in which a number of database-independent primitives are embedded -- addresses this request to the General Mapping Manager.

The request is interpreted by the General Mapping Manager (GMM) which splits up the IM request into requests for the proper database managers.

If Multimedia data are involved, a request is sent to the Multimedia HIFI Manager (MHM); if relational data are instead involved, the request is processed by the Relational HIFI Manager (RHM).

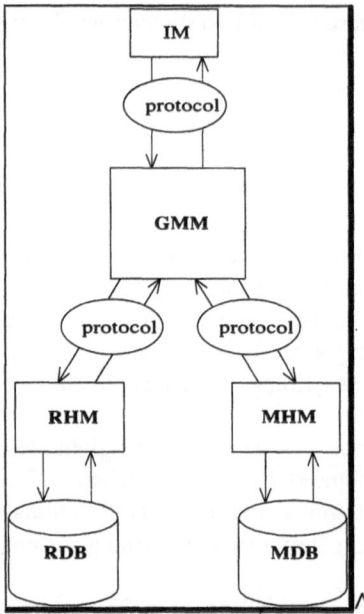

Figure 1: HIFI Execution Level

The RHM, after evaluating the complexity of the query, calculates accordingly the criteria for the query strategy, and finally produces and executes the query statement.

In order to perform its tasks, the MHM makes use of a set of definitions derived from the repository. It may try to satisfy the GMM request using information already available in its own buffer. If this is not possible, a query is issued to the multimedia database.

The data selected either by RHM or by MHM are then reorganised, by the GMM in order to build the wished HDM+ Objects which are finally returned to the IM.

3 Real-life Applications

To demonstrate the validity of the HIFI approach, three different prototype applications have been developed in the project [HIFI93c]: the first belonging to the banking world, the second to the industrial environment, the third involving a cultural institution.

The banking application provides financial consultants and salespeople with a means making it easier to customize the new banking services.

In order to effectively carry out his work, the salesperson must access a number of information contained in the bank databases: the current situation of the customer account, the available financial services, the monetary trends. In other words, he must have an exhaustive knowledge of customers, services, and general economic situation. As those information are scattered, and for many aspects, unrelated, in the bank information system, the HIFI application provides him an easy-to-use interactive navigation environment.

The medical application aims to develop an interactive hospital information system both for patients and for the medical staff. The information system is restricted in two dimensions: the type of users and the type of the domain. For this pilot application patient and medical staff have been selected as users while a orthopedics has been selected as domain. The data to be interfaced are stored in an SQL database. Additional data describe specific medical knowledge, e.g. what is the impact of the medical treatment of a certain patient. Data are potentially multimedia.

The Benaki Museum application aims at implementing an electronic exhibit on "Gold of Greece". The Benaki Museum owns perhaps the best representative collection of Greek jewelry in the world. The "Gold of Greece" exhibition organised by the Benaki Museum in collaboration with the Dallas Museum of Art, has already generated great interest in the North American and European museums where it appeared during the last two years. Benaki does not envisage hosting the exhibition in Athens in the near future. Hence the opportunity of the electronic exhibit .

The exhibition and its documentation are organised chronologically. For each period, a short introductory text provides the historical, cultural and technological context for the examination of each of the artefacts exhibited. A longer text provides additional scholarly information.

Acknowledgements: HIFI is being developed by a Consortium consisting of four Partners (Systems & Management - Italy, Epsilon - Greece, Siemens - Germany, Syntax Sistemi Software - Italy) and four Associated Partners (Benaki Museum - Greece, GMD/IPSI - Germany, Music/Forth - Greece, Politecnico di Milano - Italy).

References

[Cav93a]   Cavallaro U., Paolini P. "HIFI: Hypertext Interface For Information - Relational and Multimedia Databases" in "The Electronic Libraries", Apr. 1993, Vol 11, no. 2, p. 65-72

[Cav93b]   Cavallaro U., Garzotto F., Paolini P., Totaro D. "HIFI: Hypertext Interface For Information Systems" in "IEEE Software", Nov. 1993, Vol. 10, no. 6, p.48-51

[Chr92]   Christodoulakis S., Ailamaki A., Fragonikolakis M., Kapetanakis G., Koveos L. "An Object-oriented Architecture for Multimedia Information Systems", in "IEEE Data Engineering Bulletin", Sept. 1991

[Gar93]   Garzotto, F., Paolini, P., Schwabe, D., "HDM: a Model-based Approach to Hypermedia Application Design" in "ACM Trans. Information Systems", Jan. 1993, Vol. 11, n. 1, p. 1-26.

[HIFI93a] "HIFI - The Hypertext Interface Model" (Deliverable 2), Athens-Munich-Torino, June 1993, 80 pp.

[HIFI93b] "HIFI Tools: Specification and Design" (Deliverable 3), Athens-Munich-Torino, June 1993, 180 pp.

[HIFI93c] "HIFI Applications: Specification and Design" (Deliverable 5), Athens-Munich-Torino, June 1993, 240 pp.

[Sch92]   Schwabe, D., Caloini, A., Garzotto, F., Paolini, P., "Hypertext Development using a Model-based Approach", in "Software Practice and Experience" November 1992, Vol. 22, n. 11, p. 937-962

The ESPRIT Project HIFI Medical Application

Karin Hertwig
Siemens AG, Munich, Germany

Abstract. The medical application HYNECOS deals with hypertext navigation on an electronic patient record in the orthopedic ward section. Additionally, specific ward data (such as ward plans etc.) and textbook knowledge (e.g. [KSW92]) may be accessed. The final version of HYNECOS will base on different database systems like RDBMSs, OODBMSs, and document management systems. Different user groups (in the moment: doctors, nurses; planned: students, patients) will access this information pool with the intention to satisfy their specific information, navigation, and access needs.

1 Problems and requirements

One of the main problems occurring during the development of HYNECOS origins from the area's high level of heterogeneity. Medical information bases on heterogeneous information sources (e.g. relational databases, document management systems, multimedia data pools, text files containing background information etc.). Different user groups are involved to create and/or access the same information pool (patients, doctors, nurses, administration, students). This implies new problems like data security, decentralised data collection, multiple data registration, consistency problems, and the need to provide different views of the different information.

The creation and/or access of information happens for different purposes (e.g. to gain actual patient information data from the databases, to generate or inspect statistics, to achieve background information, CBT, combination with knowledge based systems, to get help for a certain task. In order to support openness, a satisfying medical information system must run on different target systems (Toolbook, Frame Maker, Guide...) and on different platforms (mainframes, UNIX servers, workstations, PCs, notebooks etc.).

The majority of suppliers and target users of HYNECOS are not accustomed to ambitious computer systems. Therefore, (see [STh92]), it is necessary for the system developers to collaborate closely with representatives of all involved user groups. This implies a lot of difficulties during the whole development process, but it represents the only means which helps to achieve a satisfying user acceptance of the system.

Another serious problem which occurred during the development of the first HYNECOS version was to find a common language which could help reducing misunderstandings between the areas of medicine and information technologies. Therefore it was (and will be in the future, too) absolutely necessary to perform enough discussions and interviews in order to understand each other.

2 Description of the medical application

As a result of our interviews and discussions, for our first HYNECOS version we decided to confine ourselves to the two user groups of doctors and nurses.

On the orthopedic ward section for doctors and nurses, essentially information about the patients (=> patient records), ward specific information, information about the staff, and theoretic background (=> lexicon") knowledge seem to be important. This information is interlinked on a high degree.

Patient data consists of basic data, course data (consisting of cases, diagnosises and tables for anamnesis, diagnostic results, and therapy measures), and medical reports. Basic data includes an "abstract" about the patient (containing a photo and the most important patient data at one glance) and other general data about the patient (e.g. personal data or specialties). The information sub category course data consists of such kind of patient information which is necessary to document the course of the diseases (i.e. date and character of the topical anamnesis, diagnostic measures, operations, treatment measures, nursing actions, diagnosises and cases belonging to a certain patient). Graphics showing the course of certain diagnostic measures (e.g. temperature, blood-pressure, pulse, mobility) may be attached to such a description. Reports and letters (e.g. diagnosis reports, operation reports, medical letters between different physicians) form the last type of information belonging to a patient.

Staff data contains a collection of helpful information about the staff of the clinic. There are individual photos of doctors and nurses, important telephone numbers, responsibilities and department names.

Ward data consists of general information, ward plans and ward tables. Ward plans illustrate the current bed occupation of a certain ward. Ward tables visualise the various (nursing or therapy) activities occurring on a ward for the different patients. For both ward tables and ward plans there are overviews and detailed views available.

Lexicon knowledge represents a theoretic basis for the actual events on a ward. It consists of entries for both diagnosis descriptions and method descriptions. All entries contain a general description, specialties, tables, and pictures. Attached to a diagnosis description the reader can find lists of suitable diagnostic methods and therapy proposals. In the reverse case, each method description may contain a list of all possible diagnosises.

Both doctors and nurses want to access this information for different purposes (e.g. individual visits, staff exchange, to-do-lists for nurses, decisions about therapies). Generally, every doctor and every nurse must be able to access all information about their patients. But for normal purposes they prefer to use different variants of the system supporting their (role and situation) specific needs.

There was one point, which turned out to be essential for the representatives of both user groups. Instead of getting an expert system telling them what to do they would prefer to work with an information system giving them all required information but leaving the decision what to do up to them.

3 Model of the medical application

As mentioned before, we used a model-based approach, namely HDM+ (Hypertext Design Mode), see [CGP93]), to fix the structural and navigation specific characteristics of HYNECOS. In the following section a simplified form of HDM has been chosen to represent the model.

In order to classify the different characteristics of a hypertext system, we distinguish between entity types and link types. Entity types represent the structural aspects of a system, link types represent its navigation possibilities

Entity types correspond to the nodes of a hypertext system and contain structured data. In order to define adequate entity types for a system, it is necessary to divide the whole available information into expressive classes. Other than entity types of a data model, these information classes do not have to contain disjunctive information or data. On the contrary, by defining them, the system engineer considers already the different access requirements and purposes by combining the same information to different supersets. Within a second step, these entity types are further divided by using hierarchical structures.

As a result of our discussions and data analysis, we divided the information pool of HYNECOS into the following information categories which represent the entity types of the system:

```
- patient      => basic data
                      => overview
                      => personal data
               => course
                      => cases
                      => diagnosises
                      => anamnesis
                                     => general questions
                                     => former diseases
```

```
                                        => family diseases
                                        => risk factors

- patient            => diagnostic results
                                        => current anamnesis
                                        => clinical results
                                        => apparatus results
                                        => invasive results
                                        => consultations
                     => therapy
                                        => operations
                                        => conservative
                                        => care
            => reports
                     => medical letters
                     => operation reports

- staff     => basic data
                     => overview
                     => personal data
                     => competencies

- ward      => ward plans
            => ward tables

- lexicon   => diagnosis descriptions
                     => overview
                     => diagnostic methods
                     => therapy methods
                     => specialties
                     => prognosis
                     => tables
                     => pictures
            => method descriptions
                     => overview
                     => indication
                     => proceeding
                     => complications
                     => specialties
                     => tables
                     => pictures
```

Link types represent the connections and navigation possibilities between the different entity types.

A so-called topic relation matrix (see [ThS92]) visualises link types of HYNECOS. They base on the high level relations between the different entity types.

==>	patient	staff	ward	diagnosis_ dsc	method_dsc
patient		is_treated_ by	lies_at	suffers_ at	is_treated_ with_method
staff	treats_ patient		workes_at	treats_ diagnosis	uses_method
ward	treats_ patient	employs_ staff		treats_ diagnosis	uses_method
diagno-sis_dsc	belongs_ to_patient	is_treated_ by_staff	is_treated_ at_ward		is_treated_ with_method
method_ dsc	is_used_ for_patient	is_used_ at_staff	is_used_ at_ward	is_used_ for_ diagnosis	

Table 1

4 The user interface of HYNECOS

"The simpler the user interface (together with a constant functionality), the more reliable the user acceptance."

In order to follow to this theory, every template of HYNECOS (except of full-screen images) consists of the following visualisation elements:

The navigation bar is situated on the top of each page and serves for browsing and structural navigation purposes within the system. It consists of one index column (left side) and three local navigation columns. Each index of the index column corresponds to one of the four entity types patient, staff, ward, and lexicon. By double-clicking on one of these indices, the user can access the desired index page from each arbitrary page. For navigating within the hierarchical structure of an entity type the user can browse through the information hierarchy by successively clicking on the desired subtypes (from the left to the right side). As long as no new selection happens the user may browse arbitrarily though the upper navigation line without changing his current position.

The button bar is situated on the bottom of each page and serves for non-structural navigation purposes. It always contains a help button with a general explanation of the orientation possibilities, a telephone list of the clinic, and an undo-button. On some pages it additionally contains a search-button, an index-button, and some other buttons for leaving forwards and backwards.

The marginal column is situated on the left side of each page and offers additional navigation facilities. If necessary, it may contain sorting criteria and keyword-based text references to other pages (if these references, for visualisation reasons, are not situated within the contents window).

The contents window covers the rest of each page. Apart of the actual information, it may also provide non-structural navigation by offering "sensitive fields". In the upper part of the contents field the current position is visible.

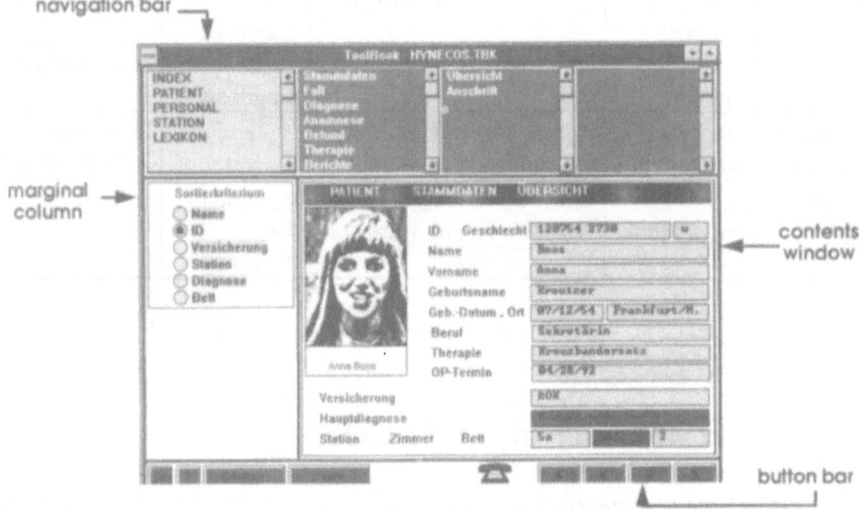

Figure 1: Patient template

The above picture 1 shows a typical example for a schema of a patient template with a (comparing to traditional hypertext applications) quite simple layout. The current position of this template is "patient - basic data - overview".

By double-clicking on one of the indices the user will get to an index page and be able to choose either a certain patient, a certain staff member, a specific ward or a lexicon entry. After having chosen such an instance he can start navigating within its individual data structures.

In the following picture 2 the structure of the patient subtype "diagnostic results" is visualised. This template shows a list of laboratory results of a patient. It is reached by hierarchically clicking on "diagnostic results - apparatus results - laboratory". This strategy also works when the user wants to change to another index (picture 3):

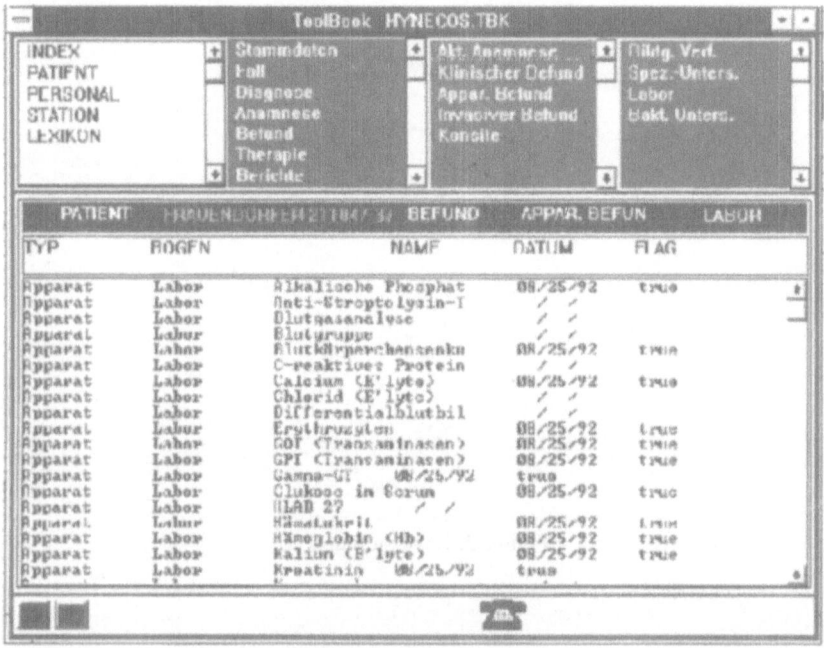

Figure 2: Diagnostic results

The following steps have been necessary to navigate to the former template:
a) Double-clicking on the "index lexicon" and choosing "Gonarthrose"
b) Navigating hierarchically through the information of "Gonarthrose"'

Non-structural navigation happens by clicking on a button. In the left column so-called key-words can be selected in order to navigate to the actual explanation (e.g. within the lexicon). By clicking on "Arthrose" in the lower part of the left margin the user can reach another lexicon page explaining the topic "Arthrose". Another possibility is clicking on sensitive fields such as the beds in our patient example. The result can be seen on the next template (figure 4) which shows the plan of the ward where the patient stays.

Each template possesses the same "pixel-exact" profile. Therefore the learning process for new users will be very quick.

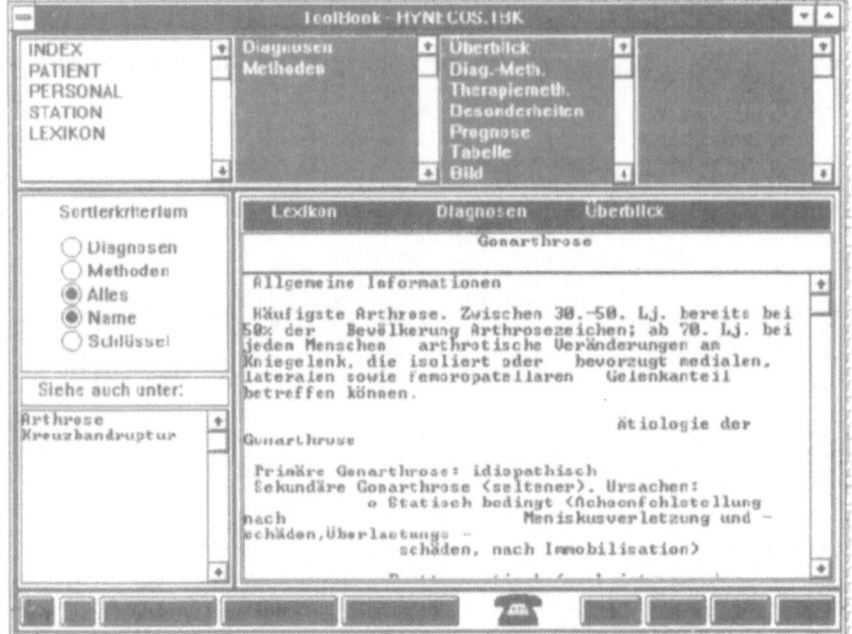

Figure 3: Lexicon Index

5 Methodological approach

The development of HYNECOS happens in a close cooperation with the Orthopedic Clinic of Heidelberg, one of the most important orthopedic clinics in Germany. Together with professional consultants and software developers they are
going to create a global system architecture which is supposed to cover and integrate the requirements of the whole hospital.

As contribution for HIFI, the structure of HYNECOS follows to a model-based
approach (see [CGP93]). That means that there exists a scheme specifying and
typifying the structural elements (nodes and links) of the system. These structural
elements are basing on existing data models of the clinic. By using a model
based approach, the development of adequate tools will be supported.

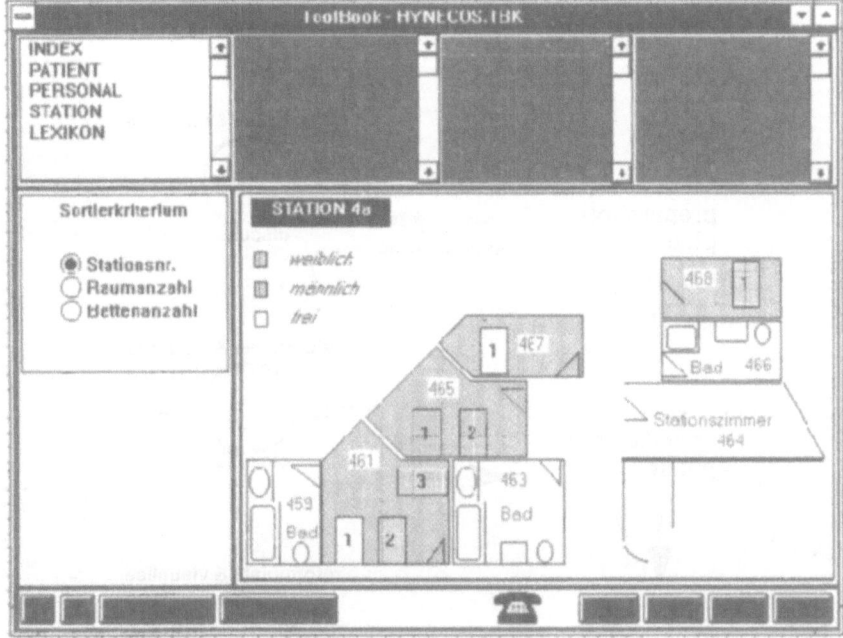

Figure 4: Ward plan

During the development of HYNECOS, together with representatives of the different user groups (doctors, nurses, students) we carried out numerous interviews and discussions in order to achieve a detailed knowledge about the required data structures and their working scenarios. We made the following experiences:

• Different experts often have different opinions about a problem and its best solution. From our experience the most efficient and diplomatic proceeding is the following:

  a) we <u>discuss</u> with all experts in order to understand the different opinions
  b) we <u>choose</u> the most suitable alternative (or a compromise) on our own
  c) we <u>reformulate</u> and <u>visualise</u> the results (sometimes we even sketch a Toolbook page)
  d) we <u>present</u> them to the experts as a basis for further discussions

• This cyclic process may happen at each phase of the development process of the application, even at the preparation phase. Nevertheless it includes specification of a solution, a concrete model, and even considerations about the layout of the user interface. The following picture shows this process:

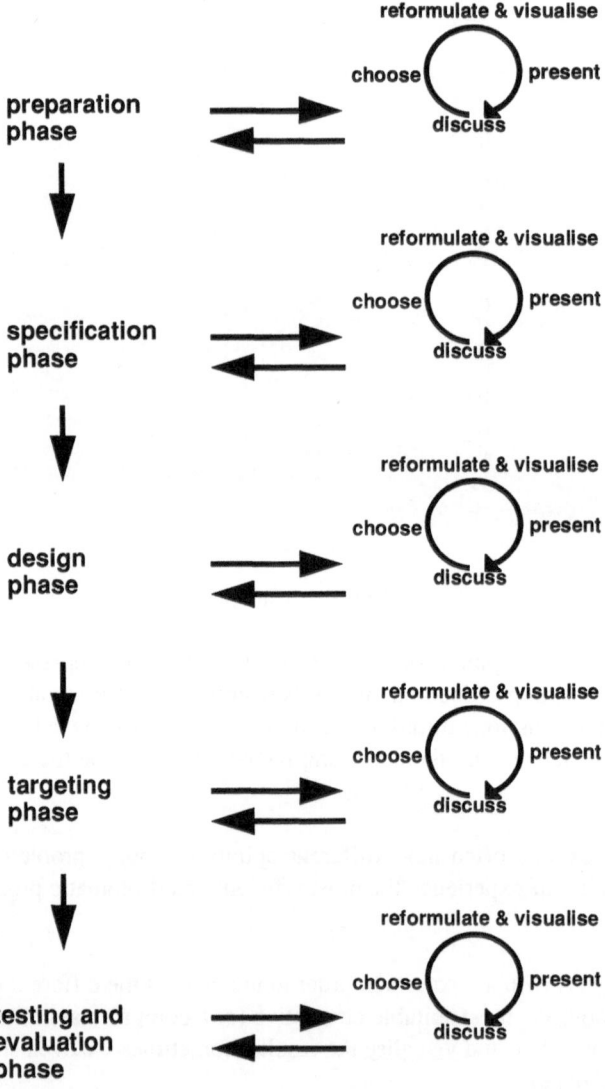

Figure 5: Cyclic design process

6 Outlook

First discussions made clear that in general, doctors and nurses refuse to accept expert systems which force the user to a certain action. What they really want are information systems which support their daily work by offering all necessary information but leave the decision, what to do, to the human user.

By combining actual patient information with multimedia data and background information, the existing information pool can be used for both daily life tasks and computer based training. Our next step will be the definition of a user model basing on different persons, jobs, tasks, and levels.

The current prototype version of HYNECOS has been implemented in Toolbook 1,5 and DBASE3 running under MS WINDOWS. The platform for the final HYNECOS version has not been fixed yet, but it will surely base on different databases. In the moment the problem of data security is solved by holding sensitive data locally and using lockable PCs. In the future this problem will be of increasing importance and we will try to use sufficient database mechanisms as far as possible. But of course this problem has not been solved yet and it will be necessary to consider additional mechanisms as well.

7 References

[CGP93]   U. Cavallaro, F. Garzotto, P. Paolini, M. Totaro: "HIFI - Hypertext Interface for Information: A Model-Based Approach" Contribution to Esprit Project HIFI, Torino - Milano, 1993

[GMP92]   F. Garzotto, L. Mainetti, P. Paolini, D. Zivieri:
"HDM User Manual - Version 2"
Contribution to Esprit Project HYTEA, Politecnico di Milano, 1992

[KSW92]   K.-L. Krämer, M. Stock, M. Winter: "Klinikleitfaden Orthopädie"
JungjohannVerlagsgesellschaft, Neckarsulm - Stuttgart, März 1992

[Hor89]   R. Horn: "Mapping HyperText"
Information Mapping Inc, Waltham, MA 02154, 1989

[Hor92]   R. Horn: "How high can it fly?"
Information Mapping Inc, Waltham, MA 02154, 1992

[MSS93]   K. Meusel, J. Schiff, B. Schröcksnadel: "Orientierung und Navigation in strukturierten Hyperdokumenten" Proceedings of the International Hypermedia'93 Conference, Zürich 1993

[Nie90]   J. Nielsen: "The Art of Navigating through Hypertext"
Hypertext and Hypermedia, Academic Press, 1990

[STh92]   W. Schuler, M. Thüring: "PHD: A Methodology for Pragmatical Hypertext Design", Esprit Project HYTEA, GMD Darmstadt, 1992.
Also as "Pragmatical Hypertext Design (PHD)".
GMD -Bericht Nr. 813, January 1994

HIFINBIPOP - Hypertext Interface to FINancial data in BIPOP bank (Italy)

Umberto Cavallaro, Marco Tentori
Systems & Management S.p.A., Milan, Italy

1 Introduction

HIFINBIPOP is one of the three pilot applications implemented to field-test the validity of the HIFI approach [Cav93a, Cav93b]. It is implemented as a hypertextual interface to the complex information system of Banca Popolare di Brescia (BIPOP Bank).

BIPOP Bank in northern Italy has 45 branches. Its current information system is based on nine databases. An additional database to store simple multimedia data (such as customers' pictures and their signatures) is planned.

The main goal of the new interface [HIFI93c] is to support the marketing department in planning new services to be offered to the customers, and to provide salespeople with a mean making it easier to identify potentially interesting buyers and to offer them customized banking services (vs. pre-defined ones).

To do this, general information is needed about each customer, his family, and the business he is involved with; information about recent transactions he made, about the services he uses or could buy; commercial information about sales activities (visits paid to him, results obtained, etc.); and marketing information about special market conditions, monetary trends, competitors' activities and products or services which could be successfully proposed. The navigational interface also provides an easy way for monitoring the results of the sales activities in terms of product effectiveness, market achievements, salesperson's productivity and efficiency.

The set of HIFI tools [HIFI93b] offers an easy-to-use interactive navigational approach, enabling the user to explore links among the various institutional data and to freely navigate into the existing databases. Such a flexible approach excites the creative thinking of the banker (salesperson or marketing responsible) who is given the freedom of re-producing on the "navigational engine" his usual "thinking approach" and of correlating to this approach the presentation of the real data available into the bank information system. The network of links among the various applications are built up by emulating the analogical mental process. Starting from a first-level "mental map", the user can perform hierarchical searches and zoom into details as well as explore related nodes through non-linear searches and lateral movements.

2 User requirements and application goals

BIPOP Bank has often to cope with a number of different, non-integrated technologies. This is quite usual in banking organisations as a result of their early growth: banks have been among the first organisations to use the information technology to manage large amounts of data.

In the last decades significant computer tools (both HW -- terminals, and SW -- transactional applications) have been installed with the aim of speeding up repetitive operations. This requirement is today less important due to the diffusion of self-services both at individual and corporate level which, as a result, reduce the clerical involvement in the low-level transactions.

In the modified scenario, the need has arisen to tell information from data, and to synthesise new information from the available one.

Most of the currently available software procedures (mainly based on VSAM files and DL1 hierarchical databases) cover most of the subjects usually dealt with by banking applications (inquiries, cash operations, services' management, etc.)[1]. Each of these functions is self-contained, and satisfactorily fulfills the specific need.

The system however lacks of a global view on the available functions and does not allow a flexible navigation. It is not possible, for instance, to automatically fill up the input mask of a given application with data directly coming from another functionality or to merge in a unified view the information related both

---

[1] Examples of data currently managed by the applications of the Bank information system are as follows:

- customers personal data: name, address, age, job, etc.
  Both the current and old customers are maintained into the database;
- commercial information: average revenues, personal belongings, stocks, estates, other properties;
- accounting information, such as operations performed, etc.;
  (a chronological log of all the operations is maintained);
- conditions applied to customer;
- available services;
- services delivered to the customer;
- agenda of the visits (contacts) the salesperson has paid to the customer;
- description of products and their characteristics
- "relations" currently actuvated: bank account, credit cards, "pris" account, stock account, stocks, credit certificate, etc.

to, e.g., the bank account and the stock account of a given customer.

For obvious reasons the existing information system of the Bank cannot be modified. In fact HIFINBIPOP is not intended to replace the software procedures currently in use. Rather, it is conceived to smoothly be integrated into the available hardware and software environments, in order to provide a degree of interoperability among the existing heterogeneous platforms. Under this perspective, it can be seen as a systems integration tool.

As a main requirement, HIFINBIPOP is a 'customer-centric' application, where all the financial information available to the bank (account status, revenues, investments etc. which provide the Banker with the parameters for evaluating the risk incurred with each customer) are considered as being the customer attributes (which have in turn other attributes, and so on).

This originates in a hypertextual net, connecting the related information frames by means of associative links among meaningful pieces of information. By using a unique software application allowing to manage all the information on a given customer, the banker may
- get basic information about the customer,
- take a look at the customer's photograph and signature,
- accurately evaluate the current financial situation of the customer,
- get economic/commercial information about the customer (i.e., he already owns the house he lives in, or he has started with a PRIS account because he is going to buy a new car, how he uses to invest his money, etc.)
- identify the customer with respect to a number of commercial parameter
- present a spectrum of opportunities,
- find out the most appropriate investment solutions for the customer,
- plan an agenda of visits or contacts,
- etc.

Furthermore, since consultants and salesmen often also performs cashiers' tasks, the application must be able to manage usual banking activities, such as:
- cash operations,
- services management (credit cards, debit cards, etc.), ...

As a by-product of this approach, the customer himself could access, as an end-user, part of the same application, taking advantage from the friendliness of the hypertextual approach: the already existing BIPOP self-service points could be enriched with a subset of the functionality provided by HIFINBIPOP too.

3 Constraints analysis and methodological approach.

BIPOP's databases are often redundant: for historical reasons, the hierarchical databases used by the Bank have been implemented as self-standing data structures efficiently satisfying specific needs, without taking care of data already stored in other parallel applications.

As a result, information on such entities as, e.g., "customer" may be found in several databases with different formalisms. Therefore, a heavy normalisation task had first to be carried out, for our purposes.
In addition, since HIFI tools aim at interfacing SQL databases, the original data had to be transferred into a relational schema (first phase of the design).

This was performed through 5 steps:
1) application investigation and identification of the application requirements
2) identification of the main information categories required by the application
3) analysis of the existing databases and selection of the set of required data (attributes)
4) inside each set, identification of redundancies with the aim of extracting a unique definition for each of the retained attributes
5) mapping of the chosen attributes into the Entity/Relationship Model, describing the database architecture of the HIFINBIPOP application.

The final result is a normalised relation database schema. For multimedia data a multimedia database schema has been formalised. At the end of this analysis/definition's iterative process, five main data classes have been identified: "Customer", "Product", "Relation", "Salesman", "Visit". They are described in the Appendix.

The HIFI approach defines a hypertext interface according to the user needs rather than to the structure of the underlying database, and the two levels are logically independent from each other. Therefore the hypertextual model for navigation has been subsequently designed using the HDM+ (Hypermedia Design Model, enhanced) methodology [HIFI93a], defined within the project (second phase of the design).

Each entity type has been duly exploded in components and linked to the other relevant entity types. The resulting HDM+ model represents the hypertextual net and the navigational possibilities offered to the user.

By using a proper tool (CASE repository), a mapping has finally been defined between the Entity/Relationship Model and the HDM+ Model (third phase of the design). For each object at the Interface level a correspondence has been identified and established with elements in the underlying databases (table/attributes in the relational database, objects in the multimedia database).

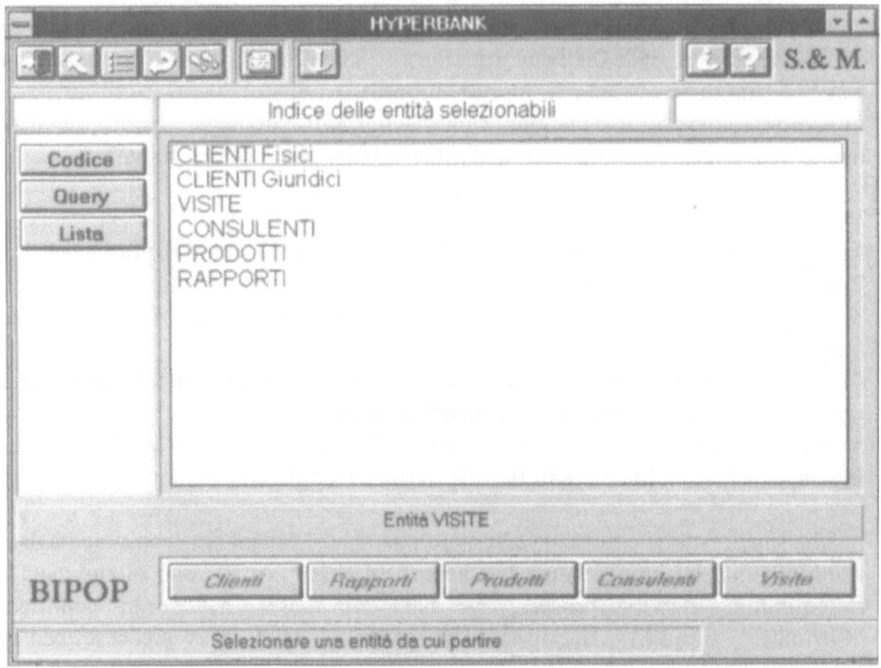

Figure 1: The main static Web index appears as default in the Index Page of the application

4 The User Interface

Special attention has been paid to the screen design and to the use of the colours and windows, in order to produce a simple yet powerful user interface, using a self-explanatory approach.

Minimal screen instructions are needed to activate the application and embark straight away on a search. Features are used consistently through the application, so that users become quickly familiar with them.

The features shown in Figure 2 are used consistently through the application, so that users become quickly familiar with them. In the main window appears the information actually retrieved from the database (in this case, the personal data of the customer): On the top are shown the system buttons, on the left the buttons for the structural navigation   (different perspectives for the same entity "Customer"), at the bottom the buttons for the applicative navigation (exploration of the other entities -- when relevant -- related to the current one:)

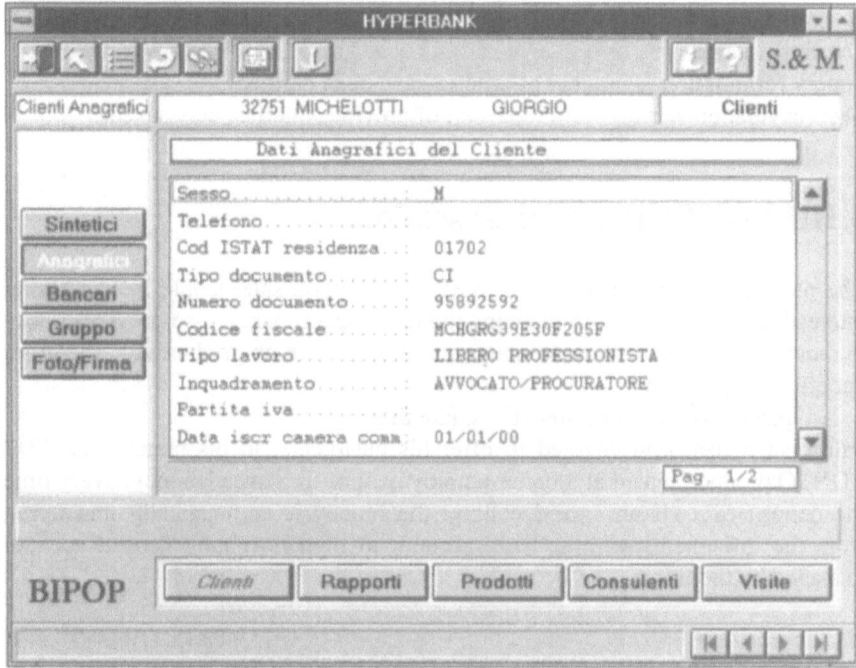

Figure 2: The main screen of the application

The system buttons are represented on the top of the screen, the buttons for the structural navigation (different perspectives on the same entity) are constantly positioned on the left hand of the screen, the buttons for the applicative navigation (exploration of data belonging to other related entities) are always represented at the bottom of the screen. They are highlighted and active only when the related functions are relevant.

The system buttons perform functionalities such as:
- help (general or contextual)
- go to start (first screen)
- go back one step
- print a document/form
- send a message
- insert an annotation
- exit from the application
- etc.

Each of the five Entity Types identified during the application investigation offers a number of different entry-point criteria; e.g., for "Customer":

- customer code
- customer name
- query formulation (a number of criteria have been defined)
- list (navigation starting from the result of previous queries, duly saved).

5 HIFINBIPOP: a typical session

The navigational interface of HIFINBIPOP supports salespeople in identifying interesting customers and in planning the daily operations; it also provides a way to monitor and supervise the sale activity, the salesperson productivity, the product effectiveness, etc.

A typical session can go something like this:

Salesman-A has been charged to offer his customers, in his branch, the TOP CONTO product, aimed at a better employment of the savers' money: every time the deposit exceeds an agreed ceiling, the money is automatically transferred from the low-interest-earning bank account to higher-yielding deposit account managed by the Bank.

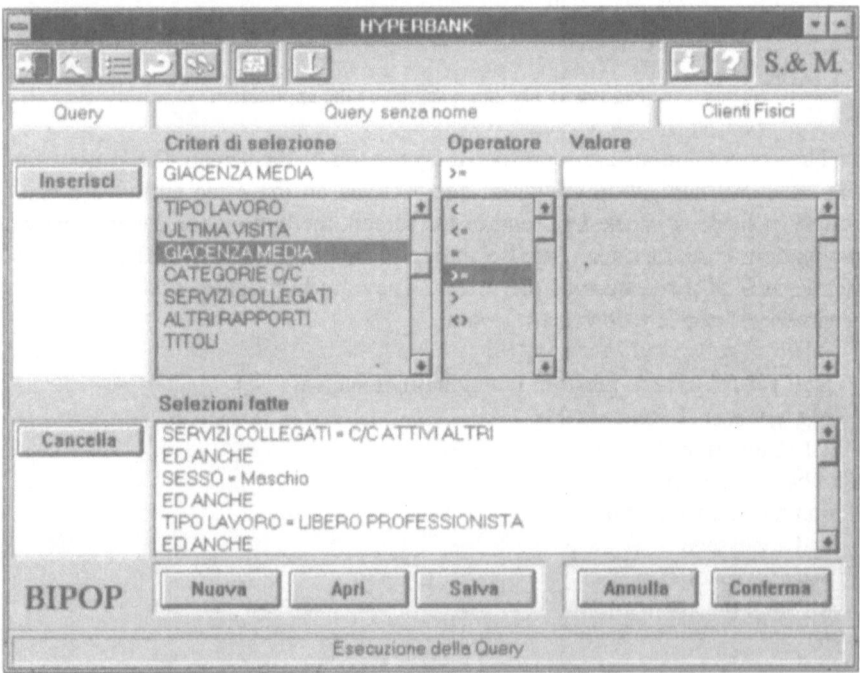

Figure 3: The point-and-click mechanism automatically builds up the query formulation which appears in the lower window and can be edited, if needed, before its execution

1. Using the point-and-click approach offered by the HIFINBIPOP interface, he formulates a query for customers with a deposit larger than 15 Million Italian Lira, on their Bank Account, and having no TOP CONTO account so far.
2. He obtains a list of 55 customers, complete with name, address and deposit amount.
3. He looks at the personal and banking data of the first ten customers
4. for each of them he goes through the visit reports and checks whether the TOP CONTO has never been proposed before
5. then he has a look at the services each of them is getting from the Bank.
6. Finally he selects 8 customers to be contacted, writes a note on his strategy and prints out synthetic data to prepare his visits.
7. The list is then saved, together with the visit plan, under a proper name chosen by the salesman (e.g., list-A) and stored for later re-use.
8. The day after recalls the proper customer cards and annotates his visit reports.
9. The marketing supervisor wants to monitor the market response to the TOP CONTO offer. A week later he gets the list of the customers who subscribed the product, with the names of the salesmen.
10. He selects Salesman-A and, after reading about the visits and their results, he writes a comment about optimised sales approach that could be attempted.
11. He selects then another salesman and starts again his navigation.
12. Sometimes later Salesman-A picks up list-A and, following the recommend-ation of the supervisor, he plans his next visits.

These steps reflects the types of navigation possible with HDM+. Steps 1 and 2 exemplifies what is done in most information systems to gather data. In step 3 the usefulness of structural navigation is shown (exploration of different per-spectives of the Entity "Customer"). Steps 4 and 5 are examples of applicative navigations (exploration of the Entities "Visits" and "Products" related to the cur-rent Entity "Customer").

6 Conclusion

HIFINBIPOP is being accepted very positively by the BIPOP personnel for its unbelievable flexibility (compared with the traditional technology), though it is revolutionising the work approach they were familiar with.

It is also seen by BIPOP management as a strategic tool for supervising the daily activities, communicating with salespeople and influencing their approach to the market.

References

[Cav93a]   Cavallaro U., Paolini P. "HIFI: Hypertext Interface For
            Information Relational and Multimedia Databases" in "The
            Electronic Libraries", April 1993, Vol 11, n! 2, p. 65-72
[Cav93b]   Cavallaro U., Garzotto F., Paolini P., Totaro D. "HIFI: Hypertext
            Interface For Information Systems" in "IEEE Software",
            November 1993, Vol. 10, n! 6, p.48-51
[HIFI93a]   HIFI - The Hypertext Interface Model (Deliverable 2), Athens-
            Munich-Torino, June 1993, 80 pp.
[HIFI93b]   HIFI Tools: Specification and Design (Deliverable 3), Athens-
            Munich-Torino, June 1993, 180 pp.
[HIFI93c]   HIFI Applications: Specification and Design (Deliverable 5),
            Athens-Munich-Torino, June 1993, 240 pp.

Appendix: Data Classes

The five identified main data classes are: "Customer", "Product", "Relation",
"Salesman", "Visit.

   "Customer" is the entity round which the whole application has been built.
The Customer is identified as a person or company needing services that the bank
can provide. It may be described as a potential Customer if it has not bought any
product so far; an active customer if it has a proper "position" as owner of specific products. It may belong to a group as a member or group-leader, owner of
accounts or delegated to ioperate on it. It may be a physical being described as
census person, or legal being described as firm. It can have a job (physical customer) or play in a specific area (legal customer, e.g.: firm). It can have meetings
with salesmen during which they discuss about banking products. When he buys
a product a "relation" is established with the bank.

   "Salesperson" describes the employee working in the Bank and giving advice
on products to the "Customers" in order to satisfy their needs. His purpose is to
sell products. He usually may work either inside a Branch waiting for Customer
who needs financial suggestions ("Branch Salesman"), or by reaching the Customer at home in order to propose, e.g., new investment opportunities ("Network
Salesman"). In order to sell products, he arranges a number of meetings with
Customer ("visits"), and when a product is sold he is involved in the "Relation"
definition.

"Product" describes a bank service that can be bought by Customer. "Products" are classified in "Categories", consisting in turn of a number of "Classes". Each single product, when purchased, originates a "Relation". Some of them require the pre-existence of other relations like "bank account relations" or "stock account relations".

"Visit" is made by a "Salesperson" to a "Customer" to discuss about his needs and the way the bank can satisfy it. A report on each visit must be filled in order to describe the conclusions of the meeting and leave traks of the work done, of the contacts established, etc.

Appendix: Addresses of the Authors

Dr. Umberto Cavallaro, Systems & Management, Via Alfieri 19,
I–10121 Torino, Italy. Phone: +39–11–561–2323 Fax: +39–11–5176304
e–mail: umberto@to.sem.it

Prof. Tom T. Carey, Dept. of Computing and Information Science,
University of Guelph, Canada N1G 2W1.
email: tcarey@snowhite.cis.uoguelph.ca

Dr. Andrew Dillon, HUSAT Research Institute, Loughborough University of
Technology, Loughborough, The Elms, Elms Grove, Leicester LE11 1RG, UK.
Phone: +44–509–611.088   Fax: +44–509–234.651
e–mail: A.P.Dillon@lut.ac.uk and adillon@ucs.indiana.edu

Klaus Eickemeyer, Siemens Nixdorf Informationssysteme AG,
Abt. SNI MR PD 134, Otto–Hahn–Ring 6, D–81739 München, Germany.
Phone: +49–89–636 40 493   Fax: +49–89–636 40 443
email: Klaus.Eickemeyer@mch.sni.de

Dr. Franca Garzotto, Dipartimento di Elettronica e Informazione,
Politecnico di Milano, Piazza L. da Vinci 32 , I–20133 Milano, Italy.
Phone: +39–2–23993520   Fax: +39–2–23993411
email: garzotto.elet.polimi.it

Heiner Gertzen, Hoechst AG, Clinical Research, P. O. Box 800320,
D–65903 Frankfurt, Germany. e–mail: gertzen@hpdesk.klifo.hoechst–ag.dbp.de

Dr.habil. Uli Glowalla, Department of Psychology, Justus Liebig University,
Otto–Behaghel–Str. 10/F, D–35394 Gießen, Germany.
Phone: +49–641–702–5403/9   Fax: +49–641–702–3811
email: glowalla@psychol.uni–giessen.d400.de

Jörg Hannemann, empirica GmbH, Communications and Technology
Research, Oxfordstr. 2, D–53111 Bonn, Germany
Phone: +49–228–985 30–0   Fax: +49–228–985 30–12
email: JOERG%emp–d.uucp@Germany.EU.net

Lynda Hardman, CWI, Kruislaan 413, P.O. Box 94079,
NL–1090 GB Amsterdam, The Netherlands.
Phone: +31–20–592 4127   Fax: +31–20–592 4199
email: Lynda.Hardman@cwi.nl

Joachim Hasebrook, Department of Psychology, Justus Liebig University,
Otto–Behaghel–Str. 10/F, D–35394 Gießen, Germany.
Phone: +49–641–702–5403/9   Fax: +49–41–702–3811
email:hasebrook@psychol.uni–giessen.d400.de

Karin Hertwig, Siemens AG, Corporate Research and Development
ZFE BT SE 56, Otto Hahn Ring 6, D–81739 München 83, Germany
Phone: +49–89–636 41 272   Fax: +49–89–636 45 111
email: Karin.Hertwig@zfe.siemens.de

Dr. Martin Hofmann, SAP AG, P.O. Box 1461, Max–Planck Str. 8,
D–69185 Walldorf (Baden), Germany.
Phone: +49–6227–34 3254   Fax: +49–6227–34 1616
email: hofman@sap–ag.de

Prof. Paul Kahn, IRIS, Brown University, 180 George Street, Box 1946,
Providence, RI 02912, USA.   e–mail: pdk@iris.brown.edu
Phone: +1–401–863–2402   Fax: +1–401–863–1758
& Dynamic Diagrams, 12 Bassett Street, Providence, RI 02903–4206, USA.
Phone: +1–401–331–2014   Fax: +1–401–331–2015

Thomas Kamps, GMD – Gesellschaft für Mathematik und Datenverarbeitung,
IPSI – Integrated Publication and Information Systems Institute,
Dolivostr. 15, D–64293 Darmstadt, Germany
Phone: +49–6151–869 904   Fax: +49–6151–869 966
email: kamps@darmstadt.gmd.de

Thomas Kirste, Computer Graphics Center (ZGDV), Wilhelminenstr. 7,
D–64283 Darmstadt Germany.
Phone: +49–6151–155–241   Fax: +49 –151–155–299
email:kirste@igd.fhg.de

Dr. Cliff McKnight, HUSAT Research Institute, Loughborough University of
Technology, Loughborough, The Elms, Elms Grove, Leicester LE11 1RG, UK.
Phone: +44–509–611.088   Fax: +44–509–234.651
email: C.Mcknight@lut.ac.uk

Klaus Meusel, Siemens AG, Corporate Research and Development
ZFE BT SE 56, Otto Hahn Ring 6, D–81730 München , Germany
Phone: +49–89–636–48 320   Fax: +49–9–636–45 111
email: Klaus.Meusel@zfe.siemens.de

Prof. Christine M. Neuwirth, Carnegie–Mellon University, Pittsburgh,
PA 15213, USA. Phone: +1–412–268–8702   Fax: +1–412–268–7989
email: cmn+@andrew.cmu.edu

Prof. Paolo Paolini, Dipartimento di Elettronica e Informazione, Politecnico
di Milano, Piazza L. da Vinci 32 , I–20133 Milano, Italy.
Phone: +39 2–239–93.520   Fax: +39 2–239–93.411
email: paolini@elet.polimi.it.

Matthias Rauterberg, Work and Organisational Psycholgy Unit, Swiss
Federal Institute of Technology (ETH), Nelkenstr. 11, CH–8092 Zürich,
Switzerland. Phone: +41–1–632–7082   e–mail: rauterberg@rzvax.ethz.ch

Klaus Reichenberger, GMD – Gesellschaft für Mathematik und Datenverarbeitung, IPSI – Integrated Publication and Information Systems Institute,
Dolivostr. 15, D–64293 Darmstadt, Germany.
Phone: +49–6151–869 908   Fax: +49–6151–869 966
email: reichen@darmstadt.gmd.de

Dr. Franz Schmalhofer, German Research Center for Artificial Intelligence,
Erwin Schrödinger Straße (Bldg. 57), D–67663 Kaiserslautern, Germany
Phone: +49–631–205 3465   Fax: +49–631–205 3210
email: schmalho@dfki.uni–kl.de

Dr. Wolfgang Schuler, GMD – Gesellschaft für Mathematik und Datenverarbeitung, IPSI – Integrated Publication and Information Systems Institute
Dolivostr. 15, D–64293 Darmstadt, Germany
Phone: +49–6151–869 915   Fax: +49–6151–869 966
email: schuler@darmstadt.gmd.de

Dr. Dr. Norbert Streitz, GMD – Gesellschaft für Mathematik und Datenverarbeitung, IPSI – Integrated Publication and Information Systems Institute,
Dolivostr. 15, D–64293 Darmstadt, Germany
Phone: +49–6151–869 919   Fax: +49–6151–869 966
email: streitz@darmstadt.gmd.de

Dr. Ulrich Thiel, GMD – Gesellschaft für Mathematik und Datenverarbeitung, IPSI – Integrated Publication and Information Systems Institute,
Dolivostr. 15, D–64293 Darmstadt, Germany
Phone: +49–6151–869 855   Fax: +49–6151–869 818
email: thiel@darmstadt.gmd.de

Dr. Manfred Thüring, empirica GmbH, Communications and Technology
Research, Oxfordstr. 2, D–53111 Bonn, Germany
Phone: +49–228–985 30–0   Fax: +49 –228–985 30–12
email: MANFRED%emp–d.uucp@Germany.EU.net

Domenico Totaro, Systems & Management, Via Farini 82,
I–20159 Milano, Italy. Phone: +39–266–80.2136   Fax: +39–266–80.3330

Kaisa Väänänen, Computer Graphics Center (ZGDV), Wilhelminenstr. 7,
D–64283 Darmstadt, Germany.
Phone: +49–6151–155–244 Fax: +49–6151–155–299
email: kaisa@igd.fhg.de